Entertainment Directory

HOUSTON
TRAVEL GUIDE
2015

SHOPS, RESTAURANTS, ATTRACTIONS & NIGHTLIFE

The Most Positively
Reviewed and Recommended
by Locals and Travelers

HOUSTON
TRAVEL GUIDE
2015

SHOPS, RESTAURANTS, ATTRACTIONS & NIGHTLIFE

HOUSTON TRAVEL GUIDE 2015
Shops, Restaurants, Arts, Entertainment & Nightlife

© Jennifer A. Emerson, 2015
© E.G.P. Editorial, 2015

Printed in USA.

ISBN-13: 978-1502462831
ISBN-10: 1502462834

Copyright © 2015
All rights reserved.

INDEX

SHOPS
Top 500 Shops - 9

RESTAURANTS
Top 500 Restaurants - 47

ARTS & ENTERTAINMENT
Top 500 Arts & Entertainment - 85

NIGHTLIFE SPOTS
Top 500 Nightlife Spots - 123

HOUSTON TRAVEL GUIDE 2015
Shops, Restaurants, Arts, Entertainment & Nightlife

This directory is dedicated to Houston Business Owners and Managers who provide the experience that the locals and tourists enjoy. Thanks you very much for all that you do and thank for being the "People Choice".

Thanks to everyone that posts their reviews online and the amazing reviews sites that make our life easier.

The places listed in this book are the most positively reviewed and recommended by locals and travelers from around the world.

Thank you for your time and enjoy the directory that is designed with locals and tourist in mind!

TOP 500 SHOPS
The Most Recommended by Locals & Trevelers
(From #1 to #500)

#1
The Galleria
Category: Shopping Center
Average price: Expensive
Area: Galleria, Uptown
Address: 5085 Westheimer Rd
Houston, TX 77056
Phone: (713) 622-0663

#2
Space Montrose
Category: Arts, Crafts, Jewelry, Art Gallery
Average price: Modest
Area: Montrose
Address: 1706 Westheimer Rd
Houston, TX 77098
Phone: (832) 649-5743

#3
Hermes of Paris
Category: Women's Clothing
Average price: Exclusive
Area: Galleria, Uptown
Address: 1800 Post Oak Blvd Ste 156
Houston, TX 77056
Phone: (713) 623-2177

#4
Jubilee
Category: Women's Clothing, Home Decor, Flowers, Gifts
Average price: Modest
Area: The Heights
Address: 321-A W 19th St
Houston, TX 77008
Phone: (713) 869-5885

#5
Hello Lucky
Category: Accessories, Women's Clothing, Art Gallery
Average price: Modest
Area: The Heights
Address: 1025 Studewood St
Houston, TX 77008
Phone: (713) 864-3556

#6
Fit Japanese Store
Category: Department Store
Average price: Inexpensive
Area: Sharpstown, Chinatown
Address: 9889 Bellaire Blvd
Houston, TX 77036
Phone: (281) 201-1360

#7
My Flaming Heart
Category: Antiques, Jewelry, Used, Vintage
Average price: Expensive
Area: Fourth Ward, Midtown
Address: 3622 Main St
Houston, TX 77002
Phone: (713) 533-1147

#8
Replay on 19th
Category: Vintage, Antiques
Average price: Modest
Area: The Heights
Address: 373 W 19th St
Houston, TX 77008
Phone: (713) 863-9344

#9
Ashton Miyako
Category: Women's Clothing, Jewelry
Average price: Modest
Area: Medical Center
Address: 1 Hermann Park Ct
Houston, TX 77021
Phone: (831) 295-1711

#10
Target Stores
Category: Department Store
Average price: Modest
Area: Braeswood Place
Address: 8500 S Main St
Houston, TX 77025
Phone: (713) 666-0967

#11
Kaboom Books
Category: Bookstore
Average price: Inexpensive
Area: The Heights
Address: 3116 Houston Ave
Houston, TX 77009
Phone: (713) 869-7600

#12
lululemon athletica
Category: Sports Wear, Women's Clothing, Yoga
Average price: Expensive
Area: Highland Village
Address: 4023 Westheimer Rd
Houston, TX 77027
Phone: (713) 621-8311

#13
Anthropologie
Category: Department Store, Women's Clothing, Home Decor
Average price: Expensive
Area: Highland Village
Address: 4066 Westheimer Rd
Houston, TX 77027
Phone: (713) 840-9428

#14
Wabash Antiques & Feed Store
Category: Antiques, Nursery, Gardening, Pet Store
Average price: Modest
Area: The Heights, Rice Military
Address: 5701 Washington Ave
Houston, TX 77007
Phone: (713) 863-8322

#15
Memorial City Mall
Category: Shopping Center
Average price: Modest
Area: Memorial
Address: 900 Gessner Rd
Houston, TX 77024
Phone: (713) 464-8640

#16
lululemon athletica
Category: Sports Wear,
Women's Clothing, Men's Clothing
Average price: Expensive
Area: Galleria, Uptown
Address: 5135 W Alabama
Houston, TX 77056
Phone: (713) 552-1681

#17
Texas Junk Company
Category: Antiques
Average price: Modest
Area: Fourth Ward, Midtown, Montrose
Address: 215 Welch St
Houston, TX 77006
Phone: (713) 524-6257

#18
Gallery M Squared
Category: Art Gallery, Venues
Average price: Modest
Area: The Heights
Address: 339 W 19th St
Houston, TX 77008
Phone: (713) 861-6070

#19
The Container Store
Category: Home Decor
Average price: Modest
Area: Galleria, Uptown
Address: 2511 Post Oak Blvd
Houston, TX 77056
Phone: (713) 960-1722

#20
Costco
Category: Wholesale Store
Average price: Modest
Area: Highland Village
Address: 3836 Richmond Ave
Houston, TX 77027
Phone: (832) 325-5850

#21
Vinal Edge Records
Category: Music, DVDs, Vinyl Records
Average price: Modest
Area: The Heights
Address: 239 W 19th St
Houston, TX 77008
Phone: (832) 618-1129

#22
More Than You Can Imagine
Category: Vintage, Women's Clothing,
Accessories
Average price: Expensive
Area: Upper Kirby
Address: 2817 Westheimer
Houston, TX 77098
Phone: (713) 668-8811

#23
Goodwill River Oaks
Category: Thrift Store
Average price: Inexpensive
Area: Montrose
Address: 2030 Westheimer
Houston, TX 77098
Phone: (713) 699-6393

#24
**Twilight Epiphany Skyspace
by James Turrell**
Category: Art Gallery
Average price: Inexpensive
Area: West University
Address: 6100 Main St
Houston, TX 77005
Phone: (713) 348-4758

#25
Nordstrom
Category: Department Store
Average price: Expensive
Area: Galleria, Uptown
Address: 5192 Hidalgo St
Houston, TX 77056
Phone: (832) 201-2700

#26
The Guild Shop
Category: Vintage, Jewelry, Women's Clothing
Average price: Modest
Area: Montrose
Address: 2009 Dunlavy St
Houston, TX 77006
Phone: (713) 528-5095

#27
Highland Village
Category: Shopping Center
Average price: Expensive
Area: Highland Village
Address: 4055 Westheimer
Houston, TX 77027
Phone: (713) 850-3100

#28
Cottage Thrift Shop
Category: Thrift Store
Average price: Inexpensive
Area: Fourth Ward, Montrose
Address: 811 Westheimer Rd
Houston, TX 77006
Phone: (713) 521-3150

#29
Top Drawer Lingerie
Category: Lingerie
Average price: Expensive
Area: Galleria, Uptown
Address: 1101 Uptown Park Blvd
Houston, TX 77056
Phone: (713) 784-8707

#30
British Isles
Category: Home Decor, Gift Shop
Average price: Modest
Area: West University
Address: 2366 Rice Blvd
Houston, TX 77005
Phone: (713) 522-6868

#31
Ten Thousand Villages
Category: Home Decor
Average price: Modest
Area: West University
Address: 2424A Rice Blvd
Houston, TX 77005
Phone: (713) 533-1000

#32
Texas Art Asylum
Category: Antiques, Art Supplies
Average price: Inexpensive
Area: EaDo
Address: 1719 Live Oak
Houston, TX 77003
Phone: (713) 224-5220

#33
Oolala
Category: Accessories, Women's Clothing, Home Decor
Average price: Modest
Area: The Heights
Address: 833 Studewood St
Houston, TX 77007
Phone: (713) 862-9800

#34
Blackbird Trading Co.
Category: Used, Vintage
Average price: Modest
Area: Montrose
Address: 1637 Westheimer
Houston, TX 77006
Phone: (713) 524-9100

#35
Walmart Supercenter
Category: Drugstore, Discount Store, Grocery
Average price: Inexpensive
Area: Spring Branch
Address: 1118 Silber Rd
Houston, TX 77055
Phone: (713) 797-2245

#36
Whole Earth Provision Co.
Category: Luggage, Outdoor Gear, Sports Wear, Home Decor
Average price: Modest
Area: Upper Kirby, Montrose
Address: 2934 S Shepherd Dr
Houston, TX 77098
Phone: (713) 526-5226

#37
Crate and Barrel
Category: Furniture Store, Home Decor, Kitchen & Bath
Average price: Expensive
Area: Highland Village
Address: 4006 Westheimer
Houston, TX 77027
Phone: (713) 490-6400

#38
Vapor-Lot
Category: Vape Shop
Average price: Modest
Area: Museum District, Upper Kirby, Montrose
Address: 3816 S Shepherd Dr
Houston, TX 77098
Phone: (832) 606-8273

#39
Goodwill
Category: Thrift Store
Average price: Inexpensive
Area: The Heights
Address: 215 W 20th St
Houston, TX 77008
Phone: (713) 970-1782

#40
Tendrils & Curls
Category: Cosmetics, Beauty Supply
Average price: Modest
Area: Montrose
Address: 2501 1/2 S Shepherd Dr
Houston, TX 77019
Phone: (713) 520-7179

#41
Hebert's Specialty Meats
Category: Meat Shop, Wholesale Store, Butcher
Average price: Modest
Area: Highland Village
Address: 4714 Richmond Ave
Houston, TX 77027
Phone: (713) 621-6328

#42
Forever 21
Category: Women's Clothing
Average price: Inexpensive
Area: Fourth Ward, Downtown
Address: 1201 Main St
Houston, TX 77002
Phone: (713) 655-1896

#43
Kuhl-Linscomb
Category: Home Decor
Average price: Expensive
Area: Upper Kirby
Address: 2424 W Alabama St
Houston, TX 77098
Phone: (713) 526-6000

#44
Texas Hookah
Category: Tobacco Shop
Average price: Modest
Area: Medical Center
Address: 8413 Almeda Rd
Houston, TX 77054
Phone: (877) 946-6524

#45
Murder by the Book
Category: Bookstore
Average price: Modest
Area: West University
Address: 2342 Bissonnet St
Houston, TX 77005
Phone: (713) 524-8597

#46
Sephora
Category: Cosmetics, Beauty Supply
Average price: Modest
Area: West University
Address: 2401 Times Blvd
Houston, TX 77005
Phone: (713) 942-0110

#47
Anthropologie
Category: Women's Clothing
Average price: Expensive
Area: Memorial
Address: 803 Town & Country Ln
Houston, TX 77024
Phone: (713) 973-0561

#48
Magick Cauldron
Category: Bookstore, Hobby Shop, Jewelry
Average price: Modest
Area: Montrose
Address: 2424 Montrose Blvd
Houston, TX 77006
Phone: (713) 523-0069

#49
Nordstrom Rack
Category: Department Store
Average price: Modest
Area: Galleria, Uptown
Address: 5000 Westheimer Rd
Houston, TX 77056
Phone: (281) 661-3600

#50
Casa Ramirez Folkart Gallery
Category: Art Gallery, Home Decor
Average price: Modest
Area: The Heights
Address: 241 W 19th St
Houston, TX 77008
Phone: (713) 880-2420

#51
BCBG Max Azria
Category: Women's Clothing
Average price: Expensive
Area: Downtown
Address: 1201 Fannin St
Houston, TX 77002
Phone: (713) 654-7752

#52
Reiner's Fine Jewelry
Category: Jewelry
Average price: Expensive
Area: River Oaks
Address: 2210 Westheimer Rd
Houston, TX 77098
Phone: (713) 520-1212

#53
Bhldn
Category: Women's Clothing, Formal Wear
Average price: Expensive
Area: Highland Village
Address: 4056 Westheimer Rd
Houston, TX 77027
Phone: (713) 599-1917

#54
Charming Charlie
Category: Accessories, Jewelry
Average price: Modest
Area: Galleria, Uptown
Address: 5085 Westheimer Road
Houston, TX 77056
Phone: (713) 623-0885

#55
DuO
Category: Women's Clothing, Men's Clothing, Accessories
Average price: Modest
Area: Montrose
Address: 1665 Westheimer Rd
Houston, TX 77098
Phone: (713) 963-8825

#56
Buffalo Exchange
Category: Vintage, Men's Clothing, Women's Clothing
Average price: Modest
Area: West University
Address: 2439 Bissonnet St
Houston, TX 77005
Phone: (713) 529-2929

#57
Marshalls
Category: Department Store
Average price: Modest
Area: River Oaks, Montrose
Address: 1540 W Gray St
Houston, TX 77019
Phone: (713) 807-8890

#58
Wish
Category: Shoe Store, Women's Clothing
Average price: Modest
Area: Montrose
Address: 1614 Westheimer Rd
Houston, TX 77006
Phone: (713) 527-0812

#59
West Elm
Category: Home Decor, Furniture Store
Average price: Modest
Area: Highland Village
Address: 3910 Westheimer Rd
Houston, TX 77027
Phone: (713) 623-2422

#60
Langford Market
Category: Women's Clothing, Accessories
Average price: Modest
Area: West University
Address: 2517 University Blvd
Houston, TX 77005
Phone: (713) 520-5575

#61
Cavender's Boot City
Category: Shoe Store
Average price: Modest
Area: South Main
Address: 2505 South Loop W
Houston, TX 77054
Phone: (713) 664-8999

#62
Em & Lee
Category: Women's Clothing
Average price: Modest
Area: River Oaks, Montrose
Address: 2021 W Gray St
Houston, TX 77019
Phone: (713) 524-8485

#63
T.j. Maxx
Category: Department Store
Average price: Modest
Area: Gulfton, Galleria, Uptown
Address: 5152 Richmond Ave
Houston, TX 77056
Phone: (713) 626-4335

#64
T.J. Maxx
Category: Department Store
Average price: Modest
Area: River Oaks, Montrose
Address: 1554 W Gray St
Houston, TX 77019
Phone: (713) 524-5582

#65
Brazos Bookstore
Category: Bookstore
Average price: Modest
Area: West University
Address: 2421 Bissonnet St
Houston, TX 77005
Phone: (713) 523-0701

#66
Yale Street Grill & Gifts
Category: Diner, Antiques
Average price: Inexpensive
Area: The Heights
Address: 2100 Yale St
Houston, TX 77008
Phone: (713) 861-3113

#67
Bliss on 19th
Category: Home Decor
Average price: Modest
Area: The Heights
Address: 235 W 19th St
Houston, TX 77008
Phone: (832) 673-0099

#68
World Market
Category: Home Decor, Beer, Wine, Spirits, Furniture Store
Average price: Modest
Area: Gulfton, Galleria, Uptown
Address: 5125 Richmond Ave
Houston, TX 77056
Phone: (713) 963-8833

#69
First Saturday Arts Market
Category: Arts, Crafts, Festival
Average price: Modest
Area: The Heights
Address: 548 W 19th St
Houston, TX 77008
Phone: (713) 802-1213

#70
Target
Category: Department Store, Grocery
Average price: Modest
Area: Highland Village, Galleria, Uptown
Address: 4323 San Felipe St
Houston, TX 77027
Phone: (713) 960-9608

#71
Third Planet
Category: Toy Store, Comic Books
Average price: Modest
Area: Upper Kirby
Address: 2718 Southwest Fwy
Houston, TX 77098
Phone: (713) 528-1067

#72
Half Price Books
Category: Books, Mags, Music, Video
Average price: Inexpensive
Area: Fourth Ward, Montrose
Address: 1011 Westheimer
Houston, TX 77006
Phone: (713) 520-1084

#73
Al's Handmade Boots
Category: Shoe Repair, Shoe Store, Leather Goods
Average price: Modest
Area: Midtown
Address: 2323 Fannin St
Houston, TX 77002
Phone: (832) 488-3000

#74
MAM Resale
Category: Thrift Store, Furniture Store, Used, Vintage
Average price: Inexpensive
Area: Spring Branch
Address: 1625 Blalock Rd
Houston, TX 77080
Phone: (713) 491-4330

#75
The Lift
Category: Bookstore, Jewelry
Average price: Modest
Area: The Heights
Address: 365 W 19th St
Houston, TX 77008
Phone: (713) 868-5438

#76
The Class Room
Category: Men's Clothing
Average price: Expensive
Area: West University
Address: 2534 Amherst St
Houston, TX 77005
Phone: (713) 874-0004

#77
Bering's
Category: Hardware Store
Average price: Expensive
Area: West University
Address: 3900 Bissonnet St
Houston, TX 77005
Phone: (713) 665-0500

#78
Frenchy's Chicken
Category: Fast Food, Cajun, Creole, Wholesale Store
Average price: Inexpensive
Area: MacGregor
Address: 3919 Scott St
Houston, TX 77004
Phone: (713) 748-2233

#79
New Living
Category: Building Supplies, Mattresses,
Average price: Modest
Area: West University
Address: 6111 Kirby Dr
Houston, TX 77005
Phone: (713) 521-1921

#80
Grace Hart
Category: Antiques, Furniture Store
Average price: Modest
Area: The Heights
Address: 313 W 19th St
Houston, TX 77008
Phone: (713) 862-1010

#81
Becker's Books
Category: Bookstore
Average price: Inexpensive
Area: Spring Branch
Address: 7405 Westview Dr
Houston, TX 77055
Phone: (713) 957-8088

#82
The Tipping Point
Category: Shoe Store, Men's Clothing, Watches
Average price: Inexpensive
Area: Fourth Ward, Downtown
Address: 1212 Main St
Houston, TX 77002
Phone: (713) 655-0443

#83
Adkins Architectural Antiques
Category: Building Supplies, Antiques, Home Decor
Average price: Modest
Area: Midtown
Address: 3515 Fannin St
Houston, TX 77004
Phone: (713) 522-6547

#84
Whole Earth Provision Co.
Category: Sports Wear, Outdoor Gear, Shoe Store
Average price: Modest
Area: Galleria, Uptown
Address: 2501 Post Oak Blvd
Houston, TX 77056
Phone: (713) 526-5440

#85
The Galaxie Jewelers
Category: Jewelry
Average price: Expensive
Area: West University
Address: 2511 Sunset Blvd
Houston, TX 77005
Phone: (713) 521-2511

#86
Sparrow and The Nest
Category: Arts, Crafts, Art Gallery, Jewelry
Average price: Modest
Area: The Heights
Address: 1020 Studewood
Houston, TX 77008
Phone: (713) 869-6378

#87
Target
Category: Department Store
Average price: Modest
Area: The Heights
Address: 2580 Shearn St
Houston, TX 77007
Phone: (713) 331-0376

#88
Retropolis
Category: Vintage, Jewelry, Women's Clothing
Average price: Modest
Area: The Heights
Address: 321 W 19th St
Houston, TX 77008
Phone: (713) 861-1950

#89
CityCentre
Category: Shopping Center
Average price: Modest
Area: Memorial
Address: 800 Town and Country Blvd
Houston, TX 77024
Phone: (713) 629-5200

#90
Tres Chic
Category: Women's Clothing, Accessories
Average price: Modest
Area: Upper Kirby
Address: 3414 Eastside St
Houston, TX 77098
Phone: (713) 528-8737

#91
Micro Center
Category: Computers
Average price: Modest
Area: Galleria, Uptown
Address: 1717 West Loop S
Houston, TX 77027
Phone: (713) 940-8500

#92
Manready Mercantile
Category: Men's Clothing, Vintage, Leather Goods
Average price: Expensive
Area: The Heights
Address: 321 W 19th St
Houston, TX 77008
Phone: (800) 554-9352

#93
Designer Exchange Consignment Resale
Category: Women's Clothing, Vintage, Personal Shopping
Average price: Inexpensive
Area: Westchase
Address: 10248 Westheimer Rd
Houston, TX 77042
Phone: (713) 782-1780

#94
Langford Market
Category: Accessories, Women's Clothing
Average price: Modest
Area: The Heights
Address: 249 W 19th St
Houston, TX 77008
Phone: (713) 880-1515

#95
DSW
Category: Shoe Store
Average price: Modest
Area: Galleria, Uptown
Address: 2477 Post Oak Boulevard
Houston, TX 77056
Phone: (713) 871-0004

#96
The Tinderbox Craft Collective
Category: Arts, Crafts
Average price: Expensive
Area: Fourth Ward, Midtown
Address: 3622 Main St
Houston, TX 77002
Phone: (713) 524-2858

#97
Poshak Hillcroft Fashion & Style
Category: Women's Clothing, Men's Clothing
Average price: Expensive
Area: Sharpstown
Address: 6620 Southwest Fwy
Houston, TX 77074
Phone: (713) 532-3232

#98
The Eye Gallery
Category: Eyewear, Opticians
Average price: Expensive
Area: Montrose
Address: 1806 Westheimer Rd
Houston, TX 77098
Phone: (713) 523-1279

#99
Montblanc
Category: Leather Goods, Accessories, Watches
Average price: Exclusive
Area: Galleria, Uptown
Address: 5085 Westheimer Road, Houston, TX 77056
Phone: (713) 960-9790

#100
Charity Guild Resale Shop
Category: Thrift Store
Average price: Inexpensive
Area: Montrose
Address: 1203 Lovett Blvd Houston, TX 77006
Phone: (713) 529-0995

#101
Fundamentally Toys
Category: Toy Store
Average price: Expensive
Area: West University
Address: 2401 Rice Blvd Houston, TX 77005
Phone: (713) 524-4400

#102
Eye Impact
Category: Optometrists, Eyewear, Opticians
Average price: Modest
Area: The Heights, Rice Military
Address: 5601 Washington Ave Houston, TX 77007
Phone: (832) 319-7732

#103
Laptops of Houston
Category: Computer Repair, Computers
Average price: Modest
Area: Westchase
Address: 10832 Westheimer Rd Houston, TX 77042
Phone: (713) 781-1855

#104
Pinot's Palette
Category: Arts, Entertainment, Arts, Crafts, Nightlife
Average price: Modest
Area: Fourth Ward, Midtown, Montrose
Address: 2406 Taft St Houston, TX 77006
Phone: (713) 523-4769

#105
Apple Store
Category: Electronics, Computers
Average price: Expensive
Area: Highland Village
Address: 4012 Westheimer Rd Houston, TX 77027
Phone: (832) 325-3500

#106
Billy Reid
Category: Women's Clothing, Men's Clothing
Average price: Expensive
Area: Upper Kirby, River Oaks
Address: 2702 Westhemier Rd Houston, TX 77098
Phone: (713) 552-0333

#107
The Hat Store
Category: Accessories
Average price: Expensive
Area: Gulfton, Galleria, Uptown
Address: 5587 Richmond Ave Houston, TX 77056
Phone: (713) 780-2480

#108
GreenStreet
Category: Music Venues, Shopping Center
Average price: Modest
Area: Downtown
Address: 1201 Fannin St Houston, TX 77002
Phone: (832) 320-1200

#109
Tuesday Morning
Category: Shopping
Average price: Inexpensive
Area: The Heights
Address: 901-A North Shepherd Drive Houston, TX 77008
Phone: (713) 868-4938

#110
Couture Blowout
Category: Women's Clothing, Discount Store, Used, Vintage
Average price: Expensive
Area: Montrose
Address: 2419 S Shepherd Dr Houston, TX 77019
Phone: (713) 533-9888

#111
The Shops at Houston Center
Category: Shopping Center
Average price: Modest
Area: Downtown
Address: 1200 McKinney St Houston, TX 77010
Phone: (713) 759-1442

#112
Rose Boutique
Category: Women's Clothing, Accessories
Average price: Modest
Area: Gulfton
Address: 5901 Hillcroft St Houston, TX 77036
Phone: (713) 952-7673

#113
Urban Outfitters
Category: Women's Clothing
Average price: Modest
Area: West University
Address: 2501 University Blvd
Houston, TX 77005
Phone: (713) 529-3023

#114
Dao Chloe Dao
Category: Women's Clothing, Accessories
Average price: Expensive
Area: West University
Address: 6127 Kirby Dr
Houston, TX 77005
Phone: (713) 807-1565

#115
Tuesday Morning
Category: Department Store
Average price: Modest
Area: Westchase
Address: 9749 Westheimer Rd
Houston, TX 77042
Phone: (713) 781-3227

#116
Reserve Supply
Category: Shoe Store, Men's Clothing
Average price: Expensive
Area: Sixth Ward
Address: 2205 Washington Ave
Houston, TX 77007
Phone: (713) 750-9582

#117
Sound Exchange
Category: Music, DVDs
Average price: Modest
Area: Montrose
Address: 1846 Richmond Ave
Houston, TX 77098
Phone: (713) 666-5555

#118
Joan Pillow
Category: Bridal
Average price: Expensive
Area: Highland Village
Address: 4001 Westheimer
Houston, TX 77027
Phone: (713) 622-1122

#119
Settlement Goods & Design
Category: Men's Clothing, Women's Clothing, Accessories
Average price: Expensive
Area: Fourth Ward, Montrose
Address: 3939 Montrose Blvd
Houston, TX 77006
Phone: (713) 701-7872

#120
310 Rosemont
Category: Women's Clothing, Men's Clothing
Average price: Expensive
Area: River Oaks, Montrose
Address: 1965 W Gray Ave
Houston, TX 77019
Phone: (713) 522-8133

#121
Francesca's Collections
Category: Jewelry, Women's Clothing
Average price: Modest
Area: Highland Village
Address: 4022 Westheimer Rd
Houston, TX 77027
Phone: (713) 961-3399

#122
Box & Box Custom Jewelry
Category: Jewelry
Average price: Modest
Area: West University
Address: 2514 Rice Blvd
Houston, TX 77005
Phone: (713) 266-7783

#123
IKEA
Category: Furniture Store, Rugs
Average price: Modest
Area: Spring Branch
Address: 7810 Katy Fwy
Houston, TX 77024
Phone: (713) 688-7867

#124
Buffalo Hardware Company
Category: Hardware Store
Average price: Modest
Area: Upper Kirby
Address: 2614 Westheimer Rd
Houston, TX 77098
Phone: (713) 524-1011

#125
DSW
Category: Shoe Store
Average price: Modest
Area: Memorial
Address: 9419 Katy Freeway
Houston, TX 77024
Phone: (713) 465-8923

#126
Nonno
Category: Women's Clothing, Men's Clothing, Accessories
Average price: Modest
Area: Montrose
Address: 1641 Westheimer Rd
Houston, TX 77006
Phone: (832) 387-2740

#127
Katie & Co.
Category: Cards, Stationery, Gift Shop
Average price: Modest
Area: The Heights
Address: 4500 Washington Ave
Houston, TX 77007
Phone: (713) 802-1345

#128
Sand Dollar Thrift Store
Category: Vintage, Thrift Store
Average price: Inexpensive
Area: The Heights
Address: 1903 Yale St
Houston, TX 77008
Phone: (713) 923-1461

#129
Fashion Plate Boutique
Category: Vintage, Women's Clothing, Men's Clothing
Average price: Expensive
Area: Museum District, Montrose
Address: 4317 Montrose Blvd
Houston, TX 77006
Phone: (713) 398-2554

#130
Premium Goods
Category: Shoe Store
Average price: Modest
Area: West University
Address: 2416 Times Blvd
Houston, TX 77005
Phone: (713) 523-8825

#131
High Fashion Home
Category: Home Decor, Furniture Store
Average price: Expensive
Area: Fourth Ward, Midtown
Address: 3100 Travis St
Houston, TX 77006
Phone: (713) 528-3838

#132
Target
Category: Discount Store
Average price: Modest
Area: Fairbanks, Northwest Crossing
Address: 13250 Northwest Freeway
Houston, TX 77040
Phone: (713) 939-7878

#133
Silverlust Jewelry
Category: Jewelry, Jewelry Repair
Average price: Modest
Area: Montrose
Address: 1338 Westheimer Rd
Houston, TX 77006
Phone: (713) 520-5440

#134
Saad's Tailors
Category: Sewing, Alterations, Men's Clothing, Bespoke Clothing
Average price: Modest
Area: Galleria, Uptown
Address: 5866 Westheimer Rd
Houston, TX 77057
Phone: (713) 785-2212

#135
Francesca's Collections
Category: Fashion
Average price: Modest
Area: Memorial
Address: 6514 Woodway Dr
Houston, TX 77057
Phone: (713) 722-0754

#136
Reeves Antiques
Category: Furniture Store
Average price: Exclusive
Area: Fourth Ward, Midtown, Montrose
Address: 2415 Taft St
Houston, TX 77006
Phone: (713) 523-5577

#137
Apple Store
Category: Computers
Average price: Expensive
Area: Galleria, Uptown
Address: 5085 Westheimer Rd
Houston, TX 77056
Phone: (713) 850-8924

#138
Intercontinental Jewelers
Category: Jewelry, Bridal
Average price: Expensive
Area: Gulfton
Address: 6222 Richmond Ave
Houston, TX 77057
Phone: (713) 785-9600

#139
Lone Star Defense & Arms
Category: Guns, Ammo
Average price: Inexpensive
Area: Spring Branch
Address: 1657 Blalock
Houston, TX 77080
Phone: (713) 465-1820

#140
Marshalls
Category: Department Store
Average price: Modest
Area: Memorial
Address: 9425 Katy Fwy
Houston, TX 77024
Phone: (713) 647-7501

#141
Marq-E Entertainment Center
Category: Shopping Center, American
Average price: Modest
Area: Spring Branch
Address: 7620 Katy Fwy
Houston, TX 77024
Phone: (713) 681-9601

#142
Emerson Rose
Category: Women's Clothing
Average price: Expensive
Area: The Heights
Address: 350 W 19th St
Houston, TX 77008
Phone: (832) 538-1487

#143
The Lego Store
Category: Toy Store
Average price: Modest
Area: Galleria, Uptown
Address: 5015 Westheimer Rd
Houston, TX 77056
Phone: (713) 439-0773

#144
Fuller's Vintage Guitar
Category: Musical Instruments
Average price: Expensive
Area: The Heights
Address: 116 North Loop
Houston, TX 77008
Phone: (713) 880-2188

#145
Williams Sonoma
Category: Kitchen & Bath, Food
Average price: Expensive
Area: Highland Village
Address: 4060 Westheimer Rd
Houston, TX 77027
Phone: (713) 212-0346

#146
Hemline
Category: Women's Clothing, Accessories
Average price: Expensive
Area: West University
Address: 2555 Amherst St
Houston, TX 77005
Phone: (713) 520-1184

#147
Houston Center
Category: Shopping Center
Average price: Modest
Area: Downtown
Address: 909 Fannin
Houston, TX 77002
Phone: (713) 654-1911

#148
Asgard Games
Category: Arcade, Hobby Shop, Toy Store
Average price: Modest
Area: Upper Kirby
Address: 3302 Shepherd Dr
Houston, TX 77098
Phone: (713) 677-0699

#149
Lush Cosmetics
Category: Cosmetics, Beauty Supply, Skin Care
Average price: Expensive
Area: Memorial
Address: 303 Memorial City
Houston, TX 77024
Phone: (713) 467-5876

#150
High Gloss
Category: Jewelry, Accessories
Average price: Expensive
Area: Galleria, Uptown
Address: 1131-06 Uptown Park Blvd
Houston, TX 77056
Phone: (713) 961-7868

#151
Heiress Boutique
Category: Women's Clothing, Accessories
Average price: Modest
Area: Montrose
Address: 1806 Westheimer Rd
Houston, TX 77098
Phone: (713) 526-1110

#152
Fly High Little Bunny
Category: Jewelry
Average price: Expensive
Area: Upper Kirby, Montrose
Address: 3120 S Shepherd Dr
Houston, TX 77098
Phone: (713) 520-9995

#153
Bed Bath & Beyond
Category: Kitchen & Bath
Average price: Modest
Area: Meyerland
Address: 4700 Beechnut St
Houston, TX 77096
Phone: (713) 666-9926

#154
Flowers Etc By Georgia
Category: Florist
Average price: Modest
Area: Montrose
Address: 1818 Waugh Dr
Houston, TX 77006
Phone: (713) 524-3989

#155
American Apparel
Category: Women's Clothing, Men's Clothing, Accessories
Average price: Modest
Area: Montrose
Address: 1665 Westheimer Rd
Houston, TX 77006
Phone: (713) 521-7171

#156
Buffalo Exchange
Category: Vintage, Men's Clothing, Women's Clothing
Average price: Modest
Area: Montrose
Address: 1618 Westheimer Rd
Houston, TX 77006
Phone: (713) 523-8701

#157
Salvation Army
Category: Thrift Store
Average price: Inexpensive
Area: Sixth Ward
Address: 2208 Washington Ave
Houston, TX 77007
Phone: (713) 425-8727

#158
A Bientot
Category: Women's Clothing, Jewelry, Cards, Stationery
Average price: Expensive
Area: River Oaks
Address: 2501 River Oaks Blvd
Houston, TX 77098
Phone: (713) 523-3997

#159
1/4 Price Books
Category: Bookstore
Average price: Modest
Area: Upper Kirby
Address: 3820 S Shepherd Dr
Houston, TX 77098
Phone: (713) 520-5009

#160
Rice University Art Gallery
Category: Museum, Art Gallery
Average price: Modest
Area: West University
Address: 6100 Main St
Houston, TX 77005
Phone: (713) 348-6069

#161
Uptown Pharmacy
Category: Drugstore
Average price: Modest
Area: Galleria, Uptown
Address: 1607 South Post Oak Lane
Houston, TX 77056
Phone: (713) 621-0621

#162
Urban Leather
Category: Leather Goods, Furniture Store
Average price: Expensive
Area: Upper Kirby
Address: 3311 Richmond Ave
Houston, TX 77098
Phone: (832) 967-0720

#163
Museum Shop at the Contemporary Arts Museum Houston
Category: Arts, Crafts
Average price: Modest
Area: Museum District
Address: 5216 Montrose Blvd
Houston, TX 77006
Phone: (713) 284-8250

#164
Museum of Fine Arts Houston
Category: Museum, Art Gallery
Average price: Inexpensive
Area: Museum District
Address: 1001 Bissonnet St
Houston, TX 77005
Phone: (713) 639-7300

#165
Today's Vision
Category: Eyewear, Opticians, Optometrists
Average price: Modest
Area: Memorial, Galleria, Uptown
Address: 5771 San Felipe
Houston, TX 77057
Phone: (713) 782-3937

#166
Lululemon Athletica
Category: Sports Wear, Women's Clothing, Yoga
Average price: Expensive
Area: Memorial
Address: 800 Town & Country Rd
Houston, TX 77024
Phone: (713) 464-1257

#167
Houston Car Stereo
Category: Electronics
Average price: Modest
Area: Gulfton
Address: 5621 Hillcroft St
Houston, TX 77036
Phone: (713) 266-6225

#168
Blue Bird Circle
Category: Vintage, Thrift Store
Average price: Modest
Area: Fourth Ward, Montrose
Address: 615 W Alabama St
Houston, TX 77006
Phone: (713) 528-0470

#169
Spring Street Studios
Category: Venues, Event Space, Art Gallery
Average price: Modest
Area: Sixth Ward
Address: 1824 Spring St
Houston, TX 77007
Phone: (713) 862-0082

#170
Forever Vapes
Category: Vape Shop
Average price: Modest
Area: The Heights
Address: 3620 Katy Fwy
Houston, TX 77007
Phone: (832) 491-1131

#171
Walmart
Category: Department Store
Average price: Inexpensive
Area: Spring Branch
Address: 7960 Longpoint Rd
Houston, TX 77055
Phone: (713) 463-6922

#172
Spa Nordstrom
Category: Massage, Skin Care, Tanning, Nail Salon, Cosmetics, Beauty Supply, Day Spa
Average price: Expensive
Area: Galleria, Uptown
Address: 5192 Hidalgo St
Houston, TX 77056
Phone: (832) 201-2750

#173
Rice Village Diamonds
Category: Jewelry, Bridal
Average price: Expensive
Area: West University
Address: 2376 Rice Blvd
Houston, TX 77005
Phone: (713) 526-1510

#174
Macy's
Category: Department Store, Men's Clothing, Women's Clothing
Average price: Modest
Area: Memorial
Address: 900 Memorial City Mall
Houston, TX 77024
Phone: (713) 461-0400

#175
Sur La Table
Category: Cooking School, Kitchen & Bath
Average price: Modest
Area: River Oaks, Montrose
Address: 1996 W Gray St
Houston, TX 77019
Phone: (713) 533-0400

#176
Pleasure Zone
Category: Swimwear, Lingerie, Costumes
Average price: Modest
Area: Gulfton, Galleria, Uptown
Address: 5705 Richmond Ave
Houston, TX 77057
Phone: (832) 251-8400

#177
Vision Source
Category: Eyewear, Opticians, Optometrists,
Average price: Modest
Area: Meyerland
Address: 9959 S Post Oak Rd
Houston, TX 77096
Phone: (713) 721-7717

#178
Erica DelGardo Jewelry Designs
Category: Jewelry
Average price: Modest
Area: The Heights
Address: 327 W 19th St
Houston, TX 77008
Phone: (713) 802-1977

#179
Last Call by Neiman Marcus
Category: Men's Clothing, Women's Clothing
Average price: Modest
Area: Galleria, Uptown
Address: 2315 Post Oak Blvd
Houston, TX 77056
Phone: (713) 993-0929

#180
Banana Republic
Category: Women's Clothing
Average price: Modest
Area: Highland Village
Address: 3920 Westheimer Rd
Houston, TX 77027
Phone: (713) 963-0320

#181
Le Creuset
Category: Kitchen & Bath
Average price: Expensive
Area: West University
Address: 5515 Kelvin Dr
Houston, TX 77005
Phone: (713) 521-4466

#182
Corazón
Category: Arts, Crafts
Average price: Expensive
Area: Montrose
Address: 2318 Waugh Dr
Houston, TX 77006
Phone: (713) 526-6591

#183
Eclectic Home
Category: Furniture Store, Home Decor
Average price: Expensive
Area: The Heights
Address: 345 W 19th St
Houston, TX 77008
Phone: (713) 869-1414

#184
Old Blue House Antiques
Category: Antiques, Jewelry
Average price: Modest
Area: Montrose
Address: 1719 Westheimer Rd
Houston, TX 77098
Phone: (832) 545-4644

#185
Zara
Category: Women's Clothing, Men's Clothing
Average price: Modest
Area: Galleria, Uptown
Address: 5085 Westheimer Rd
Houston, TX 77056
Phone: (713) 439-0995

#186
Cindie's
Category: Adult, Lingerie
Average price: Modest
Area: Montrose
Address: 3507 S Shepherd Dr
Houston, TX 77098
Phone: (713) 522-9339

#187
Target
Category: Department Store
Average price: Modest
Area: Westchase
Address: 10801 Westheimer Rd
Houston, TX 77042
Phone: (713) 782-9950

#188
Blue Leaf
Category: Furniture Store
Average price: Exclusive
Area: West University
Address: 2303 South Blvd
Houston, TX 77098
Phone: (713) 520-9975

#189
Value Village
Category: Vintage, Thrift Store, Department Store
Average price: Inexpensive
Area: Gulfton
Address: 6202 Bissonnet Street
Houston, TX 77081
Phone: (713) 685-5406

#190
Z Gallerie
Category: Home Decor, Furniture Store
Average price: Modest
Area: Highland Village
Address: 3920 Westheimer Rd
Houston, TX 77027
Phone: (713) 622-2952

#191
Jonathan Adler
Category: Home Decor, Furniture Store, Kitchen & Bath
Average price: Expensive
Area: Upper Kirby
Address: 2800 Kirby Dr
Houston, TX 77098
Phone: (713) 677-0792

#192
Target
Category: Department Store
Average price: Modest
Area: Meyerland
Address: 300 Meyerland Plaza Mall
Houston, TX 77096
Phone: (713) 292-0030

#193
Saks Fifth Avenue
Category: Department Store
Average price: Exclusive
Area: Galleria, Uptown
Address: 5115 Westheimer Rd
Houston, TX 77056
Phone: (713) 627-0500

#194
Express
Category: Accessories, Women's Clothing
Average price: Modest
Area: West University
Address: 2414 University Blvd
Houston, TX 77005
Phone: (713) 520-0669

#195
Festari For Men
Category: Men's Clothing, Bespoke Clothing
Average price: Modest
Area: Galleria, Uptown
Address: 1800 Post Oak Blvd
Houston, TX 77056
Phone: (713) 626-1234

#196
Kate Spade Saturday
Category: Women's Clothing, Accessories
Average price: Modest
Area: West University
Address: 2513 University Blvd
Houston, TX 77030
Phone: (713) 807-7396

#197
T-Mobile
Category: Electronics, Mobile Phones
Average price: Expensive
Area: Spring Branch
Address: 7670 Katy Fwy
Houston, TX 77024
Phone: (713) 686-8605

#198
Perfect Vision Eyecare & Eyewear
Category: Optometrists, Eyewear, Opticians
Average price: Modest
Area: Upper Kirby
Address: 2518 Richmond Ave
Houston, TX 77098
Phone: (713) 522-2522

#199
Express
Category: Women's Clothing, Accessories
Average price: Expensive
Area: Galleria, Uptown
Address: 5085 Westheimer Rd
Houston, TX 77056
Phone: (713) 629-7088

#200
Casa de Novia Bridal Couture
Category: Bridal
Average price: Expensive
Area: River Oaks, Montrose
Address: 2040 W Gray St, Ste 120
Houston, TX 77019
Phone: (713) 523-9090

#201
Nick Lopez Tailoring
Category: Sewing, Alterations, Bespoke Clothing
Average price: Exclusive
Area: Galleria, Uptown
Address: 2680 Sage Rd
Houston, TX 77056
Phone: (713) 621-5411

#202
Michaels
Category: Arts, Crafts, Knitting Supplies, Hobby Shop
Average price: Modest
Area: West University
Address: 3904 Bissonnet St
Houston, TX 77005
Phone: (713) 662-0913

#203
Affection Boutique
Category: Women's Clothing
Average price: Modest
Area: The Heights
Address: 2811 Washington Ave
Houston, TX 77007
Phone: (713) 370-9785

#204
Big Lots
Category: Department Store
Average price: Inexpensive
Area: The Heights
Address: 919 N Shepherd Dr
Houston, TX 77008
Phone: (713) 869-5544

#205
August Antiques
Category: Antiques
Average price: Modest
Area: The Heights
Address: 803 Heights Blvd
Houston, TX 77007
Phone: (713) 880-3353

#206
Fantasy Gifts
Category: Tobacco Shop, Gift Shop
Average price: Modest
Area: Montrose
Address: 1340 Westheimer Rd
Houston, TX 77006
Phone: (713) 526-9522

#207
The Ultimate Dressing Room
Category: Women's Clothing, Accessories
Average price: Inexpensive
Area: Braeswood Place
Address: 3280 S Loop W
Houston, TX 77025
Phone: (281) 300-7577

#208
Best Buy
Category: Computers, Appliances, Electronics
Average price: Modest
Area: Fairbanks, Northwest Crossing
Address: 13238 Northwest Fwy
Houston, TX 77040
Phone: (713) 939-8590

#209
Leopard Lounge
Category: Fashion
Average price: Modest
Area: Montrose
Address: 1657 Westheimer Rd
Houston, TX 77006
Phone: (713) 526-5100

#210
Jewelry Judge Ben Gordon
Category: Jewelry
Average price: Modest
Area: Galleria, Uptown
Address: 5433 Westheimer Rd
Houston, TX 77056
Phone: (713) 961-1432

#211
Tanglewood Flower & Garden
Category: Florist
Average price: Modest
Area: Galleria, Uptown
Address: 5550 Val Verde St
Houston, TX 77056
Phone: (713) 572-1226

#212
Orchid Express & Leasing
Category: Nursery, Gardening, Florist
Average price: Modest
Area: The Heights
Address: 111 Heights Blvd
Houston, TX 77007
Phone: (713) 526-0018

#213
Bed Bath & Beyond
Category: Home Decor, Kitchen & Bath
Average price: Modest
Area: Upper Kirby
Address: 3102 Kirby Dr
Houston, TX 77098
Phone: (713) 533-0946

#214
Crescendo Family Music Classes
Category: Performing Arts, Musical Instruments
Average price: Inexpensive
Area: The Heights
Address: 508 Pecore St
Houston, TX 77009
Phone: (832) 454-2376

#215
Guitar Lessons With Nick Rawson
Category: Musical Instruments
Average price: Inexpensive
Area: Montrose
Address: 1531 Marshall St
Houston, TX 77006
Phone: (713) 857-3039

#216
Randalls Food & Pharmacy
Category: Drugstore
Average price: Modest
Area: Fourth Ward, Midtown
Address: 2225 Louisiana St
Houston, TX 77002
Phone: (713) 331-1053

#217
My Looks by Rosie Daza
Category: Cosmetics, Beauty Supply, Makeup Artists
Average price: Modest
Area: Upper Kirby, River Oaks
Address: 2147 Westheimer
Houston, TX 77098
Phone: (713) 855-2566

#218
Chappell Jordan Clock Gallery
Category: Antiques, Home Decor
Average price: Exclusive
Area: River Oaks
Address: 2222 Westheimer Rd
Houston, TX 77098
Phone: (713) 523-0133

#219
Ace Mart Restaurant Supply
Category: Kitchen & Bath, Appliances
Average price: Modest
Area: Gulfton
Address: 5811 Chimney Rock Rd
Houston, TX 77081
Phone: (713) 662-0600

#220
Texas Star Grill Shop
Category: Appliances
Average price: Modest
Area: Museum District, West University
Address: 2045 SW Fwy
Houston, TX 77098
Phone: (832) 426-4229

#221
Briargrove Eye Center
Category: Optometrists, Eyewear, Opticians, Medical Supplies
Average price: Modest
Area: Galleria, Uptown
Address: 5874 Westheimer Rd
Houston, TX 77057
Phone: (713) 974-2020

#222
The Vapor Gypsy
Category: Vape Shop
Average price: Modest
Area: The Heights
Address: 2121 N Shepherd Dr
Houston, TX 77008
Phone: (713) 862-8273

#223
BALANI Custom Clothiers
Category: Men's Clothing
Average price: Expensive
Area: Greenway
Address: 3200 SW Fwy
Houston, TX 77027
Phone: (713) 253-9537

#224
Write Now!
Category: Cards, Stationery
Average price: Modest
Area: The Heights
Address: 3122 White Oak Dr
Houston, TX 77007
Phone: (281) 974-2138

#225
Gamestop
Category: Videos, Video Game
Average price: Modest
Area: West University
Address: 5312 Weslayan St
Houston, TX 77005
Phone: (832) 778-9666

#226
Tri Health Inc.
Category: Grocery, Health Market, Drugstore
Average price: Modest
Area: South Belt, Ellington
Address: 11025 Fuqua St
Houston, TX 77089
Phone: (713) 947-7373

#227
Christmas Rocks!
Category: Home Decor
Average price: Modest
Area: Upper Kirby
Address: 2931 Ferndale St
Houston, TX 77098
Phone: (866) 920-8226

#228
Roop Sari Palace
Category: Fabric Store, Women's Clothing, Bridal
Average price: Modest
Area: Gulfton
Address: 6655 Harwin Dr
Houston, TX 77036
Phone: (713) 278-7667

#229
Uptown Diamond
Category: Bridal, Jewelry
Average price: Expensive
Area: Galleria, Uptown
Address: 5151 San Felipe St
Houston, TX 77056
Phone: (713) 360-7922

#230
Lik Houston
Peter Lik Fine Art Gallery
Category: Art Gallery
Average price: Exclusive
Area: Galleria, Uptown
Address: 5015 Westheimer Rd
Houston, TX 77056
Phone: (713) 965-0190

#231
River Oaks Shopping Center
Category: Shopping Center
Average price: Modest
Area: River Oaks, Montrose
Address: 1964 W Gray St
Houston, TX 77019
Phone: (713) 528-4191

#232
Bike Barn
Category: Bikes, Bike Rentals
Average price: Expensive
Area: West University
Address: 5339 Weslayan St
Houston, TX 77005
Phone: (713) 529-9002

#233
Academy Sports & Outdoors
Category: Sporting Goods
Average price: Modest
Area: Upper Kirby
Address: 2404 Southwest Fwy
Houston, TX 77098
Phone: (713) 520-1795

#234
Well Done Cooking Classes
Category: Cooking School, Cooking Classes
Average price: Expensive
Area: The Heights
Address: 1208 E 29th St
Houston, TX 77009
Phone: (832) 782-3518

#235
Dubins' Fine Jewelry
Category: Jewelry
Average price: Modest
Area: Galleria, Uptown
Address: 5444 Westheimer Rd Suite 1428
Houston, TX 77056
Phone: (713) 840-0162

#236
The Bloom Room
Category: Florist
Average price: Modest
Area: South Main
Address: 8981 Interchange Dr
Houston, TX 77054
Phone: (281) 501-0768

#237
AT&T
Category: Mobile Phones
Average price: Modest
Area: West University
Address: 6027 Kirby Drive
Houston, TX 77005
Phone: (713) 526-4716

#238
Chic Warehouse
Category: Furniture Store, Home Decor, Mattresses
Average price: Modest
Area: The Heights
Address: 731 Yale St
Houston, TX 77007
Phone: (713) 822-3392

#239
Arne's Warehouse & Party Store
Category: Party Supplies, Costumes, Pet Store
Average price: Inexpensive
Area: The Heights
Address: 2830 Hicks St
Houston, TX 77007
Phone: (713) 869-8321

#240
Walgreens
Category: Drugstore, Cosmetics, Beauty Supply, Convenience Store
Average price: Inexpensive
Area: Fourth Ward, Montrose
Address: 3317 Montrose Blvd
Houston, TX 77006
Phone: (713) 520-7777

#241
Valentine Florist
Category: Florist
Average price: Modest
Area: Gulfton, Galleria, Uptown
Address: 6009 Richmond Ave
Houston, TX 77057
Phone: (713) 977-6979

#242
Soundwaves
Category: Music, DVDs, Outdoor Gear
Average price: Modest
Area: Fourth Ward, Montrose
Address: 3509 Montrose Blvd
Houston, TX 77006
Phone: (713) 520-9283

#243
Signature Eye Care at The Galleria
Category: Optometrists, Eyewear, Opticians
Average price: Modest
Area: Galleria, Uptown
Address: 5085 Westheimer Rd
Houston, TX 77056
Phone: (713) 629-1010

#244
Uptown Park
Category: Shopping Center
Average price: Exclusive
Area: Galleria, Uptown
Address: 1400 Post Oak Blvd
Houston, TX 77056
Phone: (713) 840-8474

#245
Kohl's Department Stores
Category: Cosmetics, Beauty Supply, Sports Wear, Baby Gear, Furniture
Average price: Modest
Area: Willow Meadows, Willowbend, Meyerland
Address: 4730 W Bellfort St
Houston, TX 77035
Phone: (713) 729-9118

#246
Luke's Locker
Category: Sports Wear, Shoe Store
Average price: Expensive
Area: River Oaks, Montrose
Address: 1953 W Gray St
Houston, TX 77019
Phone: (713) 529-0786

#247
Pottery Barn
Category: Furniture Store
Average price: Expensive
Area: Highland Village
Address: 4011 Westheimer Rd
Houston, TX 77027
Phone: (713) 627-8901

#248
Family Thrift Center
Category: Thrift Store
Average price: Inexpensive
Area: The Heights
Address: 920 N Durham Dr
Houston, TX 77008
Phone: (713) 868-4261

#249
Everything But Water
Category: Swimwear, Women's Clothing
Average price: Expensive
Area: Memorial
Address: 780 W Sam Houston Pkwy N
Houston, TX 77024
Phone: (713) 461-2672

#250
River Oaks Bookstore
Category: Bookstore
Average price: Modest
Area: River Oaks
Address: 3270 Westheimer Rd
Houston, TX 77098
Phone: (713) 520-0061

#251
Tootsies
Category: Women's Clothing, Accessories
Average price: Exclusive
Area: Upper Kirby
Address: 2601 Westheimer Rd.
Houston, TX 77098
Phone: (713) 629-9990

#252
Plants N Petals
Category: Florist
Average price: Expensive
Area: Highland Village
Address: 3810 Westheimer Rd
Houston, TX 77027
Phone: (713) 840-9191

#253
Tres' Bloom Floral Studio
Category: Florist, Event Planning
Average price: Modest
Area: Galleria, Uptown
Address: 6013 San Felipe St
Houston, TX 77057
Phone: (713) 952-3080

#254
Gen's Antiques
Category: Antiques
Average price: Modest
Area: The Heights
Address: 540 W 19th St
Houston, TX 77008
Phone: (713) 868-2368

#255
Aaron Brothers Art & Framing
Category: Art Supplies, Art Gallery
Average price: Modest
Area: Gulfton, Galleria, Uptown
Address: 5144 Richmond Ave
Houston, TX 77056
Phone: (713) 961-4882

#256
CVS/Pharmacy
Category: Drugstore
Average price: Inexpensive
Area: Medical Center
Address: 9838 Buffalo Speedway
Houston, TX 77025
Phone: (713) 218-4490

#257
Sam's Club
Category: Grocery, Department Store
Average price: Inexpensive
Area: Medical Center
Address: 1615 S Lp W
Houston, TX 77054
Phone: (713) 796-8599

#258
INTIMACY - Bra Fit Stylists
Category: Lingerie
Average price: Expensive
Area: Galleria, Uptown
Address: 5085 Westheimer Rd, Ste 2514
Houston, TX 77056
Phone: (832) 397-6960

#259
Burlington Coat Factory
Category: Department Store
Average price: Inexpensive
Area: Langwood
Address: 12005 NW Fwy
Houston, TX 77092
Phone: (713) 476-9500

#260
New For The Night
Category: Women's Clothing
Average price: Modest
Area: Upper Kirby
Address: 3209 Westheimer Rd
Houston, TX 77098
Phone: (713) 526-1166

#261
Athleta
Category: Sports Wear, Women's Clothing
Average price: Modest
Area: West University
Address: 2512 University Blvd
Houston, TX 77005
Phone: (713) 942-2190

#262
Gap
Category: Women's Clothing,
Men's Clothing, Children's Clothing
Average price: Modest
Area: Memorial
Address: 12850 Memorial Drive
Houston, TX 77024
Phone: (713) 932-0600

#263
Ross Dress for Less
Category: Department Store
Average price: Inexpensive
Area: Medical Center
Address: 8200 Kirby Dr
Houston, TX 77054
Phone: (832) 778-7600

#264
Aurora Studios
Category: Art Gallery
Average price: Inexpensive
Area: The Heights
Address: 129 Aurora St
Houston, TX 77008
Phone: (713) 894-4480

#265
Victoria's Secret Stores
Category: Lingerie
Average price: Modest
Area: Highland Village
Address: 3942 Westheimer Rd
Houston, TX 77027
Phone: (713) 960-0626

#266
Ross Dress for Less
Category: Department Store
Average price: Modest
Area: The Heights
Address: 1411 W 11th St
Houston, TX 77008
Phone: (713) 869-4388

#267
Loehmann's
Category: Women's Clothing, Accessories
Average price: Modest
Area: Memorial
Address: 9347 Katy Fwy
Houston, TX 77024
Phone: (713) 932-8011

#268
Sears Outlet
Category: Appliances & Repair, Appliances, Outlet Store
Average price: Modest
Area: Gulfgate, Pine Valley
Address: 5901 Griggs Rd
Houston, TX 77023
Phone: (713) 644-9351

#269
Brighton
Category: Jewelry
Average price: Expensive
Area: Highland Village
Address: 3968 Westheimer Rd
Houston, TX 77027
Phone: (713) 877-8551

#270
Bayou City Art Festival Memorial Park
Category: Performing Arts, Art Gallery
Average price: Modest
Area: River Oaks
Address: S Picnic Ln and Memorial Dr
Houston, TX 77007
Phone: (713) 521-0133

#271
Urban Soles Outpost
Category: Shoe Store
Average price: Modest
Area: The Heights
Address: 506 W 19th St
Houston, TX 77008
Phone: (713) 880-1187

#272
Today's Vision
Category: Optometrists, Eyewear, Opticians
Average price: Modest
Area: The Heights
Address: 1909 Taylor St
Houston, TX 77007
Phone: (713) 862-3937

#273
Lucy Activewear
Category: Sports Wear, Accessories, Women's Clothing
Average price: Expensive
Area: Highland Village
Address: 4052 Westheimer Rd.
Houston, TX 77027
Phone: (713) 877-0196

#274
Rienzi
Category: Museum, Art Gallery
Average price: Inexpensive
Area: River Oaks
Address: 1406 Kirby Dr
Houston, TX 77019
Phone: (713) 639-7800

#275
David Yurman
Category: Jewelry
Average price: Exclusive
Area: Galleria, Uptown
Address: 5085 Westheimer Road
Houston, TX 77056
Phone: (713) 622-5799

#276
ChefMarket
Category: Kitchen & Bath
Average price: Inexpensive
Area: West University
Address: 2542 Amherst St
Houston, TX 77005
Phone: (713) 522-2877

#277
Tiffany & Co.
Category: Jewelry
Average price: Exclusive
Area: Galleria, Uptown
Address: 5015 Westheimer Rd
Houston, TX 77056
Phone: (713) 626-0220

#278
Alabama Furniture & Accessories
Category: Furniture Store, Used, Vintage
Average price: Modest
Area: The Heights
Address: 2200 Yale St
Houston, TX 77008
Phone: (713) 862-3035

#279
Planetary Cycles
Category: Bikes
Average price: Modest
Area: Meyerland
Address: 8715-B West Loop S
Houston, TX 77096
Phone: (713) 668-2300

#280
Michael Kors
Category: Shoe Store, Leather Goods
Average price: Expensive
Area: Galleria, Uptown
Address: 5015 Westheimer Rd
Houston, TX 77056
Phone: (713) 629-7200

#281
King Dollar
Category: Department Store
Average price: Inexpensive
Area: The Heights
Address: 1511 W 18th St
Houston, TX 77008
Phone: (713) 869-9119

#282
JoS. A. Bank Clothiers
Category: Men's Clothing
Average price: Modest
Area: River Oaks, Montrose
Address: 2030 W Gray St
Houston, TX 77019
Phone: (713) 523-7077

#283
Paper Source
Category: Cards, Stationery
Average price: Modest
Area: Memorial
Address: 795 Town and Country Blvd
Houston, TX 77024
Phone: (713) 984-8619

#284
Another Place In Time
Category: Nursery, Gardening
Average price: Modest
Area: The Heights
Address: 421 W 11th St
Houston, TX 77008
Phone: (713) 864-9717

#285
Baby's 1st Furniture
Category: Baby Gear, Furniture
Average price: Expensive
Area: Gulfton, Galleria, Uptown
Address: 5575 Richmond Ave
Houston, TX 77056
Phone: (713) 785-8511

#286
Architects of Air
Category: Art Gallery
Average price: Modest
Area: Downtown
Address: 1500 McKinney
Houston, TX 77010
Phone: (713) 400-7336

#287
Urban Outfitters
Category: Fashion
Average price: Modest
Area: Memorial
Address: City Centre
Houston, TX 77024
Phone: (713) 467-1840

#288
Kate Spade
Category: Jewelry, Accessories
Average price: Expensive
Area: Highland Village
Address: 2701 Drexel Dr
Houston, TX 77027
Phone: (713) 961-9684

#289
Walgreens
Category: Drugstore, Cosmetics, Beauty Supply, Convenience Store
Average price: Modest
Area: Braeswood Place, West University
Address: 2605 W Holcombe Blvd
Houston, TX 77025
Phone: (832) 778-8106

#290
Restoration Hardware
Category: Furniture Store
Average price: Exclusive
Area: Highland Village
Address: 4030 Westheimer Rd
Houston, TX 77027
Phone: (713) 328-3100

#291
Costco
Category: Office Equipment, Electronics
Average price: Modest
Area: Memorial
Address: 1150 Bunker Hill Rd
Houston, TX 77055
Phone: (713) 576-2050

#292
Pier 1 Imports
Category: Furniture Store, Rugs
Average price: Modest
Area: River Oaks, Montrose
Address: 1927 W Gray St
Houston, TX 77019
Phone: (713) 524-1576

#293
The Menil Collection Bookstore
Category: Bookstore
Average price: Expensive
Area: Montrose
Address: 1520 Sul Ross St
Houston, TX 77006
Phone: (713) 535-3810

#294
The Children's Place
Category: Children's Clothing
Average price: Modest
Area: The Heights
Address: 1911 Taylor St
Houston, TX 77007
Phone: (713) 868-4462

#295
Kendra Scott Jewelry
Category: Jewelry
Average price: Expensive
Area: West University
Address: 2411 Times Blvd
Houston, TX 77005
Phone: (713) 965-4056

#296
Antiquarium Antique Print & Map Gallery
Category: Antiques, Art Gallery
Average price: Exclusive
Area: Upper Kirby
Address: 3021 Kirby Dr
Houston, TX 77098
Phone: (713) 622-7531

#297
Betz Gallery
Category: Art Gallery
Average price: Exclusive
Area: The Heights
Address: 2500 Summer St
Houston, TX 77007
Phone: (713) 576-6954

#298
T-Mobile
Category: Mobile Phones
Average price: Modest
Area: River Oaks, Montrose
Address: 1907 W Gray St
Houston, TX 77019
Phone: (713) 523-9131

#299
Revolution E - Electric Bike Store
Category: Bike Rentals, Bikes, Tours
Average price: Expensive
Area: Montrose
Address: 1544 Westheimer Rd
Houston, TX 77006
Phone: (713) 523-2453

#300
Moshi Moshi Gifts
Category: Toy Store, Gift Shop
Average price: Inexpensive
Area: Sharpstown, Chinatown
Address: 9108 Bellaire Blvd
Houston, TX 77036
Phone: (713) 389-8888

#301
Aker Imaging
Category: Photography Store, Services
Average price: Modest
Area: The Heights, Rice Military
Address: 4710 Lillian St
Houston, TX 77007
Phone: (713) 862-8640

#302
Houston Gold Merchants
Category: Jewelry, Pawn Shop
Average price: Modest
Area: Montrose
Address: 2011 S Shepherd Dr
Houston, TX 77019
Phone: (832) 259-7225

#303
Chippendale Eastlake Antiques
Category: Antiques
Average price: Modest
Area: The Heights
Address: 250 W 19th St
Houston, TX 77008
Phone: (713) 869-8633

#304
Unique Optical
Category: Eyewear, Opticians
Average price: Expensive
Area: West University
Address: 2431 Bissonnet St
Houston, TX 77005
Phone: (713) 522-2007

#305
Village Frame Gallery
Category: Framing
Average price: Expensive
Area: West University
Address: 2708 Bissonnet St
Houston, TX 77005
Phone: (713) 528-2288

#306
Kid To Kid Houston Galleria
Category: Toy Store, Baby Gear, Furniture, Children's Clothing
Average price: Modest
Area: Galleria, Uptown
Address: 1737 Post Oak Blvd
Houston, TX 77056
Phone: (713) 622-2545

#307
Cotton Club
Category: Women's Clothing
Average price: Modest
Area: Highland Village
Address: 3941 San Felipe St
Houston, TX 77027
Phone: (713) 465-9101

#308
Marshalls
Category: Department Store
Average price: Modest
Area: Galleria, Uptown
Address: 5000 Westheimer Rd
Houston, TX 77056
Phone: (713) 626-1334

#309
The Home Depot
Category: Nursery, Gardening, Appliances, Hardware Store
Average price: Modest
Area: Pecan Park, Gulfgate, Pine Valley
Address: 6810 Gulf Freeway
Houston, TX 77087
Phone: (713) 649-1108

#310
Plato's Closet
Category: Women's Clothing, Used, Vintage
Average price: Inexpensive
Area: Spring Branch
Address: 10516 Katy Fwy
Houston, TX 77043
Phone: (713) 464-5555

#311
Village Girls Boutique
Category: Women's Clothing
Average price: Modest
Area: West University
Address: 2509 Rice Blvd
Houston, TX 77072
Phone: (832) 368-0240

#312
Abejas Boutique
Category: Women's Clothing
Average price: Expensive
Area: West University
Address: 5600 Kirby Dr
Houston, TX 77005
Phone: (713) 522-3025

#313
Neiman Marcus
Category: Women's Clothing, Accessories, Leather Goods
Average price: Exclusive
Area: Galleria, Uptown
Address: 2600 Post Oak Blvd
Houston, TX 77056
Phone: (713) 621-7100

#314
C And D Hardware
Category: Nursery, Gardening, Hardware Store
Average price: Modest
Area: The Heights
Address: 314 E 11th St
Houston, TX 77008
Phone: (713) 861-3551

#315
Ben's Beans
Category: Coffee, Tea, Art Gallery
Average price: Inexpensive
Area: Downtown
Address: 1302 Dallas St
Houston, TX 77002
Phone: (713) 654-8856

#316
Surroundings
Category: Home Decor, Furniture Store
Average price: Expensive
Area: West University
Address: 1708 Sunset Blvd
Houston, TX 77005
Phone: (713) 527-9838

#317
Pepper Palace
Category: Herbs & Spices, Shopping Center
Average price: Modest
Area: Galleria, Uptown
Address: 5085 Westheimer Rd
Houston, TX 77056
Phone: (865) 429-4277

#318
Sig's Lagoon
Category: Vinyl Records
Average price: Modest
Area: Fourth Ward, Midtown
Address: 3622 Main St
Houston, TX 77002
Phone: (713) 533-9525

#319
Half Price Books
Category: Books, Mags, Music, Video
Average price: Inexpensive
Area: West University
Address: 2537 University Blvd.
Houston, TX 77005
Phone: (713) 524-6635

#320
Brown Book Shop
Category: Bookstore
Average price: Expensive
Area: Downtown
Address: 1517 San Jacinto St
Houston, TX 77002
Phone: (713) 652-3937

#321
Houston Junior Forum
Category: Used, Vintage
Average price: Modest
Area: The Heights
Address: 1815 Rutland St
Houston, TX 77008
Phone: (713) 868-6970

#322
Nadeau Furniture with a Soul
Category: Furniture Store, Home Decor
Average price: Modest
Area: The Heights
Address: 1502 Durham Dr
Houston, TX 77007
Phone: (713) 942-9310

#323
Academy Sports + Outdoors
Category: Sports Wear, Outdoor Gear
Average price: Modest
Area: Memorial
Address: 9734 Katy Fwy
Houston, TX 77055
Phone: (713) 827-6520

#324
Serenity Knives
Category: Kitchen & Bath
Average price: Modest
Area: The Heights
Address: 410 Harvard St
Houston, TX 77007
Phone: (832) 860-4754

#325
Bath & Body Works
Category: Cosmetics, Beauty Supply
Average price: Modest
Area: West University
Address: 2414 University Blvd
Houston, TX 77005
Phone: (713) 520-7370

#326
The Mad Potter
Category: Arts, Crafts
Average price: Modest
Area: Meyerland
Address: 4882 Beechnut St
Houston, TX 77096
Phone: (713) 664-8808

#327
Archway Gallery
Category: Art Gallery
Average price: Modest
Area: Montrose
Address: 2305 Dunlavy
Houston, TX 77006
Phone: (713) 522-2409

#328
Sur La Table
Category: Home & Garden, Do-It-Yourself Food
Average price: Expensive
Area: Memorial
Address: 803 Town & Country Blvd, Ste 123 Houston, TX 77024
Phone: (832) 201-3492

#329
West U Cycles
Category: Bikes
Average price: Modest
Area: West University
Address: 2519 Rice Blvd
Houston, TX 77005
Phone: (713) 529-0140

#330
Banana Republic Galleria
Category: Accessories, Men's Clothing, Women's Clothing
Average price: Expensive
Area: Galleria, Uptown
Address: 5135 W Alabama St
Houston, TX 77056
Phone: (713) 621-4451

#331
True Beauty Salon Spa Store
Category: Cosmetics, Beauty Supply, Hair Salon, Day Spa
Average price: Modest
Area: West University
Address: 2421 Rice Blvd
Houston, TX 77005
Phone: (713) 526-2553

#332
Wig World
Category: Cosmetics, Beauty Supply
Average price: Expensive
Area: Medical Center
Address: 8222 Kirby Dr
Houston, TX 77054
Phone: (713) 668-5558

#333
Briargrove Pharmacy & Gifts
Category: Drugstore, Cosmetics, Beauty Supply, Toy Store
Average price: Modest
Area: Memorial
Address: 6435 San Felipe St
Houston, TX 77057
Phone: (713) 783-5704

#334
Yankee Candle Company
Category: Home Decor
Average price: Modest
Area: West University
Address: 2552 University Blvd
Houston, TX 77005
Phone: (713) 522-4477

#335
Microsoft Store
Category: Electronics, Computers, Mobile Phones
Average price: Modest
Address: 5015 Westheimer Road Suite A2421 Houston, TX 77056
Phone: (713) 860-5790

#336
Robbins Brothers
The Engagement Ring Store
Category: Jewelry
Average price: Expensive
Area: Highland Village, Galleria, Uptown
Address: 2101 W Lp S
Houston, TX 77027
Phone: (713) 961-0011

#337
Audio Video Plus
Category: Videos, Video Game
Average price: Inexpensive
Area: Montrose
Address: 1225 Waugh Dr
Houston, TX 77019
Phone: (713) 526-9065

#338
Mendota
Category: Luggage, Watches
Average price: Expensive
Area: Fourth Ward, Downtown
Address: 910 Louisiana St
Houston, TX 77002
Phone: (713) 228-5600

#339
James Avery Craftsman
Category: Jewelry
Average price: Modest
Area: Memorial
Address: 704 Memorial City Shopping Center
Houston, TX 77024
Phone: (713) 932-1434

#340
Impression Bridal
Category: Bridal
Average price: Expensive
Area: Highland Village, Galleria, Uptown
Address: 3005 W Loop S
Houston, TX 77027
Phone: (713) 623-4696

#341
Dan Flavin Installation
Category: Art Gallery
Average price: Inexpensive
Area: Montrose
Address: 1500 Richmond Ave
Houston, TX 77006
Phone: (713) 520-8512

#342
Almeda Mall
Category: Shopping Center
Average price: Modest
Area: South Belt, Ellington
Address: 100 Almeda Mall
Houston, TX 77075
Phone: (713) 943-4417

#343
Crystal Children & Teacher Supply
Category: Toy Store, Music, DVDs
Average price: Modest
Area: West University
Address: 5186 Buffalo Speedway
Houston, TX 77005
Phone: (713) 669-1698

#344
Avalon Stationery & Gifts
Category: Cards, Stationery
Average price: Expensive
Area: Upper Kirby
Address: 2604 Westheimer Rd
Houston, TX 77098
Phone: (713) 528-0052

#345
Bergner and Johnson Design
Category: Florist
Average price: Expensive
Area: The Heights
Address: 519 Pecore St
Houston, TX 77009
Phone: (713) 662-3769

#346
Market Place Antiques & Collectibles
Category: Antiques
Average price: Modest
Area: Spring Branch
Address: 10910 Katy Fwy
Houston, TX 77043
Phone: (713) 464-8023

#347
Waldemars Fruit & Floral
Category: Florist
Average price: Modest
Area: Montrose
Address: 1625 W Alabama St
Houston, TX 77006
Phone: (713) 666-4400

#348
Booker Lowe Aboriginal Gallery
Category: Art Gallery
Average price: Modest
Area: The Heights, Rice Military
Address: 4623 Feagan St
Houston, TX 77007
Phone: (713) 880-1541

#349
Now & Forever Bridal Boutique
Category: Bridal
Average price: Expensive
Area: Upper Kirby
Address: 3701 Kirby Dr
Houston, TX 77098
Phone: (713) 218-0369

#350
Wireless Toyz
Category: Mobile Phones
Average price: Modest
Area: Upper Kirby, Montrose
Address: 3520 S Shepherd Dr
Houston, TX 77246
Phone: (713) 526-7200

#351
Bang & Olufsen
Category: Electronics
Average price: Expensive
Area: Upper Kirby
Address: 2800 Kirby
Houston, TX 77098
Phone: (713) 664-1188

#352
Benefit Brow Bar at Ulta
Category: Makeup Artists, Hair Removal, Cosmetics, Beauty Supply
Average price: Modest
Area: Upper Kirby
Address: 3025 Kirby Drive
Houston, TX 77098
Phone: (713) 807-7959

#353
Ann Mashburn
Category: Women's Clothing
Average price: Modest
Area: River Oaks
Address: 2515 River Oaks Blvd
Houston, TX 77098
Phone: (713) 936-9503

#354
Just In
Category: Women's Clothing, Accessories, Shoe Store
Average price: Inexpensive
Area: Gulfton, Sharpstown
Address: 5711 Hillcroft St
Houston, TX 77036
Phone: (713) 789-2322

#355
Charde Jewelers
Category: Jewelry
Average price: Modest
Area: West University
Address: 5600 Kirby Dr
Houston, TX 77005
Phone: (713) 668-6350

#356
Blooms - The Flower Shop
Category: Florist
Average price: Modest
Area: Galleria, Uptown
Address: 3028 Chimney Rock Rd
Houston, TX 77056
Phone: (713) 784-6796

#357
Soma Intimates
Category: Women's Clothing, Lingerie
Average price: Modest
Area: West University
Address: 2521 Amherst Street
Houston, TX 77005
Phone: (713) 807-8796

#358
Thread Houston
Category: Baby Gear, Furniture
Average price: Modest
Area: The Heights
Address: 249 W 19th St
Houston, TX 77008
Phone: (281) 501-0148

#359
Pickles & Ice Cream Maternity Apparel
Category: Maternity Wear
Average price: Expensive
Area: Galleria, Uptown
Address: 1800 Post Oak Blvd
Houston, TX 77056
Phone: (713) 623-2229

#360
New Element Fine Vapors
Category: Vape Shop
Average price: Modest
Area: Greenway
Address: 3995 Richmond Ave
Houston, TX 77027
Phone: (713) 840-1409

#361
Taylor Wholesale Florists
Category: Florist
Average price: Inexpensive
Area: The Heights
Address: 1601 W 21st St
Houston, TX 77008
Phone: (713) 869-7481

#362
A Classic Bloom
Category: Florist
Average price: Modest
Area: Braeswood Place, West University
Address: 2514 Dorrington St
Houston, TX 77030
Phone: (713) 664-2020

#363
Lucho Inc
Category: Men's Clothing
Average price: Exclusive
Area: Galleria, Uptown
Address: 1121 Uptown Park Blvd
Houston, TX 77056
Phone: (713) 961-3577

#364
Mattress Firm
Category: Mattresses
Average price: Modest
Area: Galleria, Uptown
Address: 5000 Westheimer
Houston, TX 77056
Phone: (713) 629-9120

#365
Vivaldi Music Academy
Category: Performing Arts, Musical Instruments,
Average price: Modest
Area: Braeswood Place, West University
Address: 3914 Gramercy St
Houston, TX 77025
Phone: (713) 858-9617

#366
The Puma Store
Category: Shoe Store
Average price: Modest
Area: Galleria, Uptown
Address: 5085 Westheimer Rd
Houston, TX 77056
Phone: (713) 623-4723

#367
Omega Boutique
Category: Watches
Average price: Expensive
Area: Galleria, Uptown
Address: 5015 Westheimer Rd
Houston, TX 77056
Phone: (713) 621-1122

#368
Art & Frame Etc
Category: Art Gallery, Framing
Average price: Modest
Area: Lazy Brook, Timbergrove
Address: 2819 W T C Jester Blvd
Houston, TX 77018
Phone: (713) 681-5077

#369
Hardy's Picture Framing
Category: Framing
Average price: Inexpensive
Area: Braeswood Place, Meyerland
Address: 8423 Stella Link Rd
Houston, TX 77025
Phone: (713) 666-1373

#370
Goodwill Industries
Category: Used, Vintage
Average price: Inexpensive
Area: Lazy Brook, Timbergrove
Address: 10903 Northwest Fwy
Houston, TX 77092
Phone: (713) 688-4088

#371
Old Navy Clothing Store
Category: Men's Clothing, Women's Clothing
Average price: Inexpensive
Area: Galleria, Uptown
Address: 5000 Westheimer Rd
Houston, TX 77056
Phone: (713) 626-5244

#372
Stella Link Shoe Service
Category: Shoe Store
Average price: Inexpensive
Area: Braeswood Place, Meyerland
Address: 4038 S Braeswood Blvd
Houston, TX 77025
Phone: (713) 667-9744

#373
Dollar Tree Stores Inc
Category: Department Store
Average price: Inexpensive
Area: Meyerland
Address: 9929 S Post Oak Rd
Houston, TX 77096
Phone: (713) 729-1670

#374
Family Thrift Center
Category: Thrift Store
Average price: Modest
Area: Spring Branch
Address: 8120 Long Point Rd
Houston, TX 77055
Phone: (713) 468-9447

#375
Compucycle
Category: Electronics
Average price: Inexpensive
Area: Langwood, Spring Branch
Address: 7700 Kempwood Dr
Houston, TX 77055
Phone: (713) 869-6700

#376
Imagination Toys
Category: Toy Store
Average price: Modest
Area: Braeswood Place, West University
Address: 3851 Bellaire Blvd
Houston, TX 77025
Phone: (713) 662-9898

#377
Taxi Taxi Clothing
Category: Used, Vintage
Average price: Inexpensive
Area: Montrose
Address: 1657 Westheimer Rd
Houston, TX 77006
Phone: (713) 528-5500

#378
High Times
Category: Tobacco Shop, Lingerie
Average price: Modest
Area: Sharpstown, Chinatown
Address: 6881 S Gessner Dr
Houston, TX 77036
Phone: (713) 777-1783

#379
Gem & Bead Gallery
Category: Jewelry, Arts, Crafts
Average price: Modest
Area: West University
Address: 2516 Times Blvd
Houston, TX 77005
Phone: (713) 520-9700

#380
Costumes & Dancewear
Category: Costumes
Average price: Modest
Area: River Oaks, Montrose
Address: 1503 Dunlavy St
Houston, TX 77006
Phone: (713) 523-4004

#381
Tangolandia-Gran
Category: Music, DVDs
Average price: Inexpensive
Area: Gulfton
Address: 6611 Chimney Rock Rd
Houston, TX 77081
Phone: (713) 661-1893

#382
Macy's
Category: Department Store, Men's Clothing, Women's Clothing
Average price: Modest
Area: Galleria, Uptown
Address: 5135 W. Alabama
Houston, TX 77056
Phone: (832) 667-4200

#383
Meyerland Jewelers
Category: Jewelry
Average price: Inexpensive
Area: Meyerland
Address: 120 Meyerland Plz
Houston, TX 77096
Phone: (713) 666-6333

#384
Aveda
Category: Cosmetics, Beauty Supply
Average price: Modest
Area: Galleria, Uptown
Address: 5135 W Alabama St Ste 7190
Houston, TX 77056
Phone: (713) 572-5500

#385
Surfhouse
Category: Sporting Goods
Average price: Modest
Area: Oak Forest, Garden Oaks
Address: 1729 W 34th St
Houston, TX 77018
Phone: (713) 686-3300

#386
J.Crew
Category: Men's Clothing, Women's Clothing, Accessories
Average price: Expensive
Area: Highland Village
Address: 4037 Westheimer Road
Houston, TX 77027
Phone: (713) 552-0797

#387
Randall's Food and Pharmacy
Category: Drugstore, Grocery
Average price: Modest
Area: Montrose
Address: 2075 Westheimer Rd
Houston, TX 77098
Phone: (713) 284-1204

#388
Men's Wearhouse and Tux
Category: Men's Clothing, Formal Wear
Average price: Modest
Area: River Oaks, Montrose
Address: 1947 West Gray
Houston, TX 77019
Phone: (713) 529-6191

#389
Adam & Eve
Category: Adult
Average price: Modest
Area: Montrose
Address: 1111 Westheimer Rd
Houston, TX 77027
Phone: (713) 521-2326

#390
The Menil Collection
Category: Museum, Art Gallery
Average price: Inexpensive
Area: Montrose
Address: 1533 Sul Ross St
Houston, TX 77006
Phone: (713) 525-9400

#391
Southwest Fertilizer
Category: Nursery, Gardening
Average price: Inexpensive
Area: Gulfton
Address: 5828 Bissonnet St
Houston, TX 77081
Phone: (713) 666-1744

#392
Carter's Babies & Kids
Category: Children's Clothing, Accessories, Shoe Store
Average price: Inexpensive
Area: Memorial
Address: 12850 Memorial Dr
Houston, TX 77024
Phone: (713) 467-2057

#393
Pro-Mark Drumsticks
Category: Musical Instruments
Average price: Inexpensive
Area: Willow Meadows, Willowbend
Address: 11550 Old Main St
Houston, TX 77025
Phone: (713) 314-1100

#394
Target
Category: Department Store, Drugstore
Average price: Modest
Area: South Belt, Ellington
Address: 8503 S Sam Houston Pkwy E
Houston, TX 77089
Phone: (713) 343-8300

#395
Village Flowery
Category: Florist
Average price: Modest
Area: West University
Address: 6103 Kirby Dr
Houston, TX 77005
Phone: (713) 523-0600

#396
Sunglass Hut
Category: Eyewear, Opticians
Average price: Expensive
Area: Galleria, Uptown
Address: 5015 Westheimer Rd Ste 2495
Houston, TX 77056
Phone: (713) 961-5150

#397
Mc Eye Center & Optical
Category: Eyewear, Opticians, Optometrists
Average price: Inexpensive
Area: Midtown
Address: 3221 Fannin St
Houston, TX 77004
Phone: (713) 522-7448

#398
Value Village
Category: Thrift Store, Department Store, Used, Vintage
Average price: Inexpensive
Area: The Heights
Address: 705 W. 23rd Street
Houston, TX 77008
Phone: (713) 685-5406

#399
The Village Firefly
Category: Home Decor, Jewelry
Average price: Modest
Area: West University
Address: 2422 Rice Blvd.
Houston, TX 77005
Phone: (713) 522-2808

#400
Lily Rain
Category: Women's Clothing, Accessories
Average price: Modest
Area: West University
Address: 2414 University Blvd
Houston, TX 77005
Phone: (713) 523-1902

#401
Thompson & Hanson
Category: Nursery, Gardening
Average price: Expensive
Area: Highland Village
Address: 3600 W Alabama St
Houston, TX 77027
Phone: (713) 622-6973

#402
Jenny Kim Couture
Category: Bridal
Average price: Modest
Area: West University
Address: 2524 Amherst St
Houston, TX 77005
Phone: (713) 528-0500

#403
Gap
Category: Men's Clothing, Women's Clothing, Sports Wear
Average price: Modest
Area: West University
Address: 6225 Kirby Dr
Houston, TX 77005
Phone: (713) 942-7061

#404
Wade Wilson Art
Category: Art Gallery
Average price: Exclusive
Area: Museum District, Montrose
Address: 4411 Montrose Blvd
Houston, TX 77246
Phone: (713) 521-2977

#405
The Cutting Garden
Category: Florist
Average price: Expensive
Area: Memorial
Address: 9039 Katy Fwy
Houston, TX 77024
Phone: (713) 465-9145

#406
Purple Glaze
Category: Arts, Crafts, Hobby Shop
Average price: Modest
Area: West University
Address: 2365 Rice Blvd
Houston, TX 77005
Phone: (713) 520-6888

#407
Origins
Category: Cosmetics, Beauty Supply, Skin Care
Average price: Modest
Area: West University
Address: 2401 Times Blvd
Houston, TX 77005
Phone: (713) 942-8870

#408
Brooks Brothers
Category: Men's Clothing, Women's Clothing
Average price: Expensive
Area: Galleria, Uptown
Address: 5085 Westheimer Rd
Houston, TX 77056
Phone: (713) 627-2057

#409
Burberry
Category: Accessories, Men's Clothing, Women's Clothing
Average price: Exclusive
Area: Galleria, Uptown
Address: 5015 Westheimer Rd
Houston, TX 77056
Phone: (713) 629-6900

#410
J.Crew
Category: Men's Clothing, Women's Clothing, Accessories
Average price: Expensive
Area: Memorial
Address: 800 Town and Country Blvd
Houston, TX 77024
Phone: (713) 827-1743

#411
Vision Optique PC
Category: Optometrists, Eyewear, Opticians
Average price: Modest
Area: West University
Address: 5158 Buffalo Speedway
Houston, TX 77005
Phone: (713) 838-2020

#412
Batteries Plus
Category: Electronics
Average price: Modest
Area: Westchase
Address: 2662 S Gessner Rd
Houston, TX 77063
Phone: (713) 785-7587

#413
Sub-Zero Wolf Showroom
Category: Appliances
Average price: Exclusive
Area: Galleria, Uptown
Address: 2800 Sage Rd
Houston, TX 77056
Phone: (713) 599-0053

#414
Soho
Category: Women's Clothing, Accessories
Average price: Expensive
Area: Memorial
Address: 6592 Woodway Dr
Houston, TX 77057
Phone: (713) 467-9233

#415
LensCrafters
Category: Eyewear, Opticians, Optometrists, Ophthalmologists
Average price: Modest
Area: Galleria, Uptown
Address: 5135 W Alabama St
Houston, TX 77056
Phone: (713) 623-0855

#416
The Walking Company
Category: Shoe Store
Average price: Expensive
Area: Galleria, Uptown
Address: 5015 Westheimer Rd
Houston, TX 77056
Phone: (713) 355-6616

#417
Verizon Wireless
Category: Mobile Phones, Electronics,
Average price: Modest
Area: Galleria, Uptown
Address: 1670 Post Oak Blvd
Houston, TX 77056
Phone: (713) 960-8585

#418
Ulta Beauty
Category: Cosmetics, Beauty Supply
Average price: Modest
Area: Memorial
Address: 12850 Memorial Dr
Houston, TX 77024
Phone: (713) 331-0065

#419
Pinto Ranch Fine Western Wear
Category: Accessories, Men's Clothing, Women's Clothing
Average price: Exclusive
Area: Galleria, Uptown
Address: 1717 Post Oak Blvd
Houston, TX 77056
Phone: (713) 333-7900

#420
Today's Vision
Category: Optometrists, Eyewear, Opticians
Average price: Modest
Area: West University
Address: 2366-A Rice Blvd
Houston, TX 77005
Phone: (713) 521-2020

#421
Sam Moon
Category: Department Store
Average price: Inexpensive
Area: Memorial
Address: 9726 Katy Fwy
Houston, TX 77055
Phone: (713) 722-0073

#422
VIDEO TAPE COPY INC
Category: Videos, Video Game
Average price: Inexpensive
Area: Galleria, Uptown
Address: 3013 Fountain View Dr
Houston, TX 77057
Phone: (713) 522-6225

#423
Nordstrom Rack
Category: Men's Clothing,
Women's Clothing, Children's Clothing
Average price: Modest
Area: Memorial
Address: 9714 Katy Fwy
Houston, TX 77053
Phone: (281) 605-2705

#424
Burn Smoke Shop
Category: Tobacco Shop, Vape Shop
Average price: Modest
Area: Westchase
Address: 10218 Westheimer Rd
Houston, TX 77027
Phone: (281) 888-6929

#425
Melodrama
Category: Women's Clothing,
Jewelry, Accessories
Average price: Modest
Area: Museum District
Address: 5306 Almeda Rd
Houston, TX 77004
Phone: (713) 523-1608

#426
Clark's Shoes
Category: Shoe Store
Average price: Modest
Area: Memorial
Address: 710 Memorial City Way
Houston, TX 77024
Phone: (713) 932-7855

#427
Northwest Vision
Category: Eyewear, Opticians, Optometrists
Average price: Modest
Area: Fairbanks, Northwest Crossing
Address: 13264 Northwest Fwy
Houston, TX 77040
Phone: (713) 690-2020

#428
Shasa
Category: Women's Clothing
Average price: Modest
Area: Memorial
Address: 303 Memorial City, Ste 720
Houston, TX 77024
Phone: (713) 465-3962

#429
The Home Depot
Category: Hardware Store,
Nursery, Gardening, Appliances
Average price: Modest
Area: Memorial
Address: 8400 Katy Freeway
Houston, TX 77024
Phone: (713) 984-2741

#430
Cool Stuff
Category: Furniture Store
Average price: Expensive
Area: Montrose
Address: 1718 Westheimer Rd
Houston, TX 77098
Phone: (713) 523-5222

#431
Randalls Food & Pharmacy
Category: Grocery, Drugstore
Average price: Modest
Area: Galleria, Uptown
Address: 5161 San Felipe St
Houston, TX 77056
Phone: (713) 964-3155

#432
Lexis Florist
Category: Party Supplies, Home Decor, Bridal
Average price: Expensive
Area: Gulfton, Galleria, Uptown
Address: 6102 Skyline Dr Ste A
Houston, TX 77057
Phone: (713) 774-8080

#433
Sony Store
Category: Electronics, Computers
Average price: Expensive
Area: Galleria, Uptown
Address: 5015 Westheimer Road
Houston, TX 77056
Phone: (713) 439-7086

#434
The Houston Potters Guild Shop & Gallery
Category: Jewelry
Average price: Modest
Area: Montrose
Address: 1701 Dunlavy St
Houston, TX 77006
Phone: (713) 528-7687

#435
Hobby Lobby
Category: Hobby Shop,
Home Decor, Art Supplies
Average price: Modest
Area: Spring Branch, Memorial
Address: 10516 Katy Fwy Suite F
Houston, TX 77043
Phone: (713) 467-6503

#436
Pier 1 Imports
Category: Furniture Store, Home Decor
Average price: Modest
Area: Meyerland
Address: 110 Meyerland Plaza Mall
Houston, TX 77096
Phone: (713) 662-2974

#437
The Limited
Category: Women's Clothing
Average price: Modest
Area: Memorial
Address: 746 Memorial City Mall
Houston, TX 77024
Phone: (713) 932-7009

#438
Apple Store
Category: Electronics, Computers
Average price: Expensive
Area: Memorial
Address: 379 Memorial City
Houston, TX 77024
Phone: (713) 986-2476

#439
Smoochee's
Category: Adult
Average price: Expensive
Area: The Heights
Address: 3333 Katy Freeway
Houston, TX 77007
Phone: (713) 869-6600

#440
Dillard's
Category: Department Store
Average price: Modest
Area: Galleria, Uptown
Address: 4925 Westheimer Rd
Houston, TX 77056
Phone: (713) 622-1200

#441
The Salvation Army
Category: Thrift Store, Used, Vintage
Average price: Inexpensive
Area: Gulfton
Address: 6150 Bissonnet St
Houston, TX 77081
Phone: (713) 778-1161

#442
Sprint Store
Category: Mobile Phones
Average price: Modest
Area: Montrose
Address: 2036 Westheimer Rd
Houston, TX 77098
Phone: (713) 781-6989

#443
Houston Piano Company
Category: Musical Instruments
Average price: Expensive
Area: The Heights
Address: 1600 W 13th St
Houston, TX 77008
Phone: (832) 685-7080

#444
Northwest Mall
Category: Shopping Center
Average price: Inexpensive
Area: Lazy Brook, Timbergrove
Address: 242 Northwest Mall
Houston, TX 77092
Phone: (713) 290-8142

#445
Reggae Bodega
Category: Jewelry
Average price: Inexpensive
Area: Museum District
Address: 4816 Almeda Rd
Houston, TX 77004
Phone: (713) 269-0241

#446
Yelp's Holiday Bazaart!
Category: Shopping, Local Flavor
Average price: Inexpensive
Area: Braeswood Place, Medical Center
Address: 4715 Main
Houston, TX 77004
Phone: (832) 274-7060

#447
Richard Ullman OD
Category: Optometrists, Eyewear, Opticians,
Average price: Modest
Area: The Heights
Address: 2106 Yale St
Houston, TX 77008
Phone: (713) 864-5421

#448
Victoria's Secret Stores
Category: Lingerie
Average price: Modest
Area: West University
Address: 2414 University Blvd
Houston, TX 77005
Phone: (713) 526-1054

#449
Marlo Miller Boutique
Category: Women's Clothing, Accessories
Average price: Expensive
Area: Galleria, Uptown
Address: 1920 Fountainview Dr
Houston, TX 77057
Phone: (713) 532-8771

#450
Stein Mart
Category: Women's Clothing,
Department Store, Accessories
Average price: Modest
Area: Meyerland
Address: 290 Meyerland Plaza Mall
Houston, TX 77096
Phone: (713) 665-6000

#451
The Monogram Shop
Category: Gift Shop, Screen Printing
Average price: Modest
Area: Memorial, Galleria, Uptown
Address: 5860 H San Felipe St
Houston, TX 77057
Phone: (832) 251-8771

#452
Forever 21
Category: Women's Clothing
Average price: Inexpensive
Area: Galleria, Uptown
Address: 5085 Westheimer Rd
Houston, TX 77056
Phone: (713) 622-7951

#453
Planet Vintage
Category: Costumes, Used, Vintage
Average price: Modest
Area: Montrose
Address: 2602 Waugh Dr
Houston, TX 77006
Phone: (713) 526-8910

#454
Pearle Vision
Category: Eyewear, Opticians
Average price: Modest
Area: Memorial
Address: 9738 Katy Freeway
Houston, TX 77055
Phone: (713) 468-2424

#455
Walmart Neighborhood Market
Category: Grocery, Drugstore, Discount Store
Average price: Inexpensive
Area: Fondren Southwest
Address: 9700 Hillcroft St
Houston, TX 77096
Phone: (713) 283-7186

#456
Verizon Wireless
Category: Mobile Phones, Electronics,
Average price: Exclusive
Area: Montrose
Address: 2071 Westheimer Rd
Houston, TX 77098
Phone: (713) 522-2810

#457
Natural Resources Salon
Category: Cosmetics,
Beauty Supply, Hair Salon
Average price: Modest
Area: West University
Address: 5313 Morningside Dr
Houston, TX 77005
Phone: (713) 528-7102

#458
Bebe
Category: Women's Clothing, Accessories
Average price: Expensive
Area: Galleria, Uptown
Address: 5015 Westheimer Rd
Houston, TX 77056
Phone: (713) 622-2113

#459
JCPenney
Category: Department Store, Women's
Clothing, Baby Gear, Furniture, Men's Clothing
Average price: Modest
Area: Meyerland
Address: 730 Meyerland Plaza Mall
Houston, TX 77096
Phone: (713) 666-3861

#460
Walgreens
Category: Drugstore, Cosmetics, Beauty
Supply, Convenience Store
Average price: Modest
Area: Memorial
Address: 6360 San Felipe St
Houston, TX 77057
Phone: (713) 278-2616

#461
Cheeky Vintage
Category: Used, Vintage
Average price: Modest
Area: Upper Kirby
Address: 2134 Richmond Avenue
Houston, TX 77098
Phone: (713) 533-1121

#462
Soccer 4 All
Category: Sports Wear
Average price: Modest
Area: West University
Address: 2425 Rice Blvd
Houston, TX 77005
Phone: (713) 522-0441

#463
Soma Intimates
Category: Lingerie, Women's Clothing
Average price: Modest
Area: Highland Village
Address: 4036 Westheimer
Houston, TX 77027
Phone: (713) 871-9439

#464
Ross Store, Inc.
Category: Men's Clothing,
Women's Clothing, Children's Clothing
Average price: Inexpensive
Area: West University
Address: 3908 Bissonnet St
Houston, TX 77005
Phone: (713) 665-4456

#465
The Mad Potter
Category: Arts, Crafts
Average price: Modest
Area: Memorial
Address: 1341 S Voss Rd
Houston, TX 77057
Phone: (713) 278-7300

#466
Just A Dollar
Category: Convenience Store, Discount Store
Average price: Inexpensive
Area: Fourth Ward, Downtown
Address: 901 Main St
Houston, TX 77002
Phone: (713) 659-3933

#467
West Houston Assistance Ministries Second Blessing Store
Category: Vintage, Thrift Store
Average price: Inexpensive
Area: Westchase
Address: 3100 Rogerdale Rd
Houston, TX 77042
Phone: (713) 780-2727

#468
Best Buy
Category: Mobile Phones,
Appliances & Repair, Appliances
Average price: Modest
Area: Meyerland
Address: 100 Meyerland Plz Mall
Houston, TX 77096
Phone: (713) 295-2040

#469
Best Buy
Category: Appliances, Electronics
Average price: Modest
Area: Memorial
Address: 9670 Old Katy Rd
Houston, TX 77055
Phone: (713) 647-6004

#470
Southland Hardware
Category: Hardware Store
Average price: Modest
Area: Montrose
Address: 1822 Westheimer Rd
Houston, TX 77098
Phone: (713) 529-4743

#471
Jo-Ann Fabrics & Crafts
Category: Fabric Store, Hobby Shop
Average price: Modest
Area: West University
Address: 5520 Weslayan St.
Houston, TX 77005
Phone: (713) 666-3328

#472
Swoon Apparel + Accessories
Category: Women's Clothing, Accessories
Average price: Modest
Area: Galleria, Uptown
Address: 5886 San Felipe St
Houston, TX 77057
Phone: (713) 781-7966

#473
Bath & Body Works
Category: Cosmetics, Beauty Supply
Average price: Inexpensive
Area: Galleria, Uptown
Address: 5085 Westheimer Rd
Houston, TX 77056
Phone: (713) 993-9566

#474
Pearle Vision
Category: Eyewear, Opticians
Average price: Exclusive
Area: Galleria, Uptown
Address: 5015 Westheimer Road
Houston, TX 77056
Phone: (713) 623-4181

#475
Camera Care Center
Category: Photography Store, Services
Average price: Modest
Area: Upper Kirby
Address: 2113 Richmond Ave
Houston, TX 77098
Phone: (713) 521-1441

#476
CVS/Pharmacy
Category: Drugstore
Average price: Modest
Area: Gulfton, Galleria, Uptown
Address: 5204 Richmond Ave
Houston, TX 77056
Phone: (713) 961-0874

#477
Dyson Service Center
Category: Appliances & Repair, Appliances
Average price: Modest
Area: Lazy Brook, Timbergrove
Address: 5200 Mitchelldale St
Houston, TX 77092
Phone: (713) 683-1602

#478
Men's Wearhouse
Category: Men's Clothing, Formal Wear
Average price: Expensive
Area: Galleria, Uptown
Address: 5602 Westheimer Rd
Houston, TX 77056
Phone: (713) 784-1185

#479
Onsite Cellular Repair Houston
Category: Electronics Repair, Mobile Phones
Average price: Expensive
Area: West University
Address: 3229 SW Fwy
Houston, TX 77027
Phone: (713) 750-9885

#480
Grace Anna's Boutique
Category: Women's Clothing
Average price: Modest
Area: West University
Address: 5501 Kelvin St
Houston, TX 77005
Phone: (713) 808-9599

#481
White House Black Market
Category: Women's Clothing
Average price: Expensive
Area: West University
Address: 2414 University Blvd, Suite 150
Houston, TX 77005
Phone: (713) 526-6380

#482
Tuesday Morning Inc
Category: Department Store
Average price: Inexpensive
Area: West University
Address: 5442 Weslayan St
Houston, TX 77005
Phone: (713) 666-0674

#483
Sas Factory Shoe Store
Category: Shoe Store
Average price: Expensive
Area: Memorial
Address: 9363 Katy Fwy
Houston, TX 77024
Phone: (713) 464-6656

#484
MYCO Furniture
Category: Furniture Store
Average price: Inexpensive
Area: Alief
Address: 9500 W Sam Houston Pkwy S
Houston, TX 77099
Phone: (713) 493-2526

#485
Houston Re-Market
Category: Arts, Crafts, Thrift Store
Average price: Modest
Area: Midtown
Address: 1502 Alabama St
Houston, TX 77004
Phone: (832) 721-3571

#486
Lewis & Maese Auction Company
Category: Antiques
Average price: Modest
Area: The Heights
Address: 1505 Sawyer St
Houston, TX 77007
Phone: (713) 880-0891

#487
Mattress Firm
Category: Mattresses
Average price: Inexpensive
Area: The Heights
Address: 1901 Taylor St.
Houston, TX 77007
Phone: (713) 862-1887

#488
Erica Jewelry
Category: Jewelry
Average price: Modest
Area: Montrose
Address: 1718 Westheimer Rd
Houston, TX 77098
Phone: (713) 529-7555

#489
Watercolor Art Society
Category: Art Gallery
Average price: Inexpensive
Area: Montrose
Address: 1601 W Alabama St
Houston, TX 77006
Phone: (713) 942-9966

#490
Randalls Food & Pharmacy
Category: Grocery, Drugstore
Average price: Modest
Area: West University
Address: 5586 Weslayan St
Houston, TX 77005
Phone: (713) 668-9820

#491
Walgreens
Category: Drugstore, Cosmetics, Beauty Supply, Convenience Store
Average price: Inexpensive
Area: Galleria, Uptown
Address: 5200 Westheimer Rd
Houston, TX 77056
Phone: (713) 623-0643

#492
Donald J Pliner
Category: Leather Goods, Shoe Store
Average price: Expensive
Area: Highland Village
Address: 4033 Westheimer Rd
Houston, TX 77027
Phone: (713) 961-0600

#493
The Baseball School & Batting Cages
Category: Sporting Goods, Batting Cages
Average price: Expensive
Area: Montrose
Address: 2019 W Alabama St
Houston, TX 77098
Phone: (713) 527-8338

#494
713 INC Art & Apparel
Category: Art Gallery
Average price: Modest
Area: Second Ward
Address: 4739 Canal St
Houston, TX 77011
Phone: (713) 545-6030

#495
The Amish Craftsman
Category: Furniture Store
Average price: Expensive
Area: The Heights, Rice Military
Address: 5555 Washington Ave
Houston, TX 77007
Phone: (713) 862-3444

#496
Breen's Florist
Category: Florist
Average price: Modest
Area: Spring Branch
Address: 1050 N Post Oak
Houston, TX 77055
Phone: (713) 668-2376

#497
Mercado Mexico
Category: Home Decor
Average price: Expensive
Area: Upper Kirby
Address: 2210 Richmond Ave
Houston, TX 77098
Phone: (713) 528-6101

#498
Sloan-Hall
Category: Jewelry, Accessories, Women's Clothing
Average price: Exclusive
Area: River Oaks
Address: 2620 Westheimer Rd
Houston, TX 77098
Phone: (713) 942-0202

#499
Old Navy Clothing Store
Category: Men's Clothing, Women's Clothing
Average price: Inexpensive
Area: Meyerland
Address: 4700 Beechnut St
Houston, TX 77096
Phone: (713) 349-9122

#500
CVS/Pharmacy
Category: Drugstore
Average price: Modest
Area: The Heights, Rice Military
Address: 5401 Washington Ave
Houston, TX 77007
Phone: (713) 861-3883

TOP 500 RESTAURANTS
The Most Recommended by Locals & Trevelers
(From #1 to #500)

Houston Travel Guide 2015 / Shops, Restaurants, Arts, Entertainment & Nightlife

#1
Local Foods
Cuisines: Sandwiches, American
Average price: Modest
Area: West University
Address: 2424 Dunstan Rd
Houston, TX 77005
Phone: (713) 521-7800

#2
Stanton's City Bites
Cuisines: Burgers, American, Bar
Average price: Inexpensive
Area: Sixth Ward
Address: 1420 Edwards St
Houston, TX 77007
Phone: (713) 227-4893

#3
M&M Grill
Cuisines: Mediterranean, Mexican, Burgers
Average price: Inexpensive
Area: Medical Center
Address: 6921 Almeda Rd
Houston, TX 77021
Phone: (713) 747-8226

#4
Vietnam Poblano
Cuisines: Vietnamese, Sandwiches
Average price: Inexpensive
Area: Spring Branch
Address: 1411 Gessner Rd
Houston, TX 77080
Phone: (832) 649-8955

#5
Little Jimmy's Deli
Cuisines: Deli, Sandwiches
Average price: Inexpensive
Area: Greenway
Address: 3837 Richmond Ave
Houston, TX 77027
Phone: (713) 622-7827

#6
Tacos Tierra Caliente
Cuisines: Mexican, Food Truck
Average price: Inexpensive
Area: Montrose
Address: 1919 W Alabama St
Houston, TX 77098
Phone: (713) 584-9359

#7
Luna Pizzeria
Cuisines: Pizza, Salad, Sandwiches
Average price: Inexpensive
Area: Upper Kirby
Address: 3435 Kirby Dr
Houston, TX 77098
Phone: (832) 767-6338

#8
Local Foods
Cuisines: Sandwiches, Gluten-Free, American
Average price: Modest
Area: River Oaks
Address: 2555 Kirby Dr
Houston, TX 77019
Phone: (713) 255-4440

#9
Doshi House Café
Cuisines: Coffee, Tea, Vegetarian, Vegan
Average price: Inexpensive
Area: Third Ward
Address: 3419 Dowling St
Houston, TX 77004
Phone: (713) 528-0060

#10
The Breakfast Klub
Cuisines: Breakfast & Brunch, Southern
Average price: Modest
Area: Fourth Ward, Midtown
Address: 3711 Travis St
Houston, TX 77002
Phone: (713) 528-8561

#11
Pappa Geno's
Cuisines: Sandwiches, Cheesesteaks, Burgers
Average price: Inexpensive
Area: Lazy Brook/Timbergrove
Address: 1801 Ella Blvd
Houston, TX 77008
Phone: (713) 863-1222

#12
Luigi's Pizzeria
Cuisines: Pizza, Italian, Ice Cream
Average price: Inexpensive
Area: Midtown
Address: 3700 Almeda Rd
Houston, TX 77004
Phone: (281) 793-3333

#13
Houston Panini & Provisions
Cuisines: Grocery, Sandwiches, Farmers Market
Average price: Inexpensive
Area: Oak Forest/Garden Oaks
Address: 1727 W 34th St
Houston, TX 77018
Phone: (713) 681-4500

#14
Baby Barnaby's Café
Cuisines: Breakfast & Brunch, Café
Average price: Inexpensive
Area: Fourth Ward, Montrose
Address: 602 Fairview St
Houston, TX 77006
Phone: (713) 522-4229

Houston Travel Guide 2015 / Shops, Restaurants, Arts, Entertainment & Nightlife

#15
The Afghan Village
Cuisines: Pakistani, Afghan
Average price: Modest
Area: Gulfton
Address: 6413 Hillcroft St
Houston, TX 77081
Phone: (713) 808-9005

#16
Hughie's Tavern & Grille
Cuisines: Vietnamese, Asian Fusion, Sandwiches
Average price: Inexpensive
Area: Lazy Brook/Timbergrove
Address: 1802 W 18th St
Houston, TX 77008
Phone: (713) 869-1830

#17
Taco Keto
Cuisines: Mexican, Food Stand
Average price: Inexpensive
Area: EaDo, Eastwood
Address: 1401 Cullen Blvd
Houston, TX 77023
Phone: (713) 224-1898

#18
Bombay Pizza Co.
Cuisines: Pizza, Indian, Vegetarian
Average price: Modest
Area: Fourth Ward, Downtown
Address: 914 Main St
Houston, TX 77002
Phone: (713) 654-4444

#19
Gatlin's Barbecue
Cuisines: Barbeque
Average price: Modest
Area: The Heights
Address: 1221 W 19th St
Houston, TX 77008
Phone: (713) 869-4227

#20
benjy's
Cuisines: Lounge, American
Average price: Modest
Area: West University
Address: 2424 Dunstan Rd
Houston, TX 77005
Phone: (713) 522-7602

#21
Bocca Deli
Cuisines: Deli, Ice Cream, Sandwiches
Average price: Inexpensive
Area: Northside Village
Address: 4707 Irvington Blvd
Houston, TX 77009
Phone: (832) 582-7225

#22
Down the Street
Cuisines: Cocktail Bar, Tapas
Average price: Modest
Area: The Heights
Address: 5746 Larkin St
Houston, TX 77007
Phone: (713) 880-3508

#23
Happy Fatz
Cuisines: Desserts, Hot Dogs, Coffee, Tea
Average price: Inexpensive
Area: The Heights
Address: 3510 White Oak Dr
Houston, TX 77007
Phone: (713) 426-3554

#24
Backstreet Café
Cuisines: American, Breakfast & Brunch
Average price: Modest
Area: River Oaks, Montrose
Address: 1103 S Shepherd Dr
Houston, TX 77019
Phone: (713) 521-2239

#25
Fainmous BBQ
Cuisines: Barbeque
Average price: Inexpensive
Area: Meyerland
Address: 10400 S Post Oak
Houston, TX 77035
Phone: (713) 728-9663

#26
Aladdin Mediterranean Cuisine
Cuisines: Mediterranean
Average price: Modest
Area: Fourth Ward, Montrose
Address: 912 Westheimer Rd
Houston, TX 77006
Phone: (713) 942-2321

#27
Hearsay Gastro Lounge
Cuisines: Lounge, American
Average price: Modest
Area: Downtown
Address: 218 Travis St
Houston, TX 77002
Phone: (713) 225-8079

#28
Conscious Café
Cuisines: Coffee, Tea, Sandwiches, Vegetarian
Average price: Inexpensive
Area: Third Ward
Address: 2612 Scott St
Houston, TX 77004
Phone: (713) 658-9191

#29
Ray's Real Pit BBQ Shack
Cuisines: Barbeque
Average price: Modest
Area: MacGregor
Address: 4529 Old Spanish Trl
Houston, TX 77021
Phone: (713) 748-4227

#30
Ambrosia
Cuisines: Tapas, Pizza, Asian Fusion
Average price: Modest
Area: Museum District, Montrose
Address: 2003 Lexington St
Houston, TX 77098
Phone: (832) 649-4636

#31
A 2nd Cup
Cuisines: Café
Average price: Inexpensive
Area: The Heights
Address: 1035 E 11th St
Houston, TX 77009
Phone: (281) 382-6161

#32
Bowl Café
Cuisines: Sandwiches, Vegetarian, Salad
Average price: Inexpensive
Area: Fourth Ward, Museum District, Montrose
Address: 607 Richmond Ave
Houston, TX 77006
Phone: (832) 582-7218

#33
Roost
Cuisines: American
Average price: Modest
Area: Montrose
Address: 1972 Fairview St
Houston, TX 77019
Phone: (713) 523-7667

#34
Mockingbird Bistro
Cuisines: French, American
Average price: Expensive
Area: Montrose
Address: 1985 Welch St
Houston, TX 77019
Phone: (713) 533-0200

#35
The Original Marini's Empanada House
Cuisines: Latin American, Argentine
Average price: Inexpensive
Area: Westchase
Address: 10001 Westheimer Rd
Houston, TX 77042
Phone: (713) 266-2729

#36
Benjy's
Cuisines: American, Lounge, Breakfast & Brunch
Average price: Modest
Area: The Heights, Rice Military
Address: 5922 Washington Ave
Houston, TX 77007
Phone: (713) 868-1131

#37
Tacos La Bala
Cuisines: Mexican
Average price: Inexpensive
Area: Gulfton
Address: 5800 Bellaire Blvd
Houston, TX 77081
Phone: (713) 839-8226

#38
Zabak's Mediterranean Cafe
Cuisines: Greek, Mediterranean
Average price: Inexpensive
Area: Galleria/Uptown
Address: 5901-G Westheimer Rd
Houston, TX 77057
Phone: (713) 977-7676

#39
District 7 Grill Midtown
Cuisines: American
Average price: Modest
Area: Fourth Ward, Midtown, Downtown, Montrose
Address: 501 Pierce St
Houston, TX 77002
Phone: (713) 751-0660

#40
Tacos A Go-Go
Cuisines: Mexican, Tex-Mex
Average price: Inexpensive
Area: Fourth Ward, Midtown
Address: 3704 Main St
Houston, TX 77002
Phone: (713) 807-8226

#41
Niko Niko's Greek & American Cafe
Cuisines: Greek, Mediterranean
Average price: Modest
Area: Montrose
Address: 2520 Montrose Blvd
Houston, TX 77006
Phone: (713) 528-4976

#42
Gusto Gourmet
Cuisines: Venezuelan, Mediterranean
Average price: Modest
Area: Upper Kirby
Address: 3306 S Shepherd
Houston, TX 77098
Phone: (713) 344-0892

#43
Kasra Persian Grill
Cuisines: Persian, Iranian
Average price: Modest
Area: Westchase
Address: 9741 Westheimer Rd
Houston, TX 77042
Phone: (713) 975-1810

#44
Fadi's Mediterranean Grill
Cuisines: Greek, Mediterranean, Middle Eastern
Average price: Modest
Area: Meyerland
Address: 4738 Beechnut St
Houston, TX 77096
Phone: (713) 666-4644

#45
Chilantro
Cuisines: Food Stand, Asian Fusion, Korean
Average price: Inexpensive
Area: West University
Address: Moving Target
Houston, TX 77005
Phone: (512) 568-0256

#46
Torchy's Tacos
Cuisines: Tex-Mex, Mexican, Breakfast & Brunch
Average price: Inexpensive
Area: Montrose
Address: 2411 S Shepherd Dr
Houston, TX 77019
Phone: (713) 595-8226

#47
Gelazzi
Cuisines: Desserts, Gelato, Italian
Average price: Inexpensive
Area: The Heights
Address: 3601 White Oak Dr
Houston, TX 77007
Phone: (713) 597-6257

#48
District 7 Grill
Cuisines: American
Average price: Modest
Area: EaDo
Address: 1508 Hutchins St
Houston, TX 77003
Phone: (713) 225-4950

#49
CRISP
Cuisines: Italian, Wine Bar
Average price: Modest
Area: The Heights
Address: 2220 Bevis St
Houston, TX 77008
Phone: (713) 360-0222

#50
Fusion Taco
Cuisines: Asian Fusion, Mexican
Average price: Modest
Area: Downtown
Address: 801 Congress
Houston, TX 77002
Phone: (713) 422-2882

#51
Wild Kitchen
Cuisines: Cajun, Creole, Burgers
Average price: Inexpensive
Area: Braeswood Place, Meyerland
Address: 8806 Stella Link Rd
Houston, TX 77025
Phone: (832) 778-9555

#52
Torchy's Tacos
Cuisines: Breakfast & Brunch, Tex-Mex
Average price: Inexpensive
Area: West University
Address: 2400 Times Blvd
Houston, TX 77005
Phone: (713) 487-0067

#53
Moon Tower Inn
Cuisines: Dive Bar, Hot Dogs
Average price: Inexpensive
Area: Second Ward
Address: 3004 Canal St
Houston, TX 77003
Phone: (832) 266-0105

#54
Caracol
Cuisines: Seafood, Mexican
Average price: Expensive
Area: Galleria/Uptown
Address: 2200 Post Oak Blvd
Houston, TX 77056
Phone: (713) 622-9996

#55
MKT BAR
Cuisines: Bar, American, Music Venues
Average price: Modest
Area: Downtown
Address: 1001 Austin St
Houston, TX 77010
Phone: (832) 360-2222

#56
Treebeards
Cuisines: Cajun, Creole, Southern, Caterer
Average price: Inexpensive
Area: Fourth Ward, Downtown
Address: 315 Travis St
Houston, TX 77002
Phone: (713) 228-2622

#57
Orange Lunch Box
Cuisines: Sandwiches, Salad, Soup
Average price: Inexpensive
Area: Memorial
Address: 1379 S Voss Rd
Houston, TX 77057
Phone: (713) 783-1626

#58
Common Bond Cafe & Bakery
Cuisines: Café, Bakery, Breakfast & Brunch
Average price: Modest
Area: Montrose
Address: 1706 Westheimer Rd
Houston, TX 77027
Phone: (713) 529-3535

#59
Ibiza
Cuisines: Wine Bar, American, Basque
Average price: Expensive
Area: Fourth Ward, Midtown
Address: 2450 Louisiana St
Houston, TX 77006
Phone: (713) 524-0004

#60
Paulie's
Cuisines: Deli, Sandwiches, Italian
Average price: Modest
Area: Montrose
Address: 1834 Westheimer Rd
Houston, TX 77098
Phone: (713) 807-7271

#61
Seasons 52
Cuisines: American, Vegetarian, Wine Bar
Average price: Modest
Area: Highland Village
Address: 4410 Westheimer Rd
Houston, TX 77027
Phone: (713) 621-5452

#62
Thai Jasmine Restaurant
Cuisines: Thai
Average price: Inexpensive
Area: South Belt/Ellington
Address: 10900 Kingspoint Rd
Houston, TX 77075
Phone: (713) 944-0360

#63
The Springbok
Cuisines: South African, Gastropub
Average price: Modest
Area: Fourth Ward, Downtown
Address: 711 Main St
Houston, TX 77030
Phone: (281) 501-9679

#64
The Blue Fish
Cuisines: Sushi Bar, Japanese, Seafood
Average price: Modest
Area: Fourth Ward, Downtown
Address: 550 Texas St
Houston, TX 77002
Phone: (713) 225-3474

#65
Truluck's
Cuisines: Seafood, Steakhouse
Average price: Expensive
Area: Galleria/Uptown
Address: 5350 Westheimer Rd
Houston, TX 77056
Phone: (713) 783-7270

#66
Pappadeaux Seafood Kitchen
Cuisines: Seafood
Average price: Modest
Area: Hobby
Address: 7800 Airport Blvd
Houston, TX 77061
Phone: (713) 847-7622

#67
Petrol Station
Cuisines: American, Bar
Average price: Modest
Area: Oak Forest/Garden Oaks
Address: 985 Wakefield Dr
Houston, TX 77018
Phone: (713) 957-2875

#68
Liberty Kitchen
Cuisines: American, Seafood, Burgers
Average price: Modest
Area: The Heights
Address: 1050 Studewood St
Houston, TX 77008
Phone: (713) 802-0533

#69
Shepherd Park Draught House
Cuisines: American, Gastropub
Average price: Modest
Area: Independence Heights, Oak Forest/Garden Oaks
Address: 3402 N Shepherd
Houston, TX 77018
Phone: (832) 767-1380

#70
Les Givral's Sandwich & Café
Cuisines: Vietnamese, Sandwiches, Barbeque
Average price: Inexpensive
Area: Fourth Ward, Midtown
Address: 2704 Milam St
Houston, TX 77006
Phone: (713) 529-1736

#71
Masraff's
Cuisines: American, Seafood
Average price: Expensive
Area: Galleria/Uptown
Address: 1753 Post Oak Blvd
Houston, TX 77056
Phone: (713) 355-1975

#72
Good Dog Houston
Cuisines: Hot Dogs
Average price: Inexpensive
Area: The Heights
Address: 903 Studewood St
Houston, TX 77008
Phone: (832) 800-3647

#73
Fat Bao
Cuisines: Asian Fusion, Ramen
Average price: Inexpensive
Area: Upper Kirby
Address: 3419 Kirby Dr
Houston, TX 77098
Phone: (713) 677-0341

#74
EurAsia Fusion Sushi
Cuisines: Asian Fusion, Japanese, Sushi Bar
Average price: Modest
Area: Spring Branch
Address: 1330 Wirt Rd
Houston, TX 77055
Phone: (832) 203-8815

#75
Oxheart
Cuisines: American
Average price: Exclusive
Area: Downtown, Warehouse District
Address: 1302 Nance St
Houston, TX 77002
Phone: (832) 830-8592

#76
Uchi
Cuisines: Sushi Bar, Japanese
Average price: Exclusive
Area: Fourth Ward, Montrose
Address: 904 Westheimer Rd
Houston, TX 77006
Phone: (713) 522-4808

#77
Vinoteca Poscol
Cuisines: Italian, Wine Bar
Average price: Modest
Area: Montrose
Address: 1609 Westheimer
Houston, TX 77006
Phone: (713) 529-2797

#78
Empire Cafe
Cuisines: Coffee, Tea, Breakfast & Brunch, American
Average price: Modest
Area: Montrose
Address: 1732 Westheimer Rd
Houston, TX 77098
Phone: (713) 528-5282

#79
Zelko Bistro
Cuisines: American, Southern
Average price: Modest
Area: The Heights
Address: 705 E 11th St
Houston, TX 77008
Phone: (713) 880-8691

#80
Barnaby's Cafe
Cuisines: American, Breakfast & Brunch, Salad
Average price: Modest
Area: Montrose
Address: 1701 S Shepherd Dr
Houston, TX 77019
Phone: (713) 520-5131

#81
The Original Ninfa's On Navigation
Cuisines: Mexican, Tex-Mex
Average price: Modest
Area: Warehouse District, Second Ward
Address: 2704 Navigation Blvd
Houston, TX 77003
Phone: (713) 228-1175

#82
Argentina Cafe
Cuisines: Latin American, Argentine, Café
Average price: Modest
Area: Galleria/Uptown
Address: 3055 Sage Rd
Houston, TX 77056
Phone: (713) 622-8877

#83
Bubba's Texas Burger Shack
Cuisines: Burgers
Average price: Inexpensive
Area: Gulfton, Galleria/Uptown
Address: 5230 Westpark Dr
Houston, TX 77056
Phone: (713) 661-1622

#84
Huynh
Cuisines: Vietnamese
Average price: Modest
Area: Downtown, EaDo
Address: 912 St. Emanuel St
Houston, TX 77003
Phone: (713) 224-8964

#85
Lucille's
Cuisines: American, Southern
Average price: Modest
Area: Museum District
Address: 5512 LaBranch
Houston, TX 77004
Phone: (713) 568-2505

#86
French Riviera Bakery & Cafe
Cuisines: Bakery, French, Coffee, Tea
Average price: Inexpensive
Area: Galleria/Uptown
Address: 3100 Chimney Rock Rd
Houston, TX 77056
Phone: (713) 783-3264

#87
Baba Yega
Cuisines: Vegetarian, Burgers, American
Average price: Modest
Area: Fourth Ward, Montrose
Address: 2607 Grant St
Houston, TX 77006
Phone: (713) 522-0042

#88
Papa Mo's Deli
Cuisines: Deli, Sandwiches, Breakfast & Brunch
Average price: Inexpensive
Area: The Heights
Address: 465B TC Jester Blvd
Houston, TX 77007
Phone: (713) 802-0043

#89
Facundo Cafe
Cuisines: Breakfast & Brunch, Burgers, Caterer
Average price: Modest
Area: Oak Forest/Garden Oaks
Address: 3103 Ella Blvd.
Houston, TX 77018
Phone: (713) 880-0898

#90
Koagie Hots
Cuisines: Cheesesteaks, Food Stand, Hot Dogs
Average price: Inexpensive
Area: Montrose
Address: 1427 Westheimer Rd
Houston, TX 77006
Phone: (602) 321-0423

#91
The Cajun Stop
Cuisines: Cajun, Creole, Seafood, Breakfast & Brunch
Average price: Modest
Area: EaDo
Address: 2130 Jefferson St
Houston, TX 77003
Phone: (713) 222-8333

#92
Number 1 Chicken Rice & Seafood
Cuisines: Chinese, Burgers, Chicken Wings
Average price: Inexpensive
Area: Museum District
Address: 4621 Almeda Rd
Houston, TX 77004
Phone: (713) 522-6093

#93
Mia's
Cuisines: American, Barbeque, Burgers
Average price: Modest
Area: Upper Kirby
Address: 3131 Argonne St
Houston, TX 77098
Phone: (713) 522-6427

#94
Izakaya Wa
Cuisines: Japanese, Tapas, Bar
Average price: Modest
Area: Memorial
Address: 12665 Memorial Dr
Houston, TX 77024
Phone: (713) 461-0155

#95
Istanbul Grill
Cuisines: Turkish, Middle Eastern, Mediterranean
Average price: Modest
Area: West University
Address: 5613 Morningside Dr
Houston, TX 77005
Phone: (713) 526-2800

#96
Zydeco Louisiana Diner
Cuisines: Cajun, Creole
Average price: Inexpensive
Area: Downtown
Address: 1119 Pease St
Houston, TX 77002
Phone: (713) 759-2001

#97
Fountain View Fish Market
Cuisines: Seafood
Average price: Inexpensive
Area: Galleria/Uptown
Address: 2912 Fountain View Dr
Houston, TX 77057
Phone: (713) 977-1436

#98
Reggae Hut
Cuisines: Caribbean
Average price: Modest
Area: Museum District
Address: 4814 Almeda Rd
Houston, TX 77004
Phone: (713) 520-7171

#99
The Community Bar
Cuisines: Lounge, Gastropub, Sports Bar
Average price: Modest
Area: Fourth Ward, Midtown
Address: 2703 Smith St
Houston, TX 77006
Phone: (713) 526-1576

#100
The Flat
Cuisines: Lounge, American
Average price: Modest
Area: Montrose
Address: 1701 Commonwealth St
Houston, TX 77006
Phone: (713) 360-7228

#101
Barnaby's Café
Cuisines: Burgers, American, Sandwiches
Average price: Modest
Area: Fourth Ward, Montrose
Address: 414 W Gray St
Houston, TX 77246
Phone: (713) 522-8898

#102
Cafe Brussels
Cuisines: Belgian, French
Average price: Modest
Area: Sixth Ward
Address: 1718 Houston Ave
Houston, TX 77007
Phone: (713) 222-6996

#103
Pollo Bravo
Cuisines: Latin American, Peruvian
Average price: Modest
Area: River Oaks, The Heights, Rice Military
Address: 5440 Memorial Dr
Houston, TX 77007
Phone: (713) 861-7866

#104
The Raven Grill
Cuisines: American
Average price: Modest
Area: Museum District, West University
Address: 1916 Bissonnet St
Houston, TX 77005
Phone: (713) 521-2027

#105
Brooklyn Meatball Co.
Cuisines: Italian, Sandwiches
Average price: Modest
Area: Fourth Ward, Downtown
Address: 930 Main St
Houston, TX 77002
Phone: (713) 632-8225

#106
Puebla's Mexican Kitchen & Bakery
Cuisines: Bakery, Mexican
Average price: Inexpensive
Area: The Heights
Address: 6320 N Main St
Houston, TX 77009
Phone: (713) 426-9062

#107
Eleven : Eleven Restaurant & Bar
Cuisines: American, Seafood, Cocktail Bar
Average price: Modest
Area: Fourth Ward, Montrose
Address: 607 W Gray St
Houston, TX 77019
Phone: (713) 529-5881

#108
Triple J's Smokehouse
Cuisines: Barbeque
Average price: Modest
Area: Trinity/Houston Gardens
Address: 6715 Homestead Rd
Houston, TX 77028
Phone: (713) 635-6381

#109
Jonathan's The Rub
Cuisines: American, Seafood, Steakhouse
Average price: Expensive
Area: Memorial
Address: 9061 Gaylord St
Houston, TX 77024
Phone: (713) 465-8200

#110
Cafe TH
Cuisines: Vietnamese, Sandwiches, Vegan
Average price: Inexpensive
Area: EaDo
Address: 2108 Pease St
Houston, TX 77003
Phone: (713) 225-4766

#111
Café Rabelais
Cuisines: French, Brasserie
Average price: Modest
Area: West University
Address: 2442 Times Blvd
Houston, TX 77005
Phone: (713) 520-8841

#112
Provisions
Cuisines: American, Bar
Average price: Modest
Area: Fourth Ward, Midtown, Montrose
Address: 807 Taft St
Houston, TX 77019
Phone: (713) 628-9020

#113
Telwink Grill
Cuisines: American, Diner, Breakfast & Brunch
Average price: Inexpensive
Area: Gulfgate/Pine Valley
Address: 4318 Telephone Rd
Houston, TX 77087
Phone: (713) 644-4933

#114
13 Celsius
Cuisines: Wine Bar, Café
Average price: Modest
Area: Midtown
Address: 3000 Caroline St
Houston, TX 77004
Phone: (713) 529-8466

#115
Jus' Mac Montrose
Cuisines: American
Average price: Inexpensive
Area: Fourth Ward, Midtown, Montrose
Address: 106 Westheimer
Houston, TX 77006
Phone: (832) 203-8340

#116
Onion Creek
Cuisines: Coffee, Tea, Bar, Breakfast & Brunch
Average price: Modest
Area: The Heights
Address: 3106 White Oak Dr
Houston, TX 77007
Phone: (713) 880-0706

#117
Korean Noodle House
Cuisines: Korean
Average price: Inexpensive
Area: Spring Branch
Address: 1415 Murray Bay St
Houston, TX 77080
Phone: (713) 463-8870

#118
Oh My Gogi! Truck
Cuisines: Korean, Asian Fusion, Food Truck
Average price: Inexpensive
Area: West University
Address: 5555 Morningside Dr
Houston, TX 77401
Phone: (281) 694-4644

#119
Thai Jin
Cuisines: Asian Fusion, Thai, Sushi Bar
Average price: Modest
Area: Spring Branch
Address: 2753 Gessner Rd
Houston, TX 77080
Phone: (713) 939-4999

#120
Dolce Vita
Cuisines: Pizza, Italian
Average price: Modest
Area: Fourth Ward, Montrose
Address: 500 Westheimer Rd
Houston, TX 77006
Phone: (713) 520-8222

#121
Brothers Taco House
Cuisines: Mexican
Average price: Inexpensive
Area: EaDo
Address: 1604 Dowling St
Houston, TX 77003
Phone: (713) 223-0091

#122
Frank's Pizza
Cuisines: Pizza, Italian, Burgers
Average price: Inexpensive
Area: Fourth Ward, Downtown
Address: 417 Travis St
Houston, TX 77002
Phone: (713) 225-5656

#123
La Guadalupana Bakery & Café
Cuisines: Mexican, Bakery
Average price: Inexpensive
Area: Montrose
Address: 2109 Dunlavy St
Houston, TX 77006
Phone: (713) 522-2301

#124
VERTS Kebap
Cuisines: German, Turkish, Sandwiches
Average price: Inexpensive
Area: The Heights
Address: 107 Yale St
Houston, TX 77007
Phone: (713) 714-8101

#125
Dish Society
Cuisines: American, Breakfast & Brunch
Average price: Modest
Area: Memorial, Galleria/Uptown
Address: 5740 San Felipe St
Houston, TX 77057
Phone: (832) 538-1060

#126
Champ Burger
Cuisines: Burgers
Average price: Inexpensive
Area: Second Ward
Address: 304 Sampson St
Houston, TX 77003
Phone: (713) 227-2094

#127
Harvest Organic Grille
Cuisines: Bar, American, Live/Raw Food
Average price: Modest
Area: Galleria/Uptown
Address: 1810 Fountain View Dr
Houston, TX 77057
Phone: (713) 243-0900

#128
Liberty Kitchen & Oysterette
Cuisines: American, Seafood,
Breakfast & Brunch
Average price: Modest
Area: Highland Village
Address: 4224 San Felipe
Houston, TX 77027
Phone: (713) 622-1010

#129
Barnaby's Café
Cuisines: Burgers, Mexican, Sandwiches
Average price: Modest
Area: Fourth Ward, Montrose
Address: 604 Fairview St
Houston, TX 77006
Phone: (713) 522-0106

#130
Sushi Miyagi
Cuisines: Sushi Bar, Japanese
Average price: Modest
Area: Chinatown, Alief
Address: 10600 Bellaire Blvd
Houston, TX 77072
Phone: (281) 933-9112

#131
888 Chinese Restaurant
Cuisines: Chinese
Average price: Modest
Area: Pecan Park, Gulfgate/Pine Valley
Address: 403 Winkler Dr
Houston, TX 77087
Phone: (713) 644-8888

#132
Gyu-Kaku Japanese BBQ
Cuisines: Japanese, Barbeque
Average price: Modest
Area: Fourth Ward, Midtown
Address: 510 Gray St
Houston, TX 77019
Phone: (713) 750-9520

#133
The Pass
Cuisines: American
Average price: Exclusive
Area: Fourth Ward, Midtown, Montrose
Address: 807 Taft St
Houston, TX 77019
Phone: (713) 628-9020

#134
Piola
Cuisines: Pizza, Italian
Average price: Modest
Area: Fourth Ward, Midtown
Address: 3201 Louisiana St
Houston, TX 77006
Phone: (713) 524-8222

#135
Kenny & Ziggy's New York Delicatessen Restaurant
Cuisines: Deli, Sandwiches, Caterer
Average price: Modest
Area: Galleria/Uptown
Address: 2327 Post Oak Blvd
Houston, TX 77056
Phone: (713) 871-8883

#136
Treebeards
Cuisines: Southern
Average price: Inexpensive
Area: Fourth Ward, Downtown
Address: 711 Louisiana St
Houston, TX 77002
Phone: (713) 224-6677

#137
Weslayan Café
Cuisines: Coffee, Tea,
Breakfast & Brunch, Sandwiches
Average price: Inexpensive
Area: Highland Village
Address: 2900 Weslayan St
Houston, TX 77027
Phone: (713) 626-3663

#138
Lankford Grocery & Market
Cuisines: Grocery, Burgers
Average price: Inexpensive
Area: Fourth Ward, Midtown, Montrose
Address: 88 Dennis St
Houston, TX 77006
Phone: (713) 522-9555

#139
Just Dinner
Cuisines: American
Average price: Expensive
Area: Montrose
Address: 1915 Dunlavy St
Houston, TX 77006
Phone: (713) 807-0077

#140
Federal American Grill
Cuisines: American, Steakhouse
Average price: Modest
Area: The Heights, Rice Military
Address: 510 Shepherd Dr
Houston, TX 77007
Phone: (713) 863-7777

#141
El Tiempo Cantina
Cuisines: Tex-Mex, Mexican
Average price: Modest
Area: Upper Kirby
Address: 3130 Richmond Ave
Houston, TX 77098
Phone: (713) 807-1600

#142
Villa Arcos
Cuisines: Mexican, Breakfast & Brunch
Average price: Inexpensive
Area: Second Ward
Address: 3009 Navigation Blvd
Houston, TX 77003
Phone: (713) 227-1743

#143
New York Bagels
Cuisines: Bagels, Breakfast & Brunch, Burgers
Average price: Inexpensive
Area: Fondren Southwest
Address: 9724 Hillcroft St
Houston, TX 77096
Phone: (713) 723-5879

#144
Hobbit Cafe
Cuisines: Breakfast & Brunch, Vegetarian
Average price: Modest
Area: Upper Kirby
Address: 2243 Richmond Ave
Houston, TX 77098
Phone: (713) 526-5460

#145
Bodega's Taco Shop
Cuisines: Mexican
Average price: Inexpensive
Area: Museum District
Address: 1200 Binz Ave
Houston, TX 77004
Phone: (713) 528-6102

#146
Goode Company Seafood
Cuisines: Seafood
Average price: Modest
Area: West University
Address: 2621 Westpark Dr
Houston, TX 77098
Phone: (713) 523-7154

#147
Hubcap Grill
Cuisines: Burgers
Average price: Inexpensive
Area: Downtown
Address: 1111 Prairie St
Houston, TX 77002
Phone: (713) 223-5885

#148
Sal Y Pimienta Kitchen
Cuisines: Latin American, Argentine
Average price: Modest
Area: Memorial
Address: 818 Town & Counrty Blvd
Houston, TX 77024
Phone: (713) 907-0412

#149
Coltivare
Cuisines: Italian, Vegetarian, Pizza
Average price: Modest
Area: The Heights
Address: 3320 White Oak Dr
Houston, TX 77007
Phone: (713) 637-4095

#150
Chief's Cajun Snack Shack
Cuisines: Burgers
Average price: Inexpensive
Area: MacGregor
Address: 5204 Live Oak St
Houston, TX 77004
Phone: (832) 203-8842

#151
True Food Kitchen
Cuisines: American, Vegan, Vegetarian
Average price: Modest
Area: Galleria/Uptown
Address: 1700 Post Oak Blvd
Houston, TX 77056
Phone: (281) 605-2505

#152
Myung Dong Restaurant
Cuisines: Korean
Average price: Modest
Area: Braeburn, Sharpstown
Address: 6415 Bissonnet St
Houston, TX 77074
Phone: (713) 779-5530

#153
Salata
Cuisines: Salad, Greek, American
Average price: Modest
Area: Highland Village
Address: 3651 Weslayan St
Houston, TX 77027
Phone: (713) 892-5800

#154
Sleepy' Po-Boys
Cuisines: American
Average price: Inexpensive
Area: Braeswood Place, Medical Center
Address: 9591 S Main St
Houston, TX 77025
Phone: (713) 662-3054

#155
Oporto Café
Cuisines: Tapas Bar, Wine Bar, Portuguese
Average price: Modest
Area: Greenway
Address: 3833 Richmond Ave
Houston, TX 77027
Phone: (713) 621-1114

#156
Laredo Taqueria
Cuisines: Mexican
Average price: Inexpensive
Area: Northside Village
Address: 113 Cavalcade St
Houston, TX 77009
Phone: (713) 695-0506

#157
Fajita Pete's
Cuisines: Caterer, Tex-Mex
Average price: Modest
Area: Braeswood Place, West University
Address: 4050 Bellaire Blvd
Houston, TX 77025
Phone: (713) 723-8100

#158
Antica Osteria
Cuisines: Italian
Average price: Expensive
Area: West University
Address: 2311 Bissonnet St
Houston, TX 77005
Phone: (713) 521-1155

#159
Witchcraft Tavern & Provision Co.
Cuisines: Pub, Burgers
Average price: Modest
Area: The Heights
Address: 1221 W 11th St
Houston, TX 77008
Phone: (832) 649-3601

#160
Garden Kitchen
Cuisines: Vegan, Live/Raw Food, Vegetarian
Average price: Modest
Area: South Main
Address: 10480 Main St
Houston, TX 77025
Phone: (832) 350-7534

#161
Black Hole Coffee House
Cuisines: American, Coffee, Tea, Breakfast & Brunch
Average price: Inexpensive
Area: Museum District, Montrose
Address: 4504 Graustark St
Houston, TX 77006
Phone: (713) 528-0653

#162
El Tiempo Cantina
Cuisines: Mexican
Average price: Modest
Area: Second Ward
Address: 2814 Navigation Blvd
Houston, TX 77003
Phone: (713) 222-6800

#163
Sweet Paris Crêperie & Cafe
Cuisines: French, Desserts, Crêperie
Average price: Modest
Area: West University
Address: 2420 Rice Blvd
Houston, TX 77005
Phone: (713) 360-6266

#164
Melange Creperie
Cuisines: Crêperie, Food Stand
Average price: Inexpensive
Area: Fourth Ward, Montrose
Address: 403 Westheimer Rd
Houston, TX 77006
Phone: (832) 724-9464

#165
Heights Asian Cafe
Cuisines: Chinese, Vietnamese
Average price: Inexpensive
Area: The Heights
Address: 2201 Yale St
Houston, TX 77008
Phone: (713) 880-9998

#166
The Brisket House
Cuisines: Barbeque
Average price: Modest
Area: Memorial, Galleria/Uptown
Address: 5775 Woodway
Houston, TX 77057
Phone: (281) 888-0331

#167
Red's Snow Wagon & More
Cuisines: Food Stand, American, Shaved Ice
Average price: Inexpensive
Area: South Acres/Crestmont Park
Address: 1309 Almeda-Genoa Rd
Houston, TX 77047
Phone: (713) 433-0164

#168
Frenchy's Chicken
Cuisines: Fast Food, Cajun, Creole, Wholesale Store
Average price: Inexpensive
Area: MacGregor
Address: 3919 Scott St
Houston, TX 77004
Phone: (713) 748-2233

#169
Saldivia's South American Grill
Cuisines: Latin American, Argentine
Average price: Modest
Area: Westchase
Address: 10234 Westheimer
Houston, TX 77042
Phone: (713) 782-9494

#170
Perbacco
Cuisines: Italian
Average price: Modest
Area: Fourth Ward, Downtown
Address: 700 Milam St
Houston, TX 77002
Phone: (713) 224-2422

#171
Darband Shishkabob
Cuisines: Persian, Iranian, Middle Eastern
Average price: Inexpensive
Area: Gulfton
Address: 5670 Hillcroft St
Houston, TX 77036
Phone: (713) 975-8350

#172
El Rey Taqueria
Cuisines: Mexican, Cuban
Average price: Inexpensive
Area: The Heights, Rice Military
Address: 910 Shepherd Dr
Houston, TX 77007
Phone: (713) 802-9145

#173
Maine-ly Sandwiches
Cuisines: Sandwiches
Average price: Modest
Area: Upper Kirby, Montrose
Address: 3310 S Shepherd Dr
Houston, TX 77098
Phone: (713) 942-2150

#174
Breakfast Burritos Anonymous
Cuisines: Food Truck, Breakfast & Brunch
Average price: Inexpensive
Area: Fourth Ward, Montrose
Address: 1953 Montrose Blvd
Houston, TX 77006
Phone: (832) 726-9222

#175
BRC Gastropub
Cuisines: Gastropub
Average price: Modest
Area: The Heights, Rice Military
Address: 519 Shepherd Dr
Houston, TX 77007
Phone: (713) 861-2233

#176
Little Pappasito's
Cuisines: Tex-Mex, Mexican
Average price: Modest
Area: Upper Kirby
Address: 2536 Richmond Ave
Houston, TX 77098
Phone: (713) 520-5066

#177
House of Bowls
Cuisines: Chinese
Average price: Inexpensive
Area: Sharpstown, Chinatown
Address: 6650 Corporate Dr
Houston, TX 77036
Phone: (713) 776-2288

#178
Tiny Boxwood's
Cuisines: Diner, Café
Average price: Modest
Area: Highland Village
Address: 3614 W Alabama St
Houston, TX 77027
Phone: (713) 622-4224

#179
Cali Sandwich & Fast Food
Cuisines: Sandwiches, Vietnamese, Salad
Average price: Inexpensive
Area: Fourth Ward, Midtown
Address: 3030 Travis St
Houston, TX 77006
Phone: (713) 520-0710

#180
Barnaby's Cafe
Cuisines: American
Average price: Modest
Area: Memorial, Galleria/Uptown
Address: 5750 Woodway Dr
Houston, TX 77057
Phone: (713) 266-0046

#181
LA Crawfish
Cuisines: Cajun, Creole, Seafood, Vietnamese
Average price: Modest
Area: Memorial
Address: 1005 Blalock Rd
Houston, TX 77055
Phone: (713) 461-8808

#182
Coco - Washington
Cuisines: Crêperie, Desserts, Coffee, Tea
Average price: Inexpensive
Area: The Heights, Rice Military
Address: 5555 Washington Ave
Houston, TX 77007
Phone: (832) 804-7985

#183
Adair Kitchen
Cuisines: American
Average price: Modest
Area: Galleria/Uptown
Address: 5161 San Felipe St
Houston, TX 77057
Phone: (713) 623-6100

#184
Papa Mio Italian Cafe
Cuisines: Italian
Average price: Inexpensive
Area: Museum District, Montrose
Address: 2006 Lexington St
Houston, TX 77098
Phone: (713) 523-2428

#185
Rudy's Country Store & Bar-B-Q
Cuisines: Barbeque
Average price: Modest
Area: Fairbanks/Northwest Crossing
Address: 14620 NW Fwy
Houston, TX 77040
Phone: (713) 462-3337

#186
The Ginger Man
Cuisines: Pub, Restaurant
Average price: Modest
Area: West University
Address: 5607 Morningside Dr
Houston, TX 77005
Phone: (713) 526-2770

#187
Beaver's
Cuisines: Barbeque, Bar, Breakfast & Brunch
Average price: Modest
Area: Sixth Ward
Address: 2310 Decatur St
Houston, TX 77007
Phone: (713) 864-2328

#188
Captain Benny's Half Shell Oyster Bar
Cuisines: Seafood, Cajun, Creole
Average price: Modest
Area: Braeswood Place
Address: 8506 S Main St
Houston, TX 77025
Phone: (713) 666-5469

#189
Relish Fine Foods
Cuisines: Specialty Food, Sandwiches, Bakery
Average price: Modest
Area: Highland Village
Address: 3951 San Felipe St
Houston, TX 77027
Phone: (713) 599-1960

#190
The Lexington Grille
Cuisines: American
Average price: Expensive
Area: Museum District, Montrose
Address: 2005 Lexington St
Houston, TX 77098
Phone: (713) 524-9877

#191
Down House
Cuisines: Bar, Café, Breakfast & Brunch
Average price: Modest
Area: The Heights
Address: 1801 Yale St
Houston, TX 77008
Phone: (713) 864-3696

#192
Corner Table
Cuisines: American
Average price: Expensive
Area: Upper Kirby
Address: 2736 Virginia St
Houston, TX 77098
Phone: (713) 568-9196

#193
Star Pizza
Cuisines: Pizza, Salad, Italian
Average price: Modest
Area: Upper Kirby
Address: 2111 Norfolk St
Houston, TX 77098
Phone: (713) 523-0800

#194
Brasil
Cuisines: Coffee, Tea, Sandwiches, Pizza
Average price: Modest
Area: Montrose
Address: 2604 Dunlavy St
Houston, TX 77006
Phone: (713) 528-1993

#195
Queen Vic Pub & Kitchen
Cuisines: Pub, Tea Room, British
Average price: Modest
Area: Upper Kirby
Address: 2712 Richmond Ave
Houston, TX 77098
Phone: (713) 533-0022

#196
Myth Kafe
Cuisines: Greek
Average price: Inexpensive
Area: Downtown
Address: 1730 Jefferson St
Houston, TX 77003
Phone: (713) 739-0990

#197
Bayou City Seafood and Pasta
Cuisines: Cajun, Creole, Seafood
Average price: Modest
Area: Highland Village, Galleria/Uptown
Address: 4730 Richmond Ave
Houston, TX 77027
Phone: (713) 621-6602

#198
Hay Merchant
Cuisines: Bar, American
Average price: Modest
Area: Montrose
Address: 1100 Westheimer Rd
Houston, TX 77006
Phone: (713) 528-9805

#199
Barry's Pizza & Italian Diner
Cuisines: Italian, Pizza
Average price: Modest
Area: Gulfton, Galleria/Uptown
Address: 6003 Richmond Ave
Houston, TX 77057
Phone: (713) 266-8692

#200
Kim Tai Restaurant
Cuisines: Vietnamese
Average price: Inexpensive
Area: Midtown
Address: 2602 Fannin St
Houston, TX 77002
Phone: (713) 652-0644

#201
Ruggles Café Bakery
Cuisines: American, Bakery, Desserts
Average price: Modest
Area: West University
Address: 2365 Rice Blvd
Houston, TX 77005
Phone: (713) 520-6662

#202
El Tiempo 1308 Cantina
Cuisines: Tex-Mex
Average price: Modest
Area: Montrose
Address: 1308 Montrose Blvd
Houston, TX 77019
Phone: (713) 807-8996

#203
Little Sheep Mongolian Hot Pot
Cuisines: Mongolian, Chinese, Hot Pot
Average price: Modest
Area: Galleria/Uptown
Address: 5901 Westheimer Rd
Houston, TX 77057
Phone: (713) 975-0687

#204
Luigi's Cucina Italiana
Cuisines: Italian
Average price: Modest
Area: Upper Kirby
Address: 3030 Audley St
Houston, TX 77098
Phone: (281) 888-9037

#205
Cook & Collins
Cuisines: American, Salad
Average price: Modest
Area: Fourth Ward, Midtown
Address: 2416 Brazos St
Houston, TX 77006
Phone: (832) 701-1973

#206
Natachee's Supper 'n Punch
Cuisines: American
Average price: Modest
Area: Fourth Ward, Midtown
Address: 3622 Main St
Houston, TX 77002
Phone: (713) 524-7203

#207
Fioza
Cuisines: Coffee, Tea, Breakfast & Brunch
Average price: Inexpensive
Area: Meyerland
Address: 9002 Chimney Rock Rd
Houston, TX 77096
Phone: (713) 729-8810

#208
Glass Wall
Cuisines: American
Average price: Expensive
Area: The Heights
Address: 933 Studewood St
Houston, TX 77008
Phone: (713) 868-7930

#209
Carter & Cooley Co.
Cuisines: Deli, Salad, Sandwiches
Average price: Inexpensive
Area: The Heights
Address: 375 W 19th St
Houston, TX 77008
Phone: (713) 864-3354

#210
MAX's Wine Dive
Cuisines: Wine Bar, American, Breakfast & Brunch
Average price: Modest
Area: The Heights, Rice Military
Address: 4720 Washington Ave
Houston, TX 77007
Phone: (713) 880-8737

#211
Sammy's Wild Game Grill
Cuisines: Hot Dogs, Burgers, Sandwiches
Average price: Modest
Area: The Heights
Address: 3715 Washington Ave
Houston, TX 77007
Phone: (713) 868-1345

#212
Pappas Burger
Cuisines: Burgers
Average price: Modest
Area: Galleria/Uptown
Address: 5815 Westheimer Rd
Houston, TX 77057
Phone: (713) 975-6082

#213
Giacomo's Cibo e Vino
Cuisines: Italian
Average price: Modest
Area: Upper Kirby
Address: 3215 Westheimer Rd
Houston, TX 77098
Phone: (713) 522-1934

#214
Costa Brava Bistro
Cuisines: Spanish, French, Tapas Bar
Average price: Expensive
Area: Bellaire
Address: 5115 Bellaire Blvd
Houston, TX 77401
Phone: (713) 839-1005

#215
Osteria Mazzantini
Cuisines: Wine Bar, Italian
Average price: Expensive
Area: Galleria/Uptown
Address: 2200 Post Oak Blvd
Houston, TX 77056
Phone: (713) 993-9898

#216
Etoile Cuisine et Bar
Cuisines: French
Average price: Expensive
Area: Galleria/Uptown
Address: 1101-11 Uptown Park Blvd
Houston, TX 77056
Phone: (832) 668-5808

#217
La Casa Del Caballo
Cuisines: Mexican, Steakhouse
Average price: Expensive
Area: Fourth Ward, Midtown, Montrose
Address: 322 Westheimer Rd
Houston, TX 77006
Phone: (832) 623-6467

#218
Eatsie Boys Cafe
Cuisines: Specialty Food, Sandwiches, Café
Average price: Modest
Area: Montrose
Address: 4100 Montrose Blvd
Houston, TX 77006
Phone: (713) 524-3737

#219
Zero's Sandwich Shop
Cuisines: Sandwiches
Average price: Inexpensive
Area: Fourth Ward, Downtown
Address: 507 Dallas St
Houston, TX 77002
Phone: (713) 739-9955

#220
Thai Bistro
Cuisines: Thai
Average price: Modest
Area: West University
Address: 3241 SW Fwy
Houston, TX 77027
Phone: (713) 669-9375

#221
Pasha
Cuisines: Turkish, Mediterranean
Average price: Modest
Area: West University
Address: 2325 University Blvd
Houston, TX 77005
Phone: (713) 592-0020

#222
Peru Cafe Express
Cuisines: Peruvian, Café
Average price: Modest
Area: Greenway, West University
Address: 3833 Southwest Fwy
Houston, TX 77027
Phone: (713) 622-7012

#223
Churrascos - Westchase
Cuisines: Latin American, Steakhouse, Seafood
Average price: Expensive
Area: Westchase
Address: 9705 Westheimer Rd
Houston, TX 77042
Phone: (713) 952-1988

#224
Chavez Mexican Cafe
Cuisines: Mexican
Average price: Inexpensive
Area: Spring Branch
Address: 2557 Gessner Rd
Houston, TX 77080
Phone: (713) 460-5392

#225
Skol Casbar & Grille
Cuisines: Bar, American
Average price: Modest
Area: Midtown
Address: 1701 Webster St
Houston, TX 77003
Phone: (713) 651-1011

#226
Carrabba's
Cuisines: Italian, Seafood
Average price: Modest
Area: Upper Kirby
Address: 3115 Kirby Dr
Houston, TX 77098
Phone: (713) 522-3131

#227
Bradley's Fine Diner
Cuisines: American
Average price: Modest
Area: The Heights
Address: 191 Heights Blvd
Houston, TX 77007
Phone: (832) 831-5939

#228
BB's Cafe
Cuisines: Cajun, Creole
Average price: Modest
Area: The Heights
Address: 2701 White Oak Dr
Houston, TX 77007
Phone: (713) 868-8000

#229
Underbelly
Cuisines: American, Wine Bar
Average price: Expensive
Area: Montrose
Address: 1100 Westheimer Rd
Houston, TX 77006
Phone: (713) 528-9800

#230
Hokkaido Japanese Restaurant
Cuisines: Japanese, Sushi Bar
Average price: Inexpensive
Area: Sharpstown, Chinatown
Address: 9108 Bellaire Blvd
Houston, TX 77036
Phone: (713) 988-8448

#231
Frank's Grill
Cuisines: Breakfast & Brunch, Burgers
Average price: Inexpensive
Area: Golfcrest/Belfort/Reveille
Address: 4702 Telephone Rd
Houston, TX 77087
Phone: (713) 649-3296

#232
Barnaby's Cafe
Cuisines: American, Breakfast & Brunch
Average price: Modest
Area: Downtown
Address: 801 Congress St
Houston, TX 77002
Phone: (713) 226-8787

#233
Torchy's Tacos
Cuisines: Mexican, Breakfast & Brunch
Average price: Inexpensive
Area: The Heights
Address: 350 W 19th St
Houston, TX 77008
Phone: (713) 595-8229

#234
Jus' Mac
Cuisines: American
Average price: Inexpensive
Area: The Heights
Address: 2617 Yale St
Houston, TX 77008
Phone: (713) 622-8646

#235
Maharaja Bhog
Cuisines: Indian, Vegetarian
Average price: Modest
Area: Westwood, Sharpstown
Address: 8338 Southwest Fwy
Houston, TX 77074
Phone: (713) 771-2464

#236
Ruggles Green | River Oaks
Cuisines: Pizza, Gluten-Free, American
Average price: Modest
Area: Upper Kirby
Address: 2311 W Alabama St
Houston, TX 77098
Phone: (713) 533-0777

#237
Fellini Caffè
Cuisines: Italian, Coffee, Tea
Average price: Inexpensive
Area: West University
Address: 5211 Kelvin Dr
Houston, TX 77005
Phone: (281) 888-6654

#238
Nippon Japanese Restaurant
Cuisines: Sushi Bar, Ramen
Average price: Modest
Area: Museum District, Montrose
Address: 4464 Montrose Blvd
Houston, TX 77006
Phone: (713) 523-3939

#239
Thien An Sandwiches
Cuisines: Vietnamese
Average price: Inexpensive
Area: Midtown
Address: 2611 San Jacinto St
Houston, TX 77004
Phone: (713) 522-7007

#240
The Boot
Cuisines: Bar, Cajun, Creole, Seafood
Average price: Modest
Area: The Heights
Address: 1206 W 20th St
Houston, TX 77008
Phone: (713) 869-2668

#241
Super Chicken
Cuisines: Peruvian, Latin American
Average price: Inexpensive
Area: Willow Meadows/Willowbend, Westbury
Address: 11107 S Post Oak Rd
Houston, TX 77035
Phone: (832) 581-2823

#242
House of Pies Restaurant & Bakery
Cuisines: Diner, Breakfast & Brunch, Bakery
Average price: Inexpensive
Area: Upper Kirby
Address: 3112 Kirby Dr
Houston, TX 77098
Phone: (713) 782-1299

#243
Pupusa Buffet
Cuisines: Latin American, Buffet
Average price: Inexpensive
Area: Gulfton, Braeburn, Sharpstown
Address: 7909 Hillcroft St
Houston, TX 77081
Phone: (713) 272-6666

#244
Dosi
Cuisines: Korean, Asian Fusion
Average price: Modest
Area: Upper Kirby
Address: 2802 S Shepherd Dr
Houston, TX 77098
Phone: (713) 521-3674

#245
Nundini Chef's Table
Cuisines: Italian, Deli
Average price: Modest
Area: The Heights
Address: 500 N Shepherd Dr
Houston, TX 77007
Phone: (713) 861-6331

#246
Spicy Pickle
Cuisines: Sandwiches, Salad, Pizza
Average price: Inexpensive
Area: Medical Center
Address: 1333 Old Spanish Trl
Houston, TX 77054
Phone: (281) 617-4777

#247
Teotihuacan Mexican Café
Cuisines: Mexican, Tex-Mex, Breakfast & Brunch
Average price: Modest
Area: The Heights
Address: 1511 Airline Dr
Houston, TX 77009
Phone: (713) 426-4420

#248
Andes Cafe
Cuisines: Venezuelan, Colombian, Peruvian
Average price: Modest
Area: Warehouse District
Address: 2311 Canal St
Houston, TX 77003
Phone: (832) 659-0063

#249
Mala Sichuan Bistro
Cuisines: Szechuan
Average price: Modest
Area: Sharpstown, Chinatown
Address: 9348 Bellaire Blvd
Houston, TX 77036
Phone: (713) 995-1889

#250
BB's Cafe
Cuisines: Cajun, Creole
Average price: Modest
Area: Montrose
Address: 2710 Montrose Blvd
Houston, TX 77006
Phone: (713) 524-4499

#251
Taqueria Del Sol
Cuisines: Tex-Mex, Mexican
Average price: Inexpensive
Area: Park Place
Address: 8114 Park Place Blvd
Houston, TX 77017
Phone: (713) 644-0535

#252
Oh My! Pocket Pies
Cuisines: Burgers, Food Stand
Average price: Inexpensive
Area: Northside Village
Address: 227 Cavalcade
Houston, TX 77009
Phone: (281) 902-9820

#253
Shri Balaji Bhavan
Cuisines: Indian, Vegetarian
Average price: Inexpensive
Area: Gulfton
Address: 5655 Hillcroft St
Houston, TX 77036
Phone: (713) 783-1126

#254
Lowbrow
Cuisines: Bar, Breakfast & Brunch
Average price: Modest
Area: Montrose
Address: 1601 W Main St
Houston, TX 77006
Phone: (281) 501-8288

#255
III Forks
Cuisines: Steakhouse
Average price: Expensive
Area: Downtown
Address: 1201 San Jacinto St
Houston, TX 77002
Phone: (713) 658-9457

#256
Sandong Noodle House
Cuisines: Chinese, Taiwanese
Average price: Inexpensive
Area: Sharpstown, Chinatown
Address: 9938 Bellaire Blvd
Houston, TX 77036
Phone: (713) 988-8802

#257
Goode's Armadillo Palace
Cuisines: Bar, Music Venues, American
Average price: Modest
Area: West University
Address: 5015 Kirby Dr
Houston, TX 77098
Phone: (713) 526-9700

#258
La Vista
Cuisines: Italian, Pizza
Average price: Modest
Area: Galleria/Uptown
Address: 1936 Fountain View Dr
Houston, TX 77057
Phone: (713) 787-9899

#259
Last Concert Café
Cuisines: Tex-Mex, Music Venues, Dive Bar
Average price: Modest
Area: Downtown, Warehouse District
Address: 1403 Nance St
Houston, TX 77002
Phone: (713) 226-8563

#260
LaMacro
Cuisines: Mexican
Average price: Inexpensive
Area: Northside Village
Address: 1822 N Main St
Houston, TX 77009
Phone: (713) 226-8226

#261
Don Café
Cuisines: Vietnamese, Sandwiches
Average price: Inexpensive
Area: Sharpstown, Chinatown
Address: 9300 Bellaire Blvd
Houston, TX 77036
Phone: (713) 777-9500

#262
Cool Runnings Jamaican Grill
Cuisines: Caribbean
Average price: Modest
Area: Fondren Southwest
Address: 8270 W Bellfort
Houston, TX 77071
Phone: (713) 777-1566

#263
Niko Niko's Market Square
Cuisines: Food Stand, Greek
Average price: Inexpensive
Area: Fourth Ward, Downtown
Address: 301 Milam
Houston, TX 77002
Phone: (713) 224-4976

#264
Super Chicken
Cuisines: Fast Food, Sandwiches, Chicken Wings
Average price: Inexpensive
Area: Greenspoint
Address: 414 N Sam Houston Pkwy E
Houston, TX 77060
Phone: (281) 448-6300

#265
Winston's On Washington
Cuisines: Bar, Breakfast & Brunch, American
Average price: Modest
Area: The Heights, Rice Military
Address: 5111 Washington Ave
Houston, TX 77007
Phone: (281) 501-9088

#266
Banana Leaf
Cuisines: Malaysian
Average price: Modest
Area: Sharpstown, Chinatown
Address: 9889 Bellaire Blvd
Houston, TX 77036
Phone: (713) 771-8118

#267
Cafe Pita
Cuisines: Mediterranean
Average price: Modest
Area: Gulfton, Galleria/Uptown
Address: 5506 Richmond Ave
Houston, TX 77056
Phone: (713) 952-9066

#268
Smashburger
Cuisines: Burgers
Average price: Inexpensive
Area: Galleria/Uptown
Address: 5381 Westheimer Rd
Houston, TX 77056
Phone: (713) 997-8357

#269
Vincent's Restaurant
Cuisines: Italian
Average price: Modest
Area: Montrose
Address: 2701 W Dallas St
Houston, TX 77019
Phone: (713) 528-4313

#270
Goode Company Barbeque
Cuisines: Barbeque, Gluten-Free
Average price: Modest
Area: West University
Address: 5109 Kirby Dr
Houston, TX 77098
Phone: (713) 522-2530

#271
Boheme
Cuisines: Wine Bar, Café, American
Average price: Modest
Area: Fourth Ward, Midtown, Montrose
Address: 307 Fairview St
Houston, TX 77006
Phone: (713) 529-1099

#272
Tacorrey
Cuisines: Mexican, Fast Food, Food Stand
Average price: Inexpensive
Area: Northside/Northline, Northside Village
Address: 63 Berry Rd
Houston, TX 77022
Phone: (832) 343-5408

#273
Asia Market
Cuisines: Ethnic Food, Thai
Average price: Inexpensive
Area: The Heights
Address: 1010 W Cavalcade St
Houston, TX 77009
Phone: (713) 863-7074

#274
Hollister Grill
Cuisines: American
Average price: Modest
Area: Spring Branch
Address: 1741 Hollister St
Houston, TX 77055
Phone: (713) 973-1741

#275
The Union Kitchen
Cuisines: American
Average price: Modest
Area: Memorial
Address: 12538 Memorial Dr
Houston, TX 77024
Phone: (713) 360-2000

#276
Xiong's Café
Cuisines: Chinese
Average price: Inexpensive
Area: Sharpstown, Chinatown
Address: 9888 Bellaire Blvd
Houston, TX 77036
Phone: (713) 771-8448

#277
Mama's Oven
Cuisines: Soul Food, Southern
Average price: Inexpensive
Area: Braeswood Place, Medical Center
Address: 9295 S Main St
Houston, TX 77025
Phone: (713) 661-3656

#278
Cafe Pita +
Cuisines: Mediterranean
Average price: Inexpensive
Area: Westchase
Address: 10852 Westheimer Rd
Houston, TX 77042
Phone: (713) 953-7237

#279
El Greco
Cuisines: Greek
Average price: Inexpensive
Area: Lawndale/Wayside
Address: 5420 Lawndale St
Houston, TX 77023
Phone: (832) 582-7918

#280
Theo's Restaurant
Cuisines: Pizza, Greek, American
Average price: Modest
Area: Fourth Ward, Montrose
Address: 812 Westheimer Rd
Houston, TX 77006
Phone: (713) 523-0425

#281
Kris Bistro and Wine Lounge
Cuisines: French, Wine Bar, Lounge
Average price: Modest
Area: Northside Village
Address: 7070 Allensby
Houston, TX 77022
Phone: (713) 358-5079

#282
Maggiano's Little Italy
Cuisines: Italian
Average price: Modest
Area: Galleria/Uptown
Address: 2019 Post Oak Blvd
Houston, TX 77056
Phone: (713) 961-2700

#283
Dry Creek Cafe
Cuisines: American, Burgers, Breakfast & Brunch
Average price: Modest
Area: The Heights
Address: 544 Yale St
Houston, TX 77007
Phone: (713) 426-2313

#284
Ponzo's Italian Food
Cuisines: Italian, Pizza
Average price: Inexpensive
Area: Fourth Ward, Midtown
Address: 2515 Bagby St
Houston, TX 77006
Phone: (713) 526-2426

#285
Mambo Seafood
Cuisines: Seafood
Average price: Inexpensive
Area: Gulfton
Address: 6697 Hillcroft St
Houston, TX 77081
Phone: (713) 541-3666

#286
Eatwell Bakery Cafe
Cuisines: Bakery, Italian, Mediterranean
Average price: Inexpensive
Area: Westchase
Address: 11150 Westheimer Rd
Houston, TX 77042
Phone: (713) 360-6600

#287
Lilo & Ella
Cuisines: Tapas, Asian Fusion
Average price: Modest
Area: The Heights
Address: 2307 Ella Blvd
Houston, TX 77008
Phone: (281) 888-5335

#288
Ninfa's Mexican Restaurant
Cuisines: Mexican
Average price: Modest
Area: Meadowbrook/Allendale
Address: 8553 Gulf Fwy
Houston, TX 77017
Phone: (713) 943-3183

#289
Shade
Cuisines: American
Average price: Modest
Area: The Heights
Address: 250 W 19th St
Houston, TX 77008
Phone: (713) 863-7500

#290
Lucky Palace Korean Restaurant
Cuisines: Korean, Barbeque
Average price: Modest
Area: Sharpstown
Address: 8508 Bellaire Blvd
Houston, TX 77036
Phone: (832) 409-6002

#291
Pho Long
Cuisines: Vietnamese
Average price: Inexpensive
Area: Lazy Brook/Timbergrove
Address: 2021 Mangum Rd
Houston, TX 77092
Phone: (713) 686-6408

#292
VERTS Kebap
Cuisines: Sandwiches, Turkish, German
Average price: Inexpensive
Area: River Oaks, Montrose
Address: 1572 W Gray St
Houston, TX 77019
Phone: (832) 804-7735

#293
Al's Quick Stop
Cuisines: Convenience Store, Fast Food
Average price: Inexpensive
Area: Montrose
Address: 2002 Waugh Dr
Houston, TX 77006
Phone: (713) 522-5170

#294
Bellissimo Ristorante
Cuisines: Italian
Average price: Modest
Area: The Heights
Address: 1848 Airline Dr
Houston, TX 77009
Phone: (832) 618-1168

#295
Plonk! Beer & Wine Bistro
Cuisines: Wine Bar, American
Average price: Modest
Area: Oak Forest/Garden Oaks
Address: 1214 W 43rd St
Houston, TX 77018
Phone: (713) 290-1070

#296
Little Bitty Burger Barn
Cuisines: Burgers
Average price: Inexpensive
Area: Oak Forest/Garden Oaks
Address: 5503 Pinemont Dr
Houston, TX 77092
Phone: (713) 683-6700

#297
Brick & Spoon
Cuisines: Breakfast & Brunch, Southern, Cajun, Creole
Average price: Modest
Area: Montrose
Address: 1312 W Alabama St
Houston, TX 77006
Phone: (832) 530-4973

#298
Hickory Hollow
Cuisines: Barbeque, Music Venues
Average price: Modest
Area: The Heights
Address: 101 Heights Blvd
Houston, TX 77007
Phone: (713) 869-6300

#299
Hubcap Grill
Cuisines: American, Burgers, Sandwiches
Average price: Inexpensive
Area: The Heights
Address: 1133 W 19th St
Houston, TX 77008
Phone: (713) 862-0555

#300
Alamo Tamale & Taco
Cuisines: Mexican
Average price: Inexpensive
Area: Northside/Northline, Northside Village
Address: 809 Berry Rd
Houston, TX 77022
Phone: (713) 692-6363

#301
Brooklyn Athletic Club
Cuisines: American
Average price: Modest
Area: Fourth Ward, Museum District, Montrose
Address: 601 Richmond Ave
Houston, TX 77006
Phone: (713) 527-4440

#302
MAX's Wine Dive
Cuisines: Wine Bar, American, Breakfast & Brunch
Average price: Modest
Area: Fourth Ward, Midtown, Montrose
Address: 214 Fairview St
Houston, TX 77006
Phone: (713) 528-9200

#303
Pondicheri
Cuisines: Indian, Bakery
Average price: Modest
Area: Upper Kirby
Address: 2800 Kirby Dr
Houston, TX 77098
Phone: (713) 522-2022

#304
Yorktown Deli & Coffee
Cuisines: Deli
Average price: Inexpensive
Area: Galleria/Uptown
Address: 2301 Yorktown St
Houston, TX 77056
Phone: (713) 552-0936

#305
Pappy's Cafe
Cuisines: American, Comfort Food, Café
Average price: Modest
Area: Memorial
Address: 9041 Katy Fwy
Houston, TX 77024
Phone: (713) 827-1811

#306
Ruggles Black
Cuisines: American, French, Asian Fusion
Average price: Expensive
Area: Upper Kirby
Address: 3939 Kirby Dr
Houston, TX 77098
Phone: (832) 530-4493

#307
Lola
Cuisines: Diner, American
Average price: Modest
Area: The Heights
Address: 1102 Yale St
Houston, TX 77008
Phone: (713) 426-5652

#308
Teotihuacan Mexican Cafe
Cuisines: Mexican
Average price: Modest
Area: Northside Village
Address: 4624 Irvington Blvd
Houston, TX 77009
Phone: (713) 695-8757

Houston Travel Guide 2015 / Shops, Restaurants, Arts, Entertainment & Nightlife

#309
Grand Lux Cafe
Cuisines: Desserts, American
Average price: Modest
Area: Galleria/Uptown
Address: 5000 Westheimer Rd
Houston, TX 77056
Phone: (713) 626-1700

#310
Triniti Restaurant
Cuisines: American
Average price: Expensive
Area: Montrose
Address: 2815 S Shepherd Dr
Houston, TX 77098
Phone: (713) 527-9090

#311
Pappasito's Cantina
Cuisines: Tex-Mex
Average price: Modest
Area: Gulfton
Address: 6445 Richmond At Hillcroft
Houston, TX 77057
Phone: (713) 784-5253

#312
Hong Kong's Cafe
Cuisines: Chinese
Average price: Inexpensive
Area: Sharpstown, Chinatown
Address: 9108 Bellaire Blvd
Houston, TX 77036
Phone: (713) 772-9633

#313
Seco's Latin Cuisine
Cuisines: Latin American
Average price: Modest
Area: West University
Address: 2536 Nottingham
Houston, TX 77005
Phone: (713) 942-0001

#314
The Golden Grill
Cuisines: Sandwiches, Food Truck
Average price: Inexpensive
Area: Fourth Ward, Montrose
Address: H-town
Houston, TX 77006
Phone: (602) 321-0423

#315
Black Walnut Café
Cuisines: American, Breakfast & Brunch, Café
Average price: Modest
Area: The Heights, Rice Military
Address: 5512 Memorial Drive
Houston, TX 77007
Phone: (713) 868-1800

#316
Asahi Sushi
Cuisines: Sushi Bar
Average price: Modest
Area: Medical Center
Address: 8236 Kirby Dr
Houston, TX 77054
Phone: (713) 664-7686

#317
Chilosos Taco House
Cuisines: Mexican, Breakfast & Brunch
Average price: Inexpensive
Area: The Heights
Address: 701 E 20th St
Houston, TX 77246
Phone: (713) 868-2273

#318
Pho Binh Trailer
Cuisines: Vietnamese
Average price: Inexpensive
Area: South Belt/Ellington
Address: 10928 Beamer Rd
Houston, TX 77089
Phone: (281) 484-3963

#319
Houston's Famous Deli
Cuisines: Caterer, Deli, Sandwiches
Average price: Inexpensive
Area: Medical Center
Address: 2130 Holly Hall St
Houston, TX 77054
Phone: (713) 799-2544

#320
E-Tao
Cuisines: Asian Fusion, Dim Sum, Thai
Average price: Modest
Area: Galleria/Uptown
Address: 5135 West Alabama
Houston, TX 77056
Phone: (713) 965-0888

#321
BB's Cafe
Cuisines: Tex-Mex, Cajun, Creole
Average price: Modest
Area: Upper Kirby
Address: 3139 Richmond Ave
Houston, TX 77098
Phone: (713) 807-1300

#322
Ruggles Green | The Heights
Cuisines: Breakfast & Brunch,
Gluten-Free, American
Average price: Modest
Area: The Heights
Address: 748 E 11th St
Houston, TX 77008
Phone: (713) 714-8460

#323
Island Sizzler Jamaican Rum Bar & Grill
Cuisines: Caribbean, Sports Bar
Average price: Inexpensive
Area: Medical Center
Address: 2114 Holly Hall St
Houston, TX 77054
Phone: (713) 378-5375

#324
Black Walnut Café
Cuisines: American, Breakfast & Brunch, Café
Average price: Modest
Area: West University
Address: 5510 Morningside Drive
Houston, TX 77005
Phone: (713) 526-5551

#325
Brook's Family BBQ
Cuisines: Barbeque
Average price: Inexpensive
Area: Third Ward
Address: 3602 Scott St
Houston, TX 77004
Phone: (713) 521-0021

#326
Zaytona
Cuisines: Mediterranean
Average price: Inexpensive
Area: Fourth Ward, Downtown
Address: 914 Main St
Houston, TX 77002
Phone: (713) 652-0933

#327
Vieng Thai
Cuisines: Thai
Average price: Modest
Area: Spring Branch
Address: 6929 Long Point Rd
Houston, TX 77055
Phone: (713) 688-9910

#328
Beer Market Co.
Cuisines: American, Beer, Wine, Spirits, Gastropub
Average price: Modest
Area: The Heights
Address: 920 Studemont St
Houston, TX 77007
Phone: (713) 426-9035

#329
Super La Mexicana
Cuisines: Mexican
Average price: Inexpensive
Area: Willow Meadows/Willowbend
Address: 10002 Stella Link Rd
Houston, TX 77025
Phone: (713) 661-2929

#330
Simply Pho
Cuisines: Vietnamese
Average price: Inexpensive
Area: Fourth Ward, Midtown
Address: 2929 Milam St
Houston, TX 77006
Phone: (713) 677-0501

#331
Pollo Bravo
Cuisines: Latin American, Peruvian
Average price: Modest
Area: Gulfton
Address: 6015 Hillcroft Ave
Houston, TX 77081
Phone: (713) 541-0069

#332
Peking Cuisine Restaurant
Cuisines: Chinese
Average price: Modest
Area: Westwood, Sharpstown
Address: 8332 SW Fwy
Houston, TX 77074
Phone: (713) 988-5838

#333
Canopy
Cuisines: American
Average price: Modest
Area: Fourth Ward, Montrose
Address: 3939 Montrose Blvd
Houston, TX 77006
Phone: (713) 528-6848

#334
The Union Kitchen
Cuisines: American
Average price: Modest
Area: Braeswood Place, West University
Address: 4057 Bellaire Blvd
Houston, TX 77025
Phone: (713) 661-0025

#335
Afrikiko Restaurant
Cuisines: African
Average price: Modest
Area: Westwood
Address: 9625 Bissonnet St
Houston, TX 77036
Phone: (713) 773-1400

#336
Cleburne Cafeteria
Cuisines: American, Southern, Comfort Food
Average price: Modest
Area: West University
Address: 3606 Bissonnet St
Houston, TX 77005
Phone: (713) 667-2386

#337
Polonia Restaurant
Cuisines: Polish
Average price: Modest
Area: Spring Branch
Address: 1900 Blalock Rd
Houston, TX 77080
Phone: (713) 464-9900

#338
Tau Bay
Cuisines: Vietnamese
Average price: Inexpensive
Area: Westwood, Sharpstown
Address: 8150 Sw Fwy
Houston, TX 77074
Phone: (713) 771-8485

#339
Lazaro's Pizza
Cuisines: Pizza
Average price: Inexpensive
Area: Inwood
Address: 9913 N Houston Rosslyn Rd
Houston, TX 77088
Phone: (713) 466-4407

#340
Maxwell Street Grill
Cuisines: Hot Dogs, American, Burgers
Average price: Inexpensive
Area: Museum District
Address: 4902 Almeda
Houston, TX 77004
Phone: (713) 239-0154

#341
Zoës Kitchen
Cuisines: Mediterranean, American, Greek
Average price: Modest
Area: Highland Village
Address: 3838 Westheimer Rd
Houston, TX 77027
Phone: (713) 621-5597

#342
Pho VN 21
Cuisines: Vietnamese
Average price: Inexpensive
Area: Gulfton
Address: 5800 Bellaire Blvd
Houston, TX 77081
Phone: (713) 663-7879

#343
Frank's Americana Revival
Cuisines: Steakhouse, American
Average price: Expensive
Area: Highland Village, River Oaks
Address: 3736 Westheimer Rd
Houston, TX 77027
Phone: (713) 572-8600

#344
Houston's
Cuisines: American, American
Average price: Modest
Area: West University
Address: 4848 Kirby Dr
Houston, TX 77098
Phone: (713) 529-2385

#345
Fiesta Tacos
Cuisines: Mexican
Average price: Inexpensive
Area: Oak Forest/Garden Oaks, Lazy Brook/Timbergrove
Address: 4620 W 34th St
Houston, TX 77092
Phone: (713) 686-6927

#346
Funky Chicken
Cuisines: American, Sandwiches
Average price: Modest
Area: The Heights
Address: 181 Heights Blvd
Houston, TX 77007
Phone: (832) 924-4655

#347
The Buffalo Grille
Cuisines: American, Breakfast & Brunch
Average price: Inexpensive
Area: West University
Address: 4080 Bissonnet St
Houston, TX 77005
Phone: (713) 661-3663

#348
Calliope's
Cuisines: Cajun, Creole
Average price: Modest
Area: Fondren Southwest
Address: 7590 W Bellfort Ave
Houston, TX 77071
Phone: (713) 773-2099

#349
Josie's Place
Cuisines: Soul Food, Southern
Average price: Inexpensive
Area: Independence Heights
Address: 7413 N Shepherd Dr
Houston, TX 77091
Phone: (713) 695-7711

#350
Josie's Place
Cuisines: Soul Food, Southern
Average price: Inexpensive
Area: Independence Heights
Address: 7413 N Shepherd Dr
Houston, TX 77091
Phone: (713) 695-7711

#351
dgn Factory
Cuisines: Indian, Vegetarian, Crêperie
Average price: Inexpensive
Area: Gulfton, Galleria/Uptown
Address: 5959 Richmond Ave
Houston, TX 77057
Phone: (713) 781-3672

#352
Guy's Meat Market
Cuisines: Meat Shop, Barbeque, Burgers
Average price: Inexpensive
Area: Medical Center
Address: 3106 Old Spanish Trl
Houston, TX 77054
Phone: (713) 747-6800

#353
Sushi Wabi
Cuisines: Japanese, Sushi Bar
Average price: Modest
Area: Greenway
Address: 3953 Richmond Ave
Houston, TX 77027
Phone: (713) 623-8818

#354
Baoz Dumpling
Cuisines: Chinese, Caterer
Average price: Inexpensive
Area: Downtown
Address: 1001 Fannin St Ste M180
Houston, TX 77002
Phone: (713) 659-3288

#355
Himalaya Restaurant & Catering
Cuisines: Indian, Pakistani, Himalayan/Nepalese
Average price: Modest
Area: Sharpstown
Address: 6652 Southwest Fwy
Houston, TX 77074
Phone: (713) 532-2837

#356
Yummy Kitchen
Cuisines: Taiwanese, Chinese
Average price: Inexpensive
Area: Sharpstown, Chinatown
Address: 9326 Bellaire Blvd
Houston, TX 77036
Phone: (713) 541-4420

#357
Dacapos
Cuisines: Sandwiches, Bakery
Average price: Modest
Area: The Heights
Address: 1141 E 11th St
Houston, TX 77009
Phone: (713) 869-9141

#358
Mikki's Café
Cuisines: Soul Food, Southern, Barbeque
Average price: Modest
Area: Fondren Southwest
Address: 10500 W Bellfort St
Houston, TX 77031
Phone: (281) 568-5115

#359
Little Matt's
Cuisines: Tex-Mex, Burgers, Sandwiches
Average price: Modest
Area: West University
Address: 6203 Edloe St
Houston, TX 77005
Phone: (713) 592-6200

#360
Miller's Cafe
Cuisines: Burgers
Average price: Inexpensive
Area: Independence Heights
Address: 3830 N Shepherd Dr
Houston, TX 77018
Phone: (713) 699-2947

#361
Revelry on Richmond
Cuisines: Gastropub, Sports Bar
Average price: Modest
Area: Museum District, Montrose
Address: 1613 Richmond Ave
Houston, TX 77006
Phone: (832) 538-0724

#362
Bohemeo's
Cuisines: Coffee, Tea, Sandwiches, Bar
Average price: Inexpensive
Area: Eastwood
Address: 708 Telephone Rd
Houston, TX 77023
Phone: (713) 923-4277

#363
Cue's Burgers & More
Cuisines: Burgers
Average price: Inexpensive
Area: Willow Meadows/Willowbend, Meyerland
Address: 10423 S Post Oak Rd
Houston, TX 77035
Phone: (713) 726-0313

#364
Empire Turkish Grill
Cuisines: Turkish
Average price: Modest
Area: Memorial
Address: 12448 Memorial Dr
Houston, TX 77024
Phone: (713) 827-7475

#365
The Modular Trailer
Cuisines: Food Stand, American
Average price: Inexpensive
Area: Braeburn
Address: 5902 Grape St
Houston, TX 77007
Phone: (713) 550-3823

#366
Boil House
Cuisines: Cajun, Creole, Seafood
Average price: Modest
Area: The Heights
Address: 606 E 11th St
Houston, TX 77008
Phone: (713) 880-3999

#367
Cottonwood
Cuisines: American
Average price: Modest
Area: Independence Heights
Address: 3422 N Shepherd Dr
Houston, TX 77018
Phone: (713) 802-0410

#368
Mandola's Deli
Cuisines: Deli, Italian, Sandwiches
Average price: Inexpensive
Area: EaDo, Eastwood
Address: 4105 Leeland St
Houston, TX 77023
Phone: (713) 223-5186

#369
Croissant-Brioche
Cuisines: Bakery, French, Coffee, Tea
Average price: Inexpensive
Area: West University
Address: 2435 Rice Blvd
Houston, TX 77005
Phone: (713) 526-9188

#370
The Grove
Cuisines: American
Average price: Modest
Area: Downtown
Address: 1611 Lamar St
Houston, TX 77010
Phone: (713) 337-7321

#371
88 Boiling Crawfish and Seafood
Cuisines: Seafood, Cajun, Creole
Average price: Modest
Area: Westchase
Address: 1910 Wilcrest Dr
Houston, TX 77042
Phone: (713) 789-8288

#372
Burger Palace
Cuisines: Burgers
Average price: Modest
Area: Galleria/Uptown
Address: 2800 Sage Rd
Houston, TX 77056
Phone: (713) 877-9700

#373
Shiv Sagar Restaurant
Cuisines: Indian
Average price: Inexpensive
Area: Sharpstown
Address: 6662 Southwest Fwy
Houston, TX 77074
Phone: (713) 977-0150

#374
Daddy and Daughter
Cuisines: Korean
Average price: Inexpensive
Area: Memorial
Address: 1302 Blalock Rd
Houston, TX 77055
Phone: (713) 449-3082

#375
Pizza L'Vino
Cuisines: Pizza, Italian
Average price: Modest
Area: River Oaks, Montrose
Address: 544 Waugh Dr
Houston, TX 77019
Phone: (713) 526-1000

#376
Hoàng Sandwich
Cuisines: Vietnamese, Sandwiches, Coffee, Tea
Average price: Inexpensive
Area: Third Ward
Address: 3509 Elgin St
Houston, TX 77004
Phone: (713) 658-9242

#377
Mai's Restaurant
Cuisines: Vietnamese
Average price: Modest
Area: Fourth Ward, Midtown
Address: 3403 Milam St
Houston, TX 77002
Phone: (713) 520-5300

#378
Mary'z Lebanese Cuisine
Cuisines: Middle Eastern, Mediterranean, Hookah Bar
Average price: Modest
Area: Gulfton, Galleria/Uptown
Address: 5825 Richmond Ave
Houston, TX 77057
Phone: (832) 251-1955

#379
Reef
Cuisines: Seafood, Lounge
Average price: Expensive
Area: Fourth Ward, Midtown
Address: 2600 Travis St
Houston, TX 77006
Phone: (713) 526-8282

#380
Del Frisco's Grille
Cuisines: Steakhouse, Burgers
Average price: Modest
Area: Upper Kirby
Address: 2800 Kirby Dr
Houston, TX 77098
Phone: (832) 623-6168

#381
Coppa Osteria
Cuisines: Italian
Average price: Modest
Area: West University
Address: 5210 Morningside
Houston, TX 77005
Phone: (713) 522-3535

#382
Two Guys Pizzeria
Cuisines: Pizza, Salad
Average price: Inexpensive
Area: Braeswood Place, West University
Address: 2250 W Holcombe Blvd
Houston, TX 77030
Phone: (713) 660-6262

#383
La Fresca Pizza
Cuisines: Pizza
Average price: Inexpensive
Area: Meyerland
Address: 5300 N Braeswood Blvd, Ste 26
Houston, TX 77096
Phone: (713) 723-7777

#384
Houston's Restaurant
Cuisines: American, Burgers
Average price: Modest
Area: Galleria/Uptown
Address: 5888 Westheimer Rd
Houston, TX 77057
Phone: (713) 975-1947

#385
Big Burger V
Cuisines: Burgers, Hot Dogs
Average price: Inexpensive
Area: Northside/Northline
Address: 11207 W Hardy Rd
Houston, TX 77076
Phone: (713) 695-4595

#386
Carniceria Aguascalientes
Cuisines: Mexican
Average price: Inexpensive
Area: Park Place
Address: 2809 Broadway St
Houston, TX 77017
Phone: (713) 641-4300

#387
Teotihuacan Mexican Restaurant
Cuisines: Mexican
Average price: Inexpensive
Area: Fondren Southwest
Address: 6579 W Bellfort St
Houston, TX 77035
Phone: (713) 726-9858

#388
El Bolillo Bakery
Cuisines: Desserts, Mexican, Bakery
Average price: Inexpensive
Area: Gulfgate/Pine Valley
Address: 2421 S Wayside Dr
Houston, TX 77023
Phone: (713) 921-3500

#389
The French House
Cuisines: Sandwiches, French
Average price: Inexpensive
Area: Galleria/Uptown
Address: 5901 Westheimer Rd
Houston, TX 77057
Phone: (713) 781-2106

#390
Avenue Grill
Cuisines: Breakfast & Brunch
Average price: Inexpensive
Area: Sixth Ward
Address: 1017 Houston Ave
Houston, TX 77007
Phone: (713) 228-5138

#391
Radical Eats
Cuisines: Vegetarian, Mexican
Average price: Modest
Area: Fourth Ward, Montrose
Address: 507 Westheimer Rd
Houston, TX 77006
Phone: (713) 697-8719

#392
Piquin Mexican Style Subs
Cuisines: Do-It-Yourself Food, Mexican
Average price: Inexpensive
Area: Fairbanks/Northwest Crossing
Address: 14185 Northwest Fwy
Houston, TX 77040
Phone: (832) 831-5061

Houston Travel Guide 2015 / Shops, Restaurants, Arts, Entertainment & Nightlife

#393
Pinewood Café
Cuisines: Café, Salad, Burgers
Average price: Inexpensive
Area: Museum District
Address: 6104 Hermann Park Dr
Houston, TX 77030
Phone: (713) 429-5238

#394
Qin's Noodle Kitchen
Cuisines: Chinese
Average price: Inexpensive
Area: Sharpstown, Chinatown
Address: 9889 Bellaire Blvd
Houston, TX 77036
Phone: (713) 772-6322

#395
Roma's Pizza
Cuisines: Pizza
Average price: Inexpensive
Area: Downtown
Address: 233 Main St
Houston, TX 77002
Phone: (713) 222-1184

#396
Michiru Sushi
Cuisines: Sushi Bar, Japanese
Average price: Modest
Area: Greenway
Address: 3800 Southwest Frwy
Houston, TX 77027
Phone: (832) 203-7082

#397
Cuchara
Cuisines: Mexican
Average price: Modest
Area: Fourth Ward, Midtown, Montrose
Address: 214 Fairview St
Houston, TX 77006
Phone: (713) 942-0000

#398
KUU Restaurant
Cuisines: Japanese, Sushi Bar, Asian Fusion
Average price: Expensive
Area: Memorial
Address: 947 Gessner Rd
Houston, TX 77024
Phone: (713) 461-1688

#399
Cedar Creek
Cuisines: Bar, American, Burgers
Average price: Modest
Area: The Heights
Address: 1034 W 20th St
Houston, TX 77008
Phone: (713) 808-9623

#400
Esther's Cajun Cafe & Soul Food
Cuisines: Soul Food, Cajun, Creole, Southern
Average price: Modest
Area: Independence Heights
Address: 5204 Yale St
Houston, TX 77091
Phone: (713) 699-1212

#401
Laredo Taqueria
Cuisines: Mexican, Tex-Mex
Average price: Inexpensive
Area: The Heights
Address: 915 Snover St
Houston, TX 77007
Phone: (713) 861-7279

#402
The Honeymoon Cafe & Bar
Cuisines: Cocktail Bar, Café, Coffee, Tea
Average price: Modest
Area: Fourth Ward, Downtown
Address: 300 Main St
Houston, TX 77002
Phone: (281) 846-6995

#403
Laurenzo's
Cuisines: American, Burgers, American
Average price: Expensive
Area: The Heights
Address: 4412 Washington Ave
Houston, TX 77007
Phone: (713) 880-5111

#404
Beaucoup Bar & Grill
Cuisines: Chicken Wings, Cajun, Creole, Burgers
Average price: Modest
Area: Medical Center
Address: 3102 Old Spanish Trl
Houston, TX 77054
Phone: (713) 747-5100

#405
Oak Leaf Smokehouse
Cuisines: Barbeque, Southern, Gluten-Free
Average price: Modest
Area: Eastwood
Address: 1000 Telephone Rd
Houston, TX 77023
Phone: (713) 487-8987

#406
Taste of Texas
Cuisines: American, Steakhouse
Average price: Expensive
Area: Memorial
Address: 10505 Katy Fwy
Houston, TX 77024
Phone: (713) 932-6901

#407
Ragin Cajun
Cuisines: Cajun, Creole, Seafood, Sports Bar
Average price: Modest
Area: Highland Village
Address: 4302 Richmond Ave
Houston, TX 77027
Phone: (713) 623-6321

#408
Xin Jiang BBQ
Cuisines: Barbeque, Chinese
Average price: Inexpensive
Area: Sharpstown, Chinatown
Address: 9260 Bellaire Blvd
Houston, TX 77036
Phone: (713) 773-9999

#409
Pax Americana
Cuisines: American
Average price: Modest
Area: Museum District, Montrose
Address: 4319 Montrose Blvd
Houston, TX 77006
Phone: (713) 239-0228

#410
Casarez
Cuisines: Mexican, Cajun, Creole
Average price: Inexpensive
Area: Edgebrook
Address: 887 Edgebrook Dr
Houston, TX 77304
Phone: (713) 947-9153

#411
Christian's Tailgate
Cuisines: Burgers, Sports Bar
Average price: Inexpensive
Area: The Heights
Address: 7340 Washington Ave
Houston, TX 77007
Phone: (713) 864-9744

#412
Hungry's Café & Bistro
Cuisines: American, Breakfast & Brunch
Average price: Modest
Area: West University
Address: 2356 Rice Blvd
Houston, TX 77005
Phone: (713) 523-8652

#413
McAlister's Deli
Cuisines: Deli, Salad, Sandwiches
Average price: Inexpensive
Area: Third Ward
Address: 4810 Calhoun Rd
Houston, TX 77204
Phone: (713) 743-9921

#414
Freebirds World Burrito
Cuisines: Mexican
Average price: Inexpensive
Area: Medical Center
Address: 8057 Kirby Dr
Houston, TX 77054
Phone: (713) 383-0700

#415
Tacos a Go-Go
Cuisines: Mexican
Average price: Inexpensive
Area: The Heights
Address: 2912 White Oak Dr
Houston, TX 77007
Phone: (713) 864-8226

#416
Gloria's Latin Cuisine
Cuisines: Tex-Mex, Dance Club, Salvadoran
Average price: Modest
Area: Fourth Ward, Midtown
Address: 2616 Louisiana St
Houston, TX 77006
Phone: (832) 360-1710

#417
Ekko's Greek American Deli
Cuisines: Greek, Deli
Average price: Inexpensive
Area: Gulfton, Galleria/Uptown
Address: 5216 Richmond Ave
Houston, TX 77056
Phone: (713) 626-5263

#418
55 Bar & Restaurant
Cuisines: Bar, American
Average price: Modest
Area: West University
Address: 5510 Morningside Dr
Houston, TX 77005
Phone: (713) 590-0610

#419
Tostaderia Madero's
Cuisines: Mexican
Average price: Inexpensive
Area: Spring Branch
Address: 9401 Clay Rd
Houston, TX 77080
Phone: (713) 996-7771

#420
Speedy Burger
Cuisines: Fast Food, Burgers
Average price: Inexpensive
Area: Northside Village
Address: 6303 Irvington Blvd
Houston, TX 77022
Phone: (713) 692-4435

#421
Yia Yia Mary's Pappas Greek Kitchen
Cuisines: Greek, Mediterranean, Fast Food
Average price: Modest
Area: Galleria/Uptown
Address: 4747 San Felipe St
Houston, TX 77056
Phone: (713) 840-8665

#422
Island Grill
Cuisines: Juice Bar, Mediterranean
Average price: Modest
Area: Braeswood Place, West University
Address: 4024 Bellaire Blvd
Houston, TX 77024
Phone: (713) 665-5388

#423
Saffron Kabob House
Cuisines: Middle Eastern, Afghan
Average price: Modest
Area: Gulfton, Sharpstown
Address: 5711 Hillcroft St
Houston, TX 77036
Phone: (713) 780-7474

#424
Escalante's
Cuisines: Tex-Mex
Average price: Modest
Area: Highland Village
Address: 4053 Westheimer Rd
Houston, TX 77027
Phone: (713) 623-4200

#425
Seoul House
Cuisines: Korean
Average price: Modest
Area: Chinatown, Alief
Address: 10603 Bellaire Blvd
Houston, TX 77072
Phone: (281) 575-8077

#426
Edloe St. Cafe & Catering
Cuisines: Deli
Average price: Modest
Area: West University
Address: 6119 Edloe St
Houston, TX 77005
Phone: (713) 666-4302

#427
Kanomwan
Cuisines: Thai
Average price: Modest
Area: Eastwood
Address: 736 1/2 Telephone Rd
Houston, TX 77023
Phone: (713) 923-4230

#428
Pluckers Wing Bar
Cuisines: Chicken Wings
Average price: Modest
Area: The Heights
Address: 1400 Shepherd Dr
Houston, TX 77007
Phone: (713) 864-9464

#429
Up Restaurant
Cuisines: American
Average price: Expensive
Area: Highland Village
Address: 3995 Westheimer Rd
Houston, TX 77027
Phone: (713) 640-5416

#430
Guadalajara Del Centro
Cuisines: Mexican, Tex-Mex
Average price: Modest
Area: Downtown
Address: 1201 San Jacinto St
Houston, TX 77002
Phone: (713) 650-0101

#431
Brother's Pizzeria
Cuisines: Pizza, Italian
Average price: Inexpensive
Area: Independence Heights
Address: 3820 N Shepherd Dr
Houston, TX 77018
Phone: (713) 692-2020

#432
Andalucia Tapas Restaurant & Bar
Cuisines: Tapas Bar, Spanish
Average price: Modest
Area: Downtown
Address: 1201 San Jacinto St
Houston, TX 77002
Phone: (832) 319-6673

#433
Omelette & Waffle Restaurant
Cuisines: Diner, Breakfast & Brunch, Mexican
Average price: Inexpensive
Area: Westwood, Sharpstown
Address: 8533 Beechnut St
Houston, TX 77036
Phone: (713) 774-0970

#434
BlackFinn American Grille
Cuisines: American, American, Sports Bar
Average price: Modest
Area: Fourth Ward, Midtown, Montrose
Address: 1910 Bagby St
Houston, TX 77002
Phone: (713) 651-9550

#435
Elevation Burger
Cuisines: Burgers, Vegetarian, American
Average price: Inexpensive
Area: Upper Kirby
Address: 3918 Kirby Drive
Houston, TX 77098
Phone: (719) 524-2909

#436
The Chelsea Grill
Cuisines: American
Average price: Modest
Area: Museum District
Address: 4621 Montrose Blvd
Houston, TX 77006
Phone: (713) 942-9857

#437
Sorrel Urban Bistro
Cuisines: American
Average price: Expensive
Area: Upper Kirby
Address: 2202 W Alabama St
Houston, TX 77098
Phone: (713) 677-0391

#438
Pink's Pizza
Cuisines: Pizza
Average price: Modest
Area: Third Ward
Address: 4701 Calhoun Rd
Houston, TX 77004
Phone: (832) 831-3145

#439
Zoës Kitchen
Cuisines: Mediterranean, Greek
Average price: Modest
Area: West University
Address: 5215 Kelvin Dr
Houston, TX 77005
Phone: (713) 528-2464

#440
Bare Bowls Kitchen
Cuisines: Breakfast & Brunch, Food Stand
Average price: Inexpensive
Area: The Heights, Rice Military
Address: 5701 Washington Ave
Houston, TX 77007
Phone: (713) 589-6526

#441
Tia Maria's
Cuisines: Mexican
Average price: Inexpensive
Area: Lazy Brook/Timbergrove
Address: 4618 Dacoma St
Houston, TX 77092
Phone: (713) 680-0825

#442
The Refinery
Cuisines: Burgers
Average price: Modest
Area: Fourth Ward, Midtown, Montrose
Address: 702 W Dallas St
Houston, TX 77019
Phone: (713) 487-0029

#443
Shan Hu Chinese Restaurant
Cuisines: Chinese
Average price: Inexpensive
Area: Hobby
Address: 7656 Bellfort St
Houston, TX 77061
Phone: (713) 640-1654

#444
Khun Kay Thai Cafe
Cuisines: Thai
Average price: Inexpensive
Area: Fourth Ward, Montrose
Address: 1209 Montrose Blvd
Houston, TX 77019
Phone: (713) 524-9614

#445
Pho Luc Lac
Cuisines: Vietnamese
Average price: Inexpensive
Area: Spring Branch
Address: 9457 Kempwood Dr
Houston, TX 77080
Phone: (713) 462-4499

#446
Goode Company Seafood
Cuisines: Seafood, Gluten-Free, Caterer
Average price: Modest
Area: Memorial
Address: 10211 Katy Fwy
Houston, TX 77024
Phone: (713) 464-7933

#447
Abdallah's Bakery
Cuisines: Middle Eastern, Bakery
Average price: Modest
Area: Gulfton
Address: 3939 Hilcroft Ave
Houston, TX 77057
Phone: (713) 952-4747

#448
Doozo Dumplings & Noodles
Cuisines: Chinese
Average price: Inexpensive
Area: Downtown
Address: 1200 McKinney St
Houston, TX 77002
Phone: (713) 571-6898

#449
Katz's Deli & Bar
Cuisines: Deli, Sandwiches, Desserts
Average price: Modest
Area: Fourth Ward, Montrose
Address: 616 Westheimer Rd
Houston, TX 77006
Phone: (713) 521-3838

#450
Thai Style
Cuisines: Thai, Fast Food
Average price: Inexpensive
Area: Chinatown
Address: 5712 S Gessner Rd
Houston, TX 77036
Phone: (713) 772-7575

#451
Aka Sushi House
Cuisines: Japanese, Sushi Bar
Average price: Modest
Area: Upper Kirby
Address: 2390 W Alabama St
Houston, TX 77098
Phone: (713) 807-7875

#452
Katch 22
Cuisines: American, Burgers, Soup
Average price: Modest
Area: The Heights, Rice Military
Address: 700 Durham Dr
Houston, TX 77007
Phone: (832) 804-7281

#453
100% Taquito
Cuisines: Mexican
Average price: Inexpensive
Area: West University
Address: 3245 Southwest Fwy
Houston, TX 77027
Phone: (713) 665-2900

#454
Bangkok Chef
Cuisines: Thai
Average price: Modest
Area: Fourth Ward, Downtown
Address: 914 Main St
Houston, TX 77002
Phone: (713) 659-1600

#455
Yapa Kitchen Fresh Take Away
Cuisines: Sandwiches, Mediterranean
Average price: Modest
Area: Braeswood Place, West University
Address: 3173 W Holcombe Blvd
Houston, TX 77025
Phone: (713) 664-9272

#456
Mango Beach
Cuisines: Food Stand, Juice Bar, Ice Cream
Average price: Inexpensive
Area: The Heights
Address: 2304 White Oak Dr
Houston, TX 77009
Phone: (713) 900-7500

#457
Ouisie's Table
Cuisines: American
Average price: Expensive
Area: Highland Village
Address: 3939 San Felipe St
Houston, TX 77027
Phone: (713) 528-2264

#458
Tango & Malbec
Cuisines: Argentine, Latin American
Average price: Expensive
Area: Galleria/Uptown
Address: 2800 Sage Rd
Houston, TX 77056
Phone: (713) 629-8646

#459
Amazon Grill
Cuisines: Latin American, Deli, Sandwiches
Average price: Modest
Area: West University
Address: 5114 Kirby Dr
Houston, TX 77098
Phone: (713) 522-5888

#460
Grotto Ristorante
Cuisines: Italian
Average price: Modest
Area: Highland Village, Galleria/Uptown
Address: 4715 Westheimer Rd
Houston, TX 77027
Phone: (713) 622-3663

#461
Salad Extraveganza
Cuisines: Salad, Juice Bar, American
Average price: Modest
Area: Greenway
Address: 3917 Richmond Ave
Houston, TX 77027
Phone: (713) 993-0091

#462
Coco - Town & Country
Cuisines: Crêperie, Coffee, Tea
Average price: Inexpensive
Area: Memorial
Address: 650 W Bough Ln
Houston, TX 77024
Phone: (713) 465-8778

#463
La Tapatia Taqueria
Cuisines: Mexican
Average price: Inexpensive
Area: Museum District, Montrose
Address: 1749 Richmond Ave
Houston, TX 77098
Phone: (713) 521-3144

#464
Pappadeaux Seafood Kitchen
Cuisines: Seafood, American, Greek
Average price: Modest
Area: South Main
Address: 2525 South Loop W
Houston, TX 77054
Phone: (713) 665-3155

#465
J. Black's Feel Good Kitchen & Lounge
Cuisines: American, Lounge
Average price: Modest
Area: The Heights
Address: 110 S Heights Blvd
Houston, TX 77007
Phone: (713) 862-7818

#466
Pizzeria Solario
Cuisines: Pizza
Average price: Modest
Area: Highland Village
Address: 3333 Weslayan
Houston, TX 77027
Phone: (713) 892-8100

#467
Go Hyang Korean Restaurant
Cuisines: Korean
Average price: Modest
Area: Spring Branch
Address: 1400 Blalock Rd
Houston, TX 77055
Phone: (713) 464-6653

#468
Boogies Chicago Style Bbq
Cuisines: Barbeque
Average price: Inexpensive
Area: Fondren Southwest
Address: 8035 W Airport Blvd
Houston, TX 77071
Phone: (713) 723-7775

#469
Sambuca Jazz Café
Cuisines: American, Lounge, Music Venues
Average price: Expensive
Area: Fourth Ward, Downtown
Address: 909 Texas St
Houston, TX 77002
Phone: (713) 224-5299

#470
Tiger Den
Cuisines: Ramen
Average price: Modest
Area: Sharpstown, Chinatown
Address: 9889 Bellaire Blvd
Houston, TX 77036
Phone: (832) 804-7755

#471
Sparrow Bar + Cookshop
Cuisines: Bar, American
Average price: Expensive
Area: Fourth Ward, Midtown
Address: 3701 Travis
Houston, TX 77002
Phone: (713) 524-6922

#472
House of Fries
Cuisines: Burgers, Sandwiches
Average price: Inexpensive
Area: Oak Forest/Garden Oaks
Address: 5322 Antoine Dr
Houston, TX 77091
Phone: (713) 682-4111

#473
Island Grill
Cuisines: Mediterranean, Juice Bar
Average price: Modest
Area: Memorial
Address: 979 Bunker Hill Rd
Houston, TX 77024
Phone: (832) 831-7071

#474
Punk's Simple Southern Food
Cuisines: Southern
Average price: Modest
Area: West University
Address: 5212 Morningside Dr
Houston, TX 77005
Phone: (713) 524-7865

#475
Ruggles Green | Citycentre
Cuisines: American, Gluten-Free, Pizza
Average price: Modest
Area: Memorial
Address: 801 Town And Country Blvd
Houston, TX 77024
Phone: (713) 464-5557

#476
Sparkle's Hamburger Spot
Cuisines: Burgers
Average price: Inexpensive
Area: EaDo
Address: 1515 Dowling St
Houston, TX 77003
Phone: (713) 225-8044

#477
Jang Guem Tofu & Bbq House
Cuisines: Korean
Average price: Modest
Area: Sharpstown, Chinatown
Address: 9896 Bellaire Blvd
Houston, TX 77036
Phone: (713) 773-2229

#478
Becks Prime
Cuisines: Fast Food, Hot Dogs, Burgers
Average price: Modest
Area: Galleria/Uptown
Address: 2615 Augusta Dr
Houston, TX 77057
Phone: (713) 266-9901

#479
Genji Japanese Restaurant & Karaoke Bar
Cuisines: Japanese, Karaoke
Average price: Modest
Area: Westchase
Address: 11124 Westheimer Rd
Houston, TX 77042
Phone: (713) 780-0827

#480
London Sizzler
Cuisines: Indian
Average price: Modest
Area: Sharpstown
Address: 6690 Southwest Fwy
Houston, TX 77074
Phone: (713) 783-2754

#481
Alexander The Great
Cuisines: Greek, Seafood
Average price: Modest
Area: Galleria/Uptown
Address: 3055 Sage Rd
Houston, TX 77056
Phone: (713) 622-2778

#482
Rock 'n' Sandwiches
Cuisines: Sandwiches, Food Truck
Average price: Inexpensive
Area: Fourth Ward, Midtown
Address: 2200 Brazos Street
Houston, TX 77006
Phone: (512) 576-5693

#483
Jenivi's Seafood Shoppe & Restaurant
Cuisines: Cajun, Creole, Seafood
Average price: Modest
Area: Westchase
Address: 10555 Westheimer Rd
Houston, TX 77042
Phone: (713) 978-5055

#484
Neeta's Indian Cuisine
Cuisines: Indian, Chinese, Vegetarian
Average price: Modest
Area: Sharpstown
Address: 6688 SW Fwy
Houston, TX 77074
Phone: (832) 251-7200

#485
Canyon Creek Cafe
Cuisines: Burgers, Bar, Breakfast & Brunch
Average price: Modest
Area: Washington Corridor
Address: 6603 Westcott St
Houston, TX 77007
Phone: (713) 864-5885

#486
Julia's Bistro
Cuisines: Latin American
Average price: Modest
Area: Fourth Ward, Midtown
Address: 3722 Main St
Houston, TX 77002
Phone: (713) 807-0090

#487
Dot Coffee Shop
Cuisines: American, Coffee, Tea
Average price: Modest
Area: Pecan Park, Gulfgate/Pine Valley
Address: 7006 Gulf Fwy
Houston, TX 77087
Phone: (713) 644-7669

#488
Chipotle Mexican Grill
Cuisines: Mexican
Average price: Inexpensive
Area: Medical Center
Address: 6600 Fannin St
Houston, TX 77030
Phone: (713) 792-9390

#489
Capellini's
Cuisines: Italian
Average price: Modest
Area: The Heights
Address: 4721 N Main St
Houston, TX 77009
Phone: (713) 869-3233

#490
Tan Tan Restaurant
Cuisines: Chinese, Vietnamese
Average price: Modest
Area: Sharpstown, Chinatown
Address: 6816 Ranchester Dr
Houston, TX 77036
Phone: (713) 771-1268

#491
Griff's
Cuisines: Sports Bar, Pub, American, Café
Average price: Inexpensive
Area: Fourth Ward, Montrose
Address: 3416 Roseland St
Houston, TX 77006
Phone: (713) 528-9912

#492
Kim Son
Cuisines: Vietnamese, Dim Sum
Average price: Modest
Area: Downtown, EaDo
Address: 2001 Jefferson St
Houston, TX 77003
Phone: (713) 222-2461

#493
Mama Yu
Cuisines: Indonesian, Chinese, Halal
Average price: Inexpensive
Area: Alief
Address: 10815 Beechnut
Houston, TX 77072
Phone: (281) 988-5470

#494
Chicago Italian Beef & Pizza
Cuisines: Hot Dogs, Burgers, Sandwiches
Average price: Inexpensive
Area: The Heights
Address: 1777 Airline Dr
Houston, TX 77009
Phone: (713) 862-2828

#495
Virgie's Bar-B-Que
Cuisines: Barbeque
Average price: Modest
Area: Carverdale
Address: 5535 Gessner Dr
Houston, TX 77041
Phone: (713) 466-6525

#496
Tinto Grill
Cuisines: Argentine, Latin American, Steakhouse
Average price: Modest
Area: Spring Branch
Address: 10085 Long Point Rd
Houston, TX 77055
Phone: (713) 461-3113

#497
Bibijo Express
Cuisines: Korean
Average price: Inexpensive
Area: Memorial
Address: 1302 Blalock
Houston, TX 77055
Phone: (713) 568-9511

#498
El Rey Taqueria
Cuisines: Cuban, Mexican
Average price: Inexpensive
Area: Memorial
Address: 9742 Katy Fwy
Houston, TX 77055
Phone: (832) 358-8100

#499
Market Square Bar & Grill
Cuisines: American
Average price: Modest
Area: Fourth Ward, Downtown
Address: 311 Travis St
Houston, TX 77002
Phone: (713) 224-6133

#500
Yard House
Cuisines: American
Average price: Modest
Area: Memorial
Address: 800 Sorella Court
Houston, TX 77024
Phone: (713) 461-9273

TOP 500
ARTS & ENTERTAINMENT
The Most Recommended by Locals & Trevelers
(From #1 to #500)

Houston Travel Guide 2015 / Shops, Restaurants, Arts, Entertainment & Nightlife

#1
Miller Outdoor Theatre
Category: Performing Arts, Music Venues
Average price: Inexpensive
Area: Museum District
Address: 6000 Hermann Park Dr
Houston, TX 77030
Phone: (281) 373-3386

#2
The Menil Collection
Category: Museum, Art Gallery
Average price: Inexpensive
Area: Montrose
Address: 1533 Sul Ross St
Houston, TX 77006
Phone: (713) 525-9400

#3
The Bell Tower On 34th
Category: Venues, Event Space
Area: Oak Forest/Garden Oaks
Address: 901 W 34th St
Houston, TX 77018
Phone: (713) 868-2355

#4
Cockrell Butterfly Center
Category: Museum
Area: Museum District
Address: 5555 Hermann Park Dr
Houston, TX 77030
Phone: (713) 639-4629

#5
Crystal Ballroom At the Rice Hotel
Category: Venues, Event Space
Area: Fourth Ward, Downtown
Address: 909 Texas St Houston, TX 77002
Phone: (713) 227-7423

#6
The Children's Museum of Houston
Category: Museum
Area: Museum District
Address: 1500 Binz St
Houston, TX 77004
Phone: (713) 522-1138

#7
Reliant Center
Category: Venues, Event Space
Area: Medical Center
Address: One Reliant Park
Houston, TX 77054
Phone: (832) 667-1400

#8
Pinot's Palette
Category: Arts, Entertainment, Arts, Crafts
Average price: Modest
Area: Fourth Ward, Midtown, Montrose
Address: 2406 Taft St
Houston, TX 77006
Phone: (713) 523-4769

#9
Asia Society Texas Center
Category: Venues, Event Space, Art Gallery
Average price: Inexpensive
Area: Museum District
Address: 1370 Southmore Blvd
Houston, TX 77004
Phone: (713) 496-9901

#10
Events
Category: Cards, Stationery, Bridal, Jewelry
Average price: Expensive
Area: River Oaks, Montrose
Address: 1966 West Gray
Houston, TX 77019
Phone: (713) 520-5700

#11
Museum of Fine Arts Houston
Category: Museum, Art Gallery
Average price: Inexpensive
Area: Museum District
Address: 1001 Bissonnet St
Houston, TX 77005
Phone: (713) 639-7300

#12
Reliant Stadium
Category: Venues, Event Space, Stadium/Arena
Area: Medical Center
Address: One Reliant Park
Houston, TX 77054
Phone: (832) 667-1400

#13
Houston Dynamo
Category: Professional Sports Team, Amateur Sports Team
Area: EaDo, Warehouse District
Address: 1001 Avenida DE Las Americas
Houston, TX 77010
Phone: (713) 276-7500

#14
Prestige Events
Category: Party & Event Planning
Area: Museum District
Address: 5428 Almeda Rd
Houston, TX 77004
Phone: (713) 520-0988

#15
SPJST Lodge 88
Category: Venues, Event Space, Social Club
Area: The Heights
Address: 1435 Beall St
Houston, TX 77008
Phone: (713) 869-5767

#16
Houston Livestock Show & Rodeo
Category: Local Flavor, Festival
Area: Medical Center
Address: 8400 Kirby Dr
Houston, TX 77054
Phone: (832) 667-1000

#17
The Orange Show
Category: Museum
Area: Gulfgate/Pine Valley
Address: 2401 Munger St
Houston, TX 77023
Phone: (713) 926-6368

#18
Plate and Bottle
Category: Winery, Gift Shop
Average price: Modest
Area: West University
Address: 5411 Morningside Dr
Houston, TX 77005
Phone: (832) 804-6941

#19
Reliant Park
Category: Stadium/Arena, Venues, Event Space
Area: Medical Center
Address: 1 Reliant Park
Houston, TX 77054
Phone: (832) 667-1400

#20
River Oaks Theatre
Category: Cinema
Area: River Oaks, Montrose
Address: 2009 W Gray St
Houston, TX 77019
Phone: (713) 524-2175

#21
The House of Dereon Media Center
Category: Music Venues, Event Space
Average price: Exclusive
Area: Midtown
Address: 2202 Crawford St
Houston, TX 77002
Phone: (713) 772-5175

#22
Sundance Cinemas
Category: Cinema
Area: Fourth Ward, Downtown
Address: 510 Texas St
Houston, TX 77002
Phone: (713) 223-3456

#23
The Corinthian
Category: Venues, Event Space
Area: Downtown
Address: 202 Fannin St
Houston, TX 77002
Phone: (713) 222-2002

#24
Space Montrose
Category: Arts, Crafts, Jewelry, Art Gallery
Average price: Modest
Area: Montrose
Address: 1706 Westheimer Rd
Houston, TX 77098
Phone: (832) 649-5743

#25
Eddie V's Prime Seafood
Category: Seafood, Steakhouse, Jazz, Blues
Average price: Expensive
Area: Upper Kirby
Address: 2800 Kirby Dr
Houston, TX 77098
Phone: (713) 874-1800

#26
Gallery M Squared
Category: Art Gallery, Venues, Event Space
Average price: Modest
Area: The Heights
Address: 339 W 19th St
Houston, TX 77008
Phone: (713) 861-6070

#27
Catering by George
Category: Caterer
Area: Northside Village
Address: 906 N Loop E
Houston, TX 77009
Phone: (713) 699-1693

#28
Fifty-Two-Twenty-Six
Category: Venues, Event Space
Area: Gulfton
Address: 5226 Elm St
Houston, TX 77081
Phone: (713) 529-2500

#29
Eddie V's Prime Seafood
Category: Steakhouse, Seafood, Jazz, Blues
Average price: Expensive
Area: Memorial
Address: 12848 Queensbury Ln
Houston, TX 77024
Phone: (832) 200-2380

#30
Avant Garden
Category: Lounge, Venues, Event Space
Average price: Modest
Area: Fourth Ward, Montrose
Address: 411 Westheimer Rd
Houston, TX 77006
Phone: (832) 519-1429

#31
Holocaust Museum Houston
Category: Museum
Area: Museum District
Address: 5401 Caroline St
Houston, TX 77004
Phone: (713) 942-8000

#32
The Music Box Theater
Category: Comedy Club, Performing Arts, Music Venues
Average price: Modest
Area: Upper Kirby
Address: 2623 Colquitt
Houston, TX 77098
Phone: (713) 522-7722

#33
Art Car Museum
Category: Museum
Area: The Heights
Address: 140 Heights Blvd
Houston, TX 77007
Phone: (713) 861-5526

#34
The Continental Club
Category: Dive Bar, Music Venues, Karaoke
Average price: Modest
Area: Fourth Ward, Midtown
Address: 3700 Main St
Houston, TX 77002
Phone: (713) 529-9899

#35
The Majestic Metro
Category: Venues, Event Space
Area: Fourth Ward, Downtown
Address: 911 Preston
Houston, TX 77002
Phone: (713) 224-7226

#36
Joystix Classic Games & Pinball
Category: Videos, Video Game, Arcade
Average price: Modest
Area: Downtown
Address: 1820 Franklin St
Houston, TX 77002
Phone: (713) 224-2225

#37
Discovery Green
Category: Park
Area: Downtown
Address: 1500 McKinney
Houston, TX 77010
Phone: (713) 400-7336

#38
Parador
Category: Venues, Event Space
Area: Museum District
Address: 2021 Binz St
Houston, TX 77004
Phone: (713) 529-3050

#39
Minute Maid Park
Category: Stadium/Arena, Music Venues
Average price: Modest
Area: Downtown
Address: 501 Crawford
Houston, TX 77002
Phone: (713) 259-8000

#40
Bonnie Blue the Rock Lady
Category: Arts, Entertainment
Area: Golfcrest/Belfort/Reveille
Address: 4105 Colgate St
Houston, TX 77087
Phone: (713) 649-6931

#41
Water 2 Wine
Category: Winery
Average price: Modest
Area: West University
Address: 3331 Westpark
Houston, TX 77005
Phone: (713) 662-9463

#42
Rockefeller Hall
Category: Venues, Event Space
Area: The Heights
Address: 3620 Washington Ave
Houston, TX 77007
Phone: (713) 869-3344

#43
Aurora Picture Show
Category: Cinema
Area: West University
Address: 2442 Bartlett St
Houston, TX 77098
Phone: (713) 868-2101

#44
Houston Rockets
Category: Professional Sports Team
Area: Downtown
Address: 1510 Polk St
Houston, TX 77002
Phone: (713) 758-7200

#45
Event Luxe & Co.
Category: Venues, Event Space,
Area: The Heights
Address: 325 Heights Blvd
Houston, TX 77007
Phone: (832) 767-0042

#46
Warehouse Live
Category: Music Venues
Average price: Modest
Area: Downtown, EaDo
Address: 813 St Emanuel St
Houston, TX 77003
Phone: (713) 225-5483

#47
Petroleum Club of Houston
Category: Venues, Event Space
Area: Fourth Ward, Downtown
Address: 800 Bell St
Houston, TX 77002
Phone: (713) 659-1431

#48
Wortham Center
Category: Performing Arts
Area: Fourth Ward, Downtown
Address: 500 Texas St
Houston, TX 77002
Phone: (713) 237-1439

#49
Keely Thorne Events
Category: Wedding Planning,
Party & Event Planning
Area: Fourth Ward, Midtown, Montrose
Address: 805 Rhode Place
Houston, TX 77019
Phone: (713) 807-8188

#50
Hobby Center
Category: Performing Arts
Area: Fourth Ward, Downtown
Address: 800 Bagby
Houston, TX 77002
Phone: (713) 315-2525

#51
Hughes Hangar
Category: Lounge, Dance Club,
Venues, Event Space
Average price: Modest
Area: The Heights
Address: 2811 Washington Ave
Houston, TX 77007
Phone: (281) 501-2028

#52
Stages Repertory Theatre
Category: Performing Arts
Area: River Oaks, Montrose
Address: 3201 Allen Pkwy
Houston, TX 77019
Phone: (713) 527-0220

#53
Meridian & Gatherings Banquet Centers
Category: Venues, Event Space
Area: Bellaire
Address: 5200/5206 Bissonnet St
Houston, TX 77401
Phone: (713) 667-8866

#54
Bayou City Art Festival Memorial Park
Category: Performing Arts, Art Gallery
Average price: Modest
Area: River Oaks
Address: S Picnic Ln and Memorial Dr
Houston, TX 77007
Phone: (713) 521-0133

#55
MJC Events
Category: Caterer
Area: Spring Branch
Address: 1050 Post Oak Rd
Houston, TX 77055
Phone: (713) 961-0911

#56
Las Velas
Category: Venues, Event Space
Area: Galleria/Uptown
Address: 5714 Fairdale Ln
Houston, TX 77057
Phone: (713) 977-5773

#57
Reliant Arena
Category: Stadium/Arena,
Venues, Event Space
Area: Medical Center
Address: 1 Reliant Park
Houston, TX 77054
Phone: (832) 667-1400

#58
Last Concert Caf'
Category: Tex-Mex, Music Venues, Dive Bar
Average price: Modest
Area: Downtown, Warehouse District
Address: 1403 Nance St
Houston, TX 77002
Phone: (713) 226-8563

Houston Travel Guide 2015 / Shops, Restaurants, Arts, Entertainment & Nightlife

#59
Colnside
Category: Venues, Event Space
Area: Sixth Ward
Address: 1919 Houston Ave
Houston, TX 77007
Phone: (713) 239-0319

#60
Rudyard's British Pub
Category: Music Venues, Pub, Comedy Club
Average price: Inexpensive
Area: Montrose
Address: 2010 Waugh Dr
Houston, TX 77006
Phone: (713) 521-0521

#61
Bayou City Outdoors
Category: Sports Club
Area: Memorial
Address: 8218 Mallie Ct
Houston, TX 77055
Phone: (713) 524-3567

#62
Hello Lucky
Category: Accessories, Women's Clothing, Art Gallery
Average price: Modest
Area: The Heights
Address: 1025 Studewood St
Houston, TX 77008
Phone: (713) 864-3556

#63
Hotel ZaZa
Category: Hotel
Average price: Expensive
Area: Museum District
Address: 5701 Main St
Houston, TX 77005
Phone: (713) 526-1991

#64
House Of Blues
Category: Music Venues, Event Space, American
Average price: Modest
Area: Downtown
Address: 1204 Caroline St
Houston, TX 77002
Phone: (888) 402-5837

#65
Houston Symphony
Category: Performing Arts, Music Venues
Average price: Modest
Area: Fourth Ward, Downtown
Address: 615 Louisiana St
Houston, TX 77002
Phone: (713) 224-7575

#66
Aerosol Warfare Studios
Category: Art Gallery
Average price: Modest
Area: EaDo
Address: 2110 Jefferson
Houston, TX 77003
Phone: (832) 748-8369

#67
Houston Museum of Natural Science
Category: Museum
Area: Museum District
Address: 5555 Hermann Park Dr
Houston, TX 77030
Phone: (713) 639-4629

#68
Royal Sonesta Hotel
Category: Hotel, Venues, Event Space
Average price: Expensive
Area: Galleria/Uptown
Address: 2222 W Loop S
Houston, TX 77027
Phone: (713) 627-7600

#69
Contemporary Arts Museum Houston
Category: Museum
Area: Museum District
Address: 5216 Montrose Blvd
Houston, TX 77006
Phone: (713) 284-8250

#70
The Original Henna Company
Category: Tattoo
Average price: Modest
Area: The Heights
Address: 1130 Yale St
Houston, TX 77008
Phone: (281) 630-8389

#71
Bayou Bend Collection & Gardens
Category: Museum, Tours
Area: River Oaks
Address: 1 Westcott St
Houston, TX 77007
Phone: (713) 639-7750

#72
Events and Adventures
Category: Social Club
Area: The Heights
Address: 344 Harvard St
Houston, TX 77007
Phone: (800) 386-0866

#73
Hope Stone, Inc.
Category: Dance Studio, Performing Arts
Area: Montrose
Address: 1210 W Clay St
Houston, TX 77019
Phone: (713) 526-1907

#74
Goode's Armadillo Palace
Category: Bar, Music Venues, American
Average price: Modest
Area: West University
Address: 5015 Kirby Dr
Houston, TX 77098
Phone: (713) 526-9700

#75
Bayou City Event Center
Category: Venues, Event Space
Area: Central Southwest, South Main
Address: 9401 Knight Rd
Houston, TX 77045
Phone: (281) 501-6720

#76
The Posh Petal - Flower Artistry
Category: Cards, Stationery, Florist
Average price: Modest
Area: Oak Forest/Garden Oaks
Address: 2126 W 34th St
Houston, TX 77018
Phone: (713) 686-8808

#77
ERJCC Houston
Category: Performing Arts, Gym
Area: Meyerland
Address: 5601 S Braeswood Blvd
Houston, TX 77096
Phone: (713) 729-3200

#78
Hickory Hollow
Category: Barbeque, Music Venues
Average price: Modest
Area: The Heights
Address: 101 Heights Blvd
Houston, TX 77007
Phone: (713) 869-6300

#79
City Kitchen
Category: Caterer
Area: Hobby
Address: 8101 Airport Blvd
Houston, TX 77061
Phone: (713) 847-8004

#80
STAGE Lounge & Live Music
Category: Bar, Music Venues, Breakfast & Brunch
Average price: Modest
Area: Sharpstown, Chinatown
Address: 9889 Bellaire Blvd
Houston, TX 77036
Phone: (281) 846-1389

#81
Pump It Up
Category: Party & Event Planning
Area: Spring Branch
Address: 7620 Katy Frwy
Houston, TX 77024
Phone: (713) 686-7867

#82
Houston Ballet
Category: Dance Studio, Opera, Ballet
Area: Fourth Ward, Downtown
Address: 601 Preston St
Houston, TX 77002
Phone: (713) 523-6300

#83
George R.
Category: Venues, Event Space
Area: Downtown
Address: 1001 Avenida de las Americas
Houston, TX 77010
Phone: (713) 853-8000

#84
McGonigel's Mucky Duck
Category: Pub, Music Venues, Irish
Average price: Modest
Area: Upper Kirby
Address: 2425 Norfolk St
Houston, TX 77098
Phone: (713) 528-5999

#85
Simpleton's Fine Catering
Category: Caterer
Area: Westchase
Address: 1251 Wilcrest Dr
Houston, TX 77042
Phone: (281) 691-4426

#86
The Rothko Chapel
Category: Museum
Area: Montrose
Address: 1409 Sul Ross St
Houston, TX 77006
Phone: (713) 524-9839

#87
Houston Sports & Social Club
Category: Social Club,
Amateur Sports Team, Sports Club
Area: The Heights
Address: 201 S Heights Blvd
Houston, TX 77007
Phone: (713) 481-2558

#88
Events Made Perfect
Category: Caterer
Area: Westchase
Address: 2119 Blue Willow Dr
Houston, TX 77042
Phone: (713) 829-8009

#89
1940 Air Terminal Museum
Category: Museum
Area: Hobby
Address: 8325 Travelair Rd
Houston, TX 77061
Phone: (713) 454-1940

#90
Twilight Epiphany Skyspace by James Turrell
Category: Art Gallery
Average price: Inexpensive
Area: West University
Address: 6100 Main St
Houston, TX 77005
Phone: (713) 348-4758

#91
Alley Theatre
Category: Performing Arts
Area: Fourth Ward, Downtown
Address: 615 Texas Ave
Houston, TX 77002
Phone: (713) 220-5700

#92
Bayou Music Center
Category: Music Venues, Event Space
Average price: Modest
Area: Fourth Ward, Downtown
Address: 520 Texas Ave
Houston, TX 77002
Phone: (713) 230-1600

#93
Ben's Beans
Category: Coffee, Tea, Art Gallery
Average price: Inexpensive
Area: Downtown
Address: 1302 Dallas St
Houston, TX 77002
Phone: (713) 654-8856

#94
Houston Engineering and Scientific Society
Category: Venues, Event Space
Area: Galleria/Uptown
Address: 5430 Westheimer Rd
Houston, TX 77056
Phone: (713) 627-2283

#95
Spring Street Studios
Category: Venues, Event Space, Art Gallery
Area: Sixth Ward
Address: 1824 Spring St
Houston, TX 77007
Phone: (713) 862-0082

#96
notsuoH
Category: Bar, Music Venues
Average price: Inexpensive
Area: Fourth Ward, Downtown
Address: 314 Main St
Houston, TX 77002
Phone: (713) 409-4750

#97
The Big Easy Social and Pleasure Club
Category: Jazz, Blues
Average price: Inexpensive
Area: West University
Address: 5731 Kirby Dr
Houston, TX 77005
Phone: (713) 523-9999

#98
Fitzgerald's
Category: Dive Bar, Music Venues
Average price: Inexpensive
Area: The Heights
Address: 2706 White Oak Dr
Houston, TX 77007
Phone: (713) 862-3838

#99
A&A Video
Category: Photographers, Videographers
Area: Fondren Southwest
Address: 10101 SW Freeway
Houston, TX 77074
Phone: (713) 772-6899

#100
Walters Downtown
Category: Music Venues, Bar
Average price: Inexpensive
Area: Northside Village
Address: 1120 Naylor St
Houston, TX 77002
Phone: (713) 222-2679

#101
Cezanne
Category: Bar, Music Venues, Jazz, Blues
Average price: Modest
Area: Montrose
Address: 4100 Montrose Blvd
Houston, TX 77006
Phone: (713) 522-9621

#102
River Oaks Garden Club Forum of Civics
Category: Venues, Event Space
Area: Upper Kirby
Address: 2503 Westheimer Rd
Houston, TX 77098
Phone: (713) 523-2483

#103
Casa Ramirez Folkart Gallery
Category: Art Gallery, Home Decor
Average price: Modest
Area: The Heights
Address: 241 W 19th St
Houston, TX 77008
Phone: (713) 880-2420

#104
Villa Rinata
Category: Venues, Event Space
Area: Galleria/Uptown
Address: 2840 Chimney Rock
Houston, TX 77057
Phone: (713) 334-7765

#105
Broadway Across America
Category: Performing Arts
Area: Fourth Ward, Downtown
Address: 800 Bagby
Houston, TX 77002
Phone: (713) 622-7469

#106
Lawndale Art Center
Category: Museum, Art Gallery
Average price: Inexpensive
Area: Museum District
Address: 4912 Main St
Houston, TX 77002
Phone: (713) 528-5858

#107
Frenetic Theater
Category: Performing Arts
Area: Second Ward
Address: 5102 Navigation Blvd
Houston, TX 77011
Phone: (832) 426-4624

#108
Sambuca Jazz Caf'
Category: American, Lounge, Music Venues
Average price: Expensive
Area: Fourth Ward, Downtown
Address: 909 Texas St
Houston, TX 77002
Phone: (713) 224-5299

#109
Kim Son Ballroom
Category: Vietnamese, Venues, Event Space
Area: Downtown, EaDo
Address: 1589 St. Emmanuel
Houston, TX 77003
Phone: (713) 222-2461

#110
14 Pews
Category: Cinema
Area: The Heights
Address: 800 Aurora St
Houston, TX 77009
Phone: (281) 888-9677

#111
Abuso Catering Co.
Category: Caterer
Area: West University
Address: 6729 Stella Link Rd
Houston, TX 77005
Phone: (713) 660-6617

#112
Howl at the Moon
Category: Music Venues, Bar
Average price: Modest
Area: Fourth Ward, Midtown
Address: 612 Hadley St
Houston, TX 77002
Phone: (713) 658-9700

#113
H-Town Casino Events
Category: Casino
Area: The Heights
Address: 2411 Washington Ave
Houston, TX 77007
Phone: (281) 727-6101

#114
Toyota Center
Category: Stadium/Arena
Area: Downtown
Address: 1510 Polk St
Houston, TX 77002
Phone: (713) 758-7200

#115
T J's Catering & Take Out
Category: Caterer
Area: Fourth Ward, Midtown, Montrose
Address: 1100 W Dallas St
Houston, TX 77019
Phone: (713) 974-5442

Houston Travel Guide 2015 / Shops, Restaurants, Arts, Entertainment & Nightlife

#116
Dionisio Winery
Category: Winery, Wine Bar
Average price: Modest
Area: EaDo
Address: 2110 Jefferson St
Houston, TX 77003
Phone: (713) 906-2499

#117
Brady's Landing
Category: Venues, Event Space, American, Seafood
Average price: Expensive
Area: Harrisburg/Manchester
Address: 8505 Cypress St.
Houston, TX 77012
Phone: (713) 928-9921

#118
First Saturday Arts Market
Category: Arts, Crafts, Festival
Average price: Modest
Area: The Heights
Address: 548 W 19th St
Houston, TX 77008
Phone: (713) 802-1213

#119
The Heights Villa
Category: Venues, Event Space
Area: The Heights
Address: 3600 Michaux St
Houston, TX 77009
Phone: (713) 405-9340

#120
MKT BAR
Category: Bar, American, Music Venues
Average price: Modest
Area: Downtown
Address: 1001 Austin St
Houston, TX 77010
Phone: (832) 360-2222

#121
Aztec Events and Tents
Category: Party Supplies
Area: The Heights
Address: 601 W 6th St
Houston, TX 77007
Phone: (713) 699-0088

#122
Firehouse Saloon
Category: Bar, Music Venues
Average price: Modest
Area: Gulfton, Galleria/Uptown
Address: 5930 Southwest Fwy
Houston, TX 77057
Phone: (281) 513-1995

#123
Photo Rental Source
Category: Videographers, Photographers
Area: Memorial
Address: 9055 Gaylord St
Houston, TX 77024
Phone: (713) 932-0264

#124
Houston Event Centers
Category: Venues, Event Space
Area: Hobby
Address: 9906 Gulf Fwy
Houston, TX 77034
Phone: (713) 987-7300

#125
Winter Street Studios
Category: Art Gallery, Real Estate
Area: Sixth Ward
Address: 2101 Winter St
Houston, TX 77007
Phone: (713) 862-0082

#126
Eventology Weddings
Category: Wedding Planning, Party & Event Planning
Area: Fourth Ward, Montrose
Address: 4119 Montrose
Houston, TX 77006
Phone: (713) 409-5737

#127
Art League of Houston
Category: Art Gallery, Art Classes
Average price: Expensive
Area: Fourth Ward, Montrose
Address: 1953 Montrose
Houston, TX 77006
Phone: (713) 523-9530

#128
Jackson & Company Caterers
Category: Caterer
Area: Fourth Ward, Montrose
Address: 707 Hawthorne St
Houston, TX 77006
Phone: (713) 523-5780

#129
Numbers Night Club
Category: Music Venues, Dance Club
Average price: Inexpensive
Area: Fourth Ward, Midtown, Montrose
Address: 300 Westheimer Rd
Houston, TX 77006
Phone: (713) 521-1121

#130
LG Entertainers
Category: Party & Event Planning
Area: Lazy Brook/Timbergrove
Address: 2855 Magnum Rd
Houston, TX 77092
Phone: (281) 235-8668

#131
Studio Movie Grill
Category: Cinema
Area: Memorial
Address: 822 Town & Country Blvd
Houston, TX 77024
Phone: (713) 461-4449

#132
Nouveau Antique Art Bar
Category: Bar, Venues, Event Space
Average price: Modest
Area: Fourth Ward, Midtown
Address: 2913 Main St
Houston, TX 77002
Phone: (713) 526-2220

#133
Magnolia Hotel Houston
Category: Hotel, Venues, Event Space
Average price: Expensive
Area: Downtown
Address: 1100 Texas St
Houston, TX 77002
Phone: (713) 221-0011

#134
Lucia's Especialidades Argentina
Category: Caterer,
Area: Downtown
Address: 907 Franklin St
Houston, TX 77002
Phone: (713) 858-4840

#135
Theatre Under The Stars
Category: Performing Arts, Dance School
Area: Fourth Ward, Downtown
Address: 800 Bagby St
Houston, TX 77002
Phone: (713) 558-2600

#136
Houston Center For Contemporary Craft
Category: Museum
Area: Museum District
Address: 4848 Main St
Houston, TX 77002
Phone: (713) 529-4848

#137
The Heritage Society
Category: Museum
Area: Fourth Ward, Downtown
Address: 1100 Bagby St
Houston, TX 77002
Phone: (713) 655-1912

#138
Green Planet Sanctuary
Category: Venues, Event Space, Massage
Average price: Modest
Area: Energy Corridor
Address: 13424-B Briar Forest
Houston, TX 77077
Phone: (281) 558-1112

#139
Neon Boots Dancehall & Saloon
Category: Country Dance Hall, Gay Bar, Music Venues
Average price: Modest
Area: Lazy Brook/Timbergrove, Spring Branch
Address: 11410 Hempstead Hwy
Houston, TX 77092
Phone: (713) 677-0828

#140
Crawdad's! Crawfish Boils & Cajun Catering
Category: Caterer, Seafood
Area: Galleria/Uptown
Address: 5868 A1 Westhiemer Rd
Houston, TX 77057
Phone: (713) 283-2401

#141
Antiquarium Antique Print & Map Gallery
Category: Antiques, Art Gallery
Average price: Exclusive
Area: Upper Kirby
Address: 3021 Kirby Dr
Houston, TX 77098
Phone: (713) 622-7531

#142
University Center Game Room
Category: Bowling, Arts, Entertainment
Area: Third Ward
Address: 4800 Calhoun Rd
Houston, TX 77004
Phone: (713) 743-5324

#143
Anderson Fair
Category: Music Venues
Average price: Modest
Area: Fourth Ward, Montrose
Address: 2007 Grant St
Houston, TX 77006
Phone: (832) 767-2785

Houston Travel Guide 2015 / Shops, Restaurants, Arts, Entertainment & Nightlife

#144
Doubletree Hotel
Category: Hotel
Average price: Expensive
Area: Fourth Ward, Downtown
Address: 400 Dallas St
Houston, TX 77002
Phone: (713) 759-0202

#145
Theatre Suburbia
Category: Performing Arts
Area: Langwood
Address: 4106 Way Out W Dr
Houston, TX 77092
Phone: (713) 682-3525

#146
Hilton Americas
Category: Hotel
Average price: Expensive
Area: Downtown
Address: 1600 Lamar St
Houston, TX 77010
Phone: (713) 739-8000

#147
Buffalo Bayou Partnership
Category: Social Club
Area: Northside Village
Address: 1113 Vine St
Houston, TX 77002
Phone: (713) 752-0314

#148
Magnolia Ballroom
Category: Venues, Event Space
Area: Downtown
Address: 715 Franklin
Houston, TX 77002
Phone: (713) 223-8508

#149
En Vogue Events
Category: Wedding Planning,
Party & Event Planning
Area: The Heights
Address: 635 W 19th St
Houston, TX 77008
Phone: (281) 414-0844

#150
Cy Twombly Gallery
Category: Museum, Tours
Area: Montrose
Address: 1501 Branard St
Houston, TX 77006
Phone: (713) 525-9400

#151
The Fedora Lounge
Category: Lounge, Jazz, Blues
Average price: Modest
Area: West University
Address: 2726 Bissonnet St
Houston, TX 77005
Phone: (832) 581-3232

#152
Laura Sponaugle Photography
Category: Photographers
Area: West University
Address: 6310 Main St
Houston, TX 77005
Phone: (281) 413-9401

#153
Kay's Lounge
Category: Dive Bar, Music Venues, Pizza
Average price: Inexpensive
Area: West University
Address: 2324 Bissonnet St
Houston, TX 77005
Phone: (713) 521-0010

#154
Main Street Theater
Category: Performing Arts
Area: Museum District
Address: 4617 Montrose Blvd
Houston, TX 77006
Phone: (713) 524-6706

#155
Edwards Marq'e Stadium 23 Cinemas
Category: Cinema
Area: Spring Branch
Address: 7600 Katy Fwy
Houston, TX 77024
Phone: (713) 263-0808

#156
Holiday Inn Express Hotel & Suites Houston-Dwtn Conv Ctr
Category: Venues, Event Space, Hotel
Average price: Modest
Area: Downtown
Address: 1810 Bell Street
Houston, TX 77003
Phone: (713) 652-9400

#157
The Houston Club
Category: Venues, Event Space, Bar
Average price: Expensive
Area: Fourth Ward, Downtown
Address: 910 Louisiana St
Houston, TX 77002
Phone: (713) 225-1661

Houston Travel Guide 2015 / Shops, Restaurants, Arts, Entertainment & Nightlife

#158
Rice University Art Gallery
Category: Museum, Art Gallery
Average price: Modest
Area: West University
Address: 6100 Main St
Houston, TX 77005
Phone: (713) 348-6069

#159
Avalon Event Rentals
Category: Party Supplies, Venues, Event Space
Area: Spring Branch
Address: 10803 Warwana Rd, Bldg C
Houston, TX 77043
Phone: (713) 974-3646

#160
Dan Electro's Guitar Bar
Category: Dive Bar, Music Venues
Average price: Inexpensive
Area: The Heights
Address: 1031 E 24th St
Houston, TX 77009
Phone: (713) 862-8707

#161
Jones Hall
Category: Performing Arts
Area: Fourth Ward, Downtown
Address: 615 Louisiana St
Houston, TX 77208
Phone: (713) 227-3974

#162
Omni Houston Hotel
Category: Caterer, Hotel
Average price: Expensive
Area: Galleria/Uptown
Address: 4 Riverway
Houston, TX 77056
Phone: (713) 396-5500

#163
Local Pour Houston
Category: Bar, American, Music Venues
Average price: Modest
Area: River Oaks, Montrose
Address: 1952 W Gray St
Houston, TX 77019
Phone: (713) 521-1881

#164
King Kong Party Rentals
Category: Party Equipment Rental
Area: Spring Branch
Address: 2231 Hoskins Dr
Houston, TX 77080
Phone: (832) 738-9999

#165
Blaffer Art Museum
Category: Art Gallery, Museum
Average price: Inexpensive
Area: Third Ward
Address: 120 Fine Arts Bldg
Houston, TX 77204
Phone: (713) 743-9521

#166
Tomas Ramos
Category: Photographers
Area: Galleria/Uptown
Address: 5714 Fairdale
Houston, TX 77057
Phone: (713) 410-1389

#167
Boondocks
Category: Dive Bar, Music Venues
Average price: Inexpensive
Area: Montrose
Address: 1417 Westheimer Ave
Houston, TX 77006
Phone: (713) 522-8500

#168
Edwards Grand Palace Stadium 24 Cinemas
Category: Cinema
Area: Greenway
Address: 3839 Weslayan St
Houston, TX 77027
Phone: (713) 871-8880

#169
Arne's Warehouse & Party Store
Category: Party Supplies, Costumes, Pet Store
Average price: Inexpensive
Area: The Heights
Address: 2830 Hicks St
Houston, TX 77007
Phone: (713) 869-8321

#170
Museum of Printing History
Category: Museum
Area: Montrose
Address: 1324 W Clay St
Houston, TX 77019
Phone: (713) 522-4652

#171
Green Plate Kitchen
Category: Food Delivery Services, Bakery, Caterer
Average price: Modest
Area: Bellaire, Galleria/Uptown
Address: 5200 W Lp S
Houston, TX 77401
Phone: (713) 665-5885

Houston Travel Guide 2015 / Shops, Restaurants, Arts, Entertainment & Nightlife

#172
Ronald McDonald House Houston
Category: Community Service
Area: Medical Center
Address: 1907 Holcombe Blvd
Houston, TX 77030
Phone: (713) 795-3500

#173
Asgard Games
Category: Arcade, Hobby Shop, Toy Store
Average price: Expensive
Area: Upper Kirby
Address: 3302 Shepherd Dr
Houston, TX 77098
Phone: (713) 677-0699

#174
Events In Bloom
Category: Party & Event Planning
Area: The Heights
Address: 633A W 19th St
Houston, TX 77008
Phone: (713) 880-1475

#175
Brilliant Lecture Series
Category: Musical Instruments, Performing Arts
Average price: Expensive
Area: Galleria/Uptown
Address: 2400 Augusta Dr
Houston, TX 77057
Phone: (713) 974-1335

#176
Obsidian Art Space
Category: Performing Arts
Area: The Heights
Address: 3522 White Oak Dr
Houston, TX 77007
Phone: (832) 889-7837

#177
Czech Center Museum
Category: Museum
Area: Museum District
Address: 4920 San Jacinto
Houston, TX 77004
Phone: (713) 528-2060

#178
My Happy Lens Photography
Category: Photographers
Area: Fourth Ward, Midtown
Address: Midtown
Houston, TX 77002
Phone: (979) 292-4466

#179
Painting Above the Bar
Category: Arts, Entertainment
Area: Midtown
Address: 3116 Telge
Houston, TX 77054
Phone: (832) 644-5532

#180
FotoFest
Category: Art Gallery
Area: Northside Village
Address: 1113 Vine St
Houston, TX 77002
Phone: (713) 223-5522

#181
Pellazio
Category: Party & Event Planning
Area: Westchase
Address: 12121 Westheimer
Houston, TX 77082
Phone: (281) 531-0008

#182
Framework
Category: Art Gallery, Framing
Average price: Expensive
Area: Lazy Brook/Timbergrove
Address: 2855 Mangum St
Houston, TX 77007
Phone: (713) 868-0011

#183
Family Bingo Center
Category: Arts, Entertainment
Area: Independence Heights
Address: 641 W Crosstimbers St
Houston, TX 77018
Phone: (713) 692-4640

#184
Houston Astros
Category: Professional Sports Team
Area: Downtown
Address: 501 Crawford
Houston, TX 77002
Phone: (713) 259-8000

#185
JW Marriott Houston
Category: Hotel
Average price: Expensive
Area: Galleria/Uptown
Address: 5150 Westheimer Road
Houston, TX 77056
Phone: (713) 961-1500

#186
Fresh Arts
Category: Art Gallery
Area: Sixth Ward
Address: 2101 Winter St
Houston, TX 77007
Phone: (713) 868-1839

#187
Residence Inn
Category: Hotel
Average price: Modest
Address: 2929 Westpark Dr
Houston, TX 77005
Phone: (713) 661-4660

#188
Crescendo Family Music Classes
Category: Performing Arts, Musical Instruments
Average price: Inexpensive
Area: The Heights
Address: 508 Pecore St
Houston, TX 77009
Phone: (832) 454-2376

#189
Write Now!
Categories: Cards, Stationery
Average price: Modest
Area: The Heights
Address: 3122 White Oak Dr
Houston, TX 77007
Phone: (281) 974-2138

#190
Da Camera
Category: Performing Arts
Area: Montrose
Address: 1427 Branard St
Houston, TX 77006
Phone: (713) 524-5050

#191
Jerry B Smith Photography
Category: Photographers
Area: Oak Forest/Garden Oaks
Address: 4418 Deer Lodge Dr
Houston, TX 77018
Phone: (713) 628-7489

#192
Beta Theater
Category: Comedy Club, Performing Arts
Average price: Inexpensive
Area: Sixth Ward
Address: 1900 Kane St
Houston, TX 77007
Phone: (713) 591-5867

#193
Flock The Houston Zoo Young Supporters
Category: Social Club
Area: Museum District
Address: 6200 Hermann Park Dr
Houston, TX 77030
Phone: (713) 533-6500

#194
Peter Lik Gallery
Category: Art Gallery
Average price: Exclusive
Area: Galleria/Uptown
Address: 5085 Westheimer Rd
Houston, TX 77056
Phone: (713) 965-0190

#195
Opulent Photography
Category: Photographers
Area: Central Southwest
Address: 13011 Pentacle Ln
Houston, TX 77085
Phone: (281) 757-6114

#196
Houston Chamber Choir
Category: Performing Arts
Area: Fourth Ward, Downtown
Address: 1117 Texas St
Houston, TX 77002
Phone: (713) 224-5566

#197
Communication Workers of America
Category: Venues, Event Space
Area: Downtown
Address: 1730 Jefferson
Houston, TX 77003
Phone: (713) 654-1115

#198
Interactive Theater
Category: Performing Arts
Area: The Heights
Address: 1548 Heights Blvd
Houston, TX 77008
Phone: (713) 862-7112

#199
Sparrow and The Nest
Category: Arts, Crafts, Art Gallery, Jewelry
Average price: Modest
Area: The Heights
Address: 1020 Studewood
Houston, TX 77008
Phone: (713) 869-6378

#200
Gaslight Gallery
Category: Tattoo, Art Gallery
Average price: Modest
Area: Montrose
Address: 1416 Westheimer Rd
Houston, TX 77006
Phone: (713) 524-3535

#201
Houston Marriott South at Hobby Airport
Category: Hotel, Venues, Event Space, Restaurant
Average price: Expensive
Area: Hobby
Address: 9100 Gulf Freeway
Houston, TX 77017
Phone: (713) 943-7979

#202
TC's Houston's Premiere Showbar
Category: Gay Bar, Performing Arts
Average price: Inexpensive
Area: Fourth Ward, Montrose
Address: 817 Fairview
Houston, TX 77006
Phone: (713) 526-2625

#203
Zoo Lights
Category: Festival, Local Flavor
Area: Museum District
Address: 6200 Hermann Park Dr
Houston, TX 77030
Phone: (713) 533-6500

#204
Bowlmor Houston
Category: Nightlife, Bowling, Arts, Entertainment
Average price: Expensive
Area: Memorial
Address: 925 Bunker Hill Rd
Houston, TX 77024
Phone: (713) 461-1207

#205
Child Advocates
Category: Community Service
Area: Upper Kirby
Address: 2401 Portsmouth St Ste 210
Houston, TX 77098
Phone: (713) 529-1396

#206
Burke Baker Planetarium
Category: Museum, Cinema
Area: Museum District
Address: 1 Hermann Circle Dr
Houston, TX 77030
Phone: (713) 639-4629

#207
Jesse H.
Category: Hotel
Average price: Modest
Area: Medical Center
Address: 1600 Holcombe Blvd
Houston, TX 77030
Phone: (713) 790-1600

#208
Dave & Buster's
Category: Arcade, American
Average price: Modest
Area: Galleria/Uptown
Address: 6010 Richmond Ave
Houston, TX 77057
Phone: (713) 952-2233

#209
Sharespace
Category: Venues, Event Space
Area: EaDo, Warehouse District
Address: 2201 Preston St
Houston, TX 77003
Phone: (832) 582-4689

#210
The Health Museum
Category: Museum
Area: Museum District
Address: 1515 Hermann Dr
Houston, TX 77004
Phone: (713) 521-1515

#211
Houston Party Tent and Event
Category: Party Equipment Rentals
Area: Lazy Brook/Timbergrove
Address: 3800 W 11th St
Houston, TX 77055
Phone: (713) 231-7375

#212
Dean's
Category: Dive Bar, Music Venues
Average price: Modest
Area: Fourth Ward, Downtown
Address: 316 Main St
Houston, TX 77002
Phone: (281) 624-5541

#213
Hotel Derek
Category: Hotel, Venues, Event Space
Average price: Expensive
Area: Highland Village, Galleria/Uptown
Address: 2525 W Loop S
Houston, TX 77027
Phone: (713) 961-3000

#214
Country Playhouse
Category: Performing Arts
Area: Memorial
Address: 12802 Queensbury Ln
Houston, TX 77024
Phone: (713) 467-4497

#215
Holiday Inn Houston Reliant Park Area
Category: Hotel, Venues, Event Space
Average price: Modest
Area: Medical Center
Address: 8111 Kirby Dr
Houston, TX 77054
Phone: (713) 790-1900

#216
Houston Maritime Museum
Category: Museum
Area: Braeswood Place, West University
Address: 2204 Dorrington St
Houston, TX 77030
Phone: (713) 666-1910

#217
Angela & Co.
Category: Party & Event Planning
Area: Downtown
Address: PO Box 7866
Houston, TX 77270
Phone: (713) 880-3613

#218
The Catastrophic Theatre
Category: Performing Arts
Area: Northside Village
Address: 1119 East Fwy
Houston, TX 77002
Phone: (713) 522-2723

#219
El Dorado Ballroom
Category: Venues, Event Space
Area: Third Ward
Address: 2310 Elgin
Houston, TX 77004
Phone: (713) 526-7662

#220
The Ensemble Theatre
Category: Performing Arts, Cultural Center
Area: Fourth Ward, Midtown
Address: 3535 Main St
Houston, TX 77002
Phone: (713) 520-0055

#221
Nutcracker Market
Category: Performing Arts, Arts, Crafts
Area: Fourth Ward, Downtown
Address: 601 Preston St
Houston, TX 77002
Phone: (713) 535-3271

#222
Hilton Houston Post Oak
Category: Hotel
Average price: Modest
Area: Galleria/Uptown
Address: 2001 Post Oak Blvd
Houston, TX 77056
Phone: (713) 961-9300

#223
Texas Rock Gym
Category: Gym, Venues, Event Space
Area: Spring Branch
Address: 1526 Campbell Rd
Houston, TX 77055
Phone: (713) 973-7625

#224
Mainstage
Category: Dance Club, Music Venues
Average price: Modest
Area: Fourth Ward, Midtown, Downtown
Address: 2016 Main St
Houston, TX 77002
Phone: (713) 751-3101

#225
Reclaimed Moments Photography
Category: Event Photography
Area: The Heights
Address: 6613 N Main St
Houston, TX 77009
Phone: (832) 649-7162

#226
Rienzi
Category: Museum, Art Gallery
Average price: Inexpensive
Area: River Oaks
Address: 1406 Kirby Dr
Houston, TX 77019
Phone: (713) 639-7800

#227
La Colombe d'Or Hotel
Category: Venues, Event Space, French, Hotel
Average price: Exclusive
Area: Fourth Ward, Montrose
Address: 3410 Montrose Blvd
Houston, TX 77006
Phone: (713) 524-7999

#228
Painting with a Twist
Category: Arts, Crafts,
Average price: Modest
Area: Westchase
Address: 10001 Westheimer Rd
Houston, TX 77042
Phone: (713) 609-9509

#229
Tinseltown 290
Category: Cinema
Area: Fairbanks/Northwest Crossing
Address: 12920 Northwest Fwy
Houston, TX 77040
Phone: (713) 329-9975

#230
The Gardens of Bammel Lane
Category: Wedding Planning,
Party & Event Planning
Area: Upper Kirby
Address: 2807 Bammel Ln
Houston, TX 77098
Phone: (713) 418-7243

Houston Travel Guide 2015 / Shops, Restaurants, Arts, Entertainment & Nightlife

#231
Super Happy Fun Land
Category: Performing Arts, Music Venues
Average price: Inexpensive
Area: EaDo, Eastwood
Address: 3801 Polk St
Houston, TX 77003
Phone: (713) 880-2100

#232
Off the Wall Gallery
Category: Art Gallery
Average price: Exclusive
Area: Galleria/Uptown
Address: 5015 Westheimer Rd, Ste 2208
Houston, TX 77056
Phone: (713) 871-0940

#233
MFAH Films
Category: Cinema
Area: Museum District
Address: 1001 Bissonnet
Houston, TX 77006
Phone: (713) 639-7515

#234
Sheraton Houston Brookhollow Hotel
Category: Hotel
Average price: Modest
Area: Lazy Brook/Timbergrove
Address: 3000 N Lp W Frwy
Houston, TX 77092
Phone: (713) 688-0100

#235
Grooves of Houston
Category: Dance Club, Music Venues, Event Space
Average price: Expensive
Area: Third Ward
Address: 2300 Pierce St
Houston, TX 77003
Phone: (713) 652-9900

#236
Betz Gallery
Category: Art Gallery
Average price: Exclusive
Area: The Heights
Address: 2500 Summer St
Houston, TX 77007
Phone: (713) 576-6954

#237
Prelude Music Classes For Children
Category: Preschools, Arts, Entertainment
Area: Highland Village
Address: 3701 W Alabama
Houston, TX 77027
Phone: (832) 803-7701

#238
Aaron Brothers Art & Framing
Category: Art Supplies, Art Gallery
Average price: Modest
Area: Gulfton, Galleria/Uptown
Address: 5144 Richmond Ave
Houston, TX 77056
Phone: (713) 961-4882

#239
Hyatt Regency Houston
Category: Hotel
Average price: Modest
Area: Fourth Ward, Downtown
Address: 1200 Louisiana Street
Houston, TX 77002
Phone: (713) 654-1234

#240
Village Frame Gallery
Category: Art Gallery, Framing
Average price: Expensive
Area: West University
Address: 2708 Bissonnet St
Houston, TX 77005
Phone: (713) 528-2288

#241
The Power Center
Category: Venues, Event Space
Area: Central Southwest
Address: 12401 S Post Oak Rd
Houston, TX 77045
Phone: (713) 723-6837

#242
NJ's
Category: Dive Bar, Music Venues
Average price: Inexpensive
Area: Oak Forest/Garden Oaks
Address: 3815 Mangum Rd
Houston, TX 77092
Phone: (713) 682-3363

#243
GreenStreet
Category: Music Venues, Shopping Center
Average price: Modest
Area: Downtown
Address: 1201 Fannin St
Houston, TX 77002
Phone: (832) 320-1200

#244
Archway Gallery
Category: Art Gallery
Average price: Modest
Area: Montrose
Address: 2305 Dunlavy
Houston, TX 77006
Phone: (713) 522-2409

#245
Architects of Air
Category: Art Gallery
Average price: Modest
Area: Downtown
Address: 1500 McKinney
Houston, TX 77010
Phone: (713) 400-7336

#246
Goode Company Catering
Category: Caterer,
Food Delivery Services, Barbeque
Area: West University
Address: 2515 N Blvd
Houston, TX 77098
Phone: (713) 224-6633

#247
**Perimeter Arts Gallery
& Custom Framing**
Category: Framing, Art Gallery
Area: West University
Address: 2365 Rice Blvd
Houston, TX 77005
Phone: (713) 521-5928

#248
Pole Position Raceway
Category: Race Track
Area: South Belt/Ellington
Address: 12552 Galveston Rd
Webster, TX 77598
Phone: (281) 581-7223

#249
Houston Texans
Category: Professional Sports Team
Area: Medical Center
Address: One Reliant Park
Houston, TX 77054
Phone: (832) 667-2002

#250
Houston Grand Opera
Category: Performing Arts, Opera, Ballet
Area: Fourth Ward, Downtown
Address: 510 Preston St
Houston, TX 77002
Phone: (281) 546-0200

#251
Tony's Catering
Category: Caterer
Area: Greenway
Address: 3755 Richmond Ave
Houston, TX 77046
Phone: (713) 622-6779

#252
Houston Auto Show
Category: Festival
Area: Medical Center
Address: 1 Reliant Park
Houston, TX 77054
Phone: (832) 667-1400

#253
City Hall Annex
Category: Landmark/Historical
Area: Fourth Ward, Downtown
Address: 900 Bagby St
Houston, TX 77002
Phone: (713) 837-0311

#254
SoundBox-Studios
Category: Performing Arts, Dance School
Area: Gulfton
Address: 5325 Glenmont
Houston, TX 77081
Phone: (713) 218-0799

#255
Four Seasons Hotel Houston
Category: Hotel
Average price: Expensive
Area: Downtown
Address: 1300 Lamar St
Houston, TX 77010
Phone: (713) 650-1300

#256
Dan Flavin Installation
Category: Art Gallery
Average price: Inexpensive
Area: Montrose
Address: 1500 Richmond Ave
Houston, TX 77006
Phone: (713) 520-8512

#257
Bella Elegante
Category: Venues, Event Space
Area: Fourth Ward, Downtown
Address: 300 Milam St
Houston, TX 77002
Phone: (713) 228-1300

#258
The Bird & The Bear
Category: American, Jazz, Blues
Average price: Expensive
Area: River Oaks
Address: 2810 Westheimer Rd
Houston, TX 77098
Phone: (713) 528-2473

Houston Travel Guide 2015 / Shops, Restaurants, Arts, Entertainment & Nightlife

#259
Vivaldi Music Academy
Category: Performing Arts, Musical Instruments
Average price: Modest
Area: Braeswood Place, West University
Address: 3914 Gramercy St
Houston, TX 77025
Phone: (713) 858-9617

#260
Moody Gallery Inc.
Category: Art Gallery
Area: Upper Kirby
Address: 2815 Colquitt St
Houston, TX 77098
Phone: (713) 526-9911

#261
The Westin Galleria Houston
Category: Hotel
Average price: Expensive
Area: Galleria/Uptown
Address: 5060 West Alabama
Houston, TX 77056
Phone: (713) 960-8100

#262
The Listening Room
Category: Music Venues
Average price: Modest
Area: The Heights
Address: 508 Pecore St
Houston, TX 77009
Phone: (713) 864-4260

#263
Arden's Picture Framing & Gallery
Category: Art Gallery, Framing
Area: Montrose
Address: 1631 W Alabama St
Houston, TX 77006
Phone: (713) 522-5281

#264
Booker Lowe Aboriginal Gallery
Category: Art Gallery
Average price: Modest
Area: The Heights, Rice Military
Address: 4623 Feagan St
Houston, TX 77007
Phone: (713) 880-1541

#265
Luxury Trio
Category: Jazz, Blues
Average price: Modest
Area: Westchase
Address: 10611 Candlewood
Houston, TX 77042
Phone: (713) 829-1553

#266
Barfield Photography
Category: Photographers
Area: Spring Branch
Address: 1312 Woodvine Dr
Houston, TX 77055
Phone: (713) 688-0148

#267
Emmit's Place
Category: Jazz, Blues, Music Venues, Lounge
Average price: Modest
Area: Willow Meadows/Willowbend
Address: 4852 Benning Dr
Houston, TX 77035
Phone: (713) 728-0012

#268
Hilton University of Houston
Category: Hotel
Average price: Expensive
Area: Third Ward
Address: 4800 Calhoun Rd
Houston, TX 77004
Phone: (713) 741-2447

#269
Art & Frame Etc
Category: Art Gallery, Framing
Average price: Modest
Area: Lazy Brook/Timbergrove
Address: 2819 W T C Jester Blvd
Houston, TX 77018
Phone: (713) 681-5077

#270
Mitsi Dancing School
Category: Performing Arts
Area: Sharpstown, Chinatown
Address: 9889 Bellaire Blvd
Houston, TX 77036
Phone: (832) 638-2185

#271
Alliance Francaise De Houston I
Category: Language Schools
Area: Fourth Ward, Montrose
Address: 427 Lovett Blvd
Houston, TX 77006
Phone: (713) 526-1121

#272
City Dance Studio
Category: Performing Arts, Dance School, Dance Studio
Area: Montrose
Address: 1307 W Clay St
Houston, TX 77019
Phone: (713) 529-6100

#273
D'lish Catering Inc.
Category: Caterer
Area: Downtown
Address: 1200 Mckinney St
Houston, TX 77010
Phone: (281) 953-5474

#274
Wag's D.J.
Category: DJs
Area: Clear Lake
Address: P.O. Box 891573
Houston, TX 77289
Phone: (281) 480-6513

#275
Pappas Catering
Category: Restaurant, Caterer
Area: Gulfton
Address: 6445 Richmond Ave
Houston, TX 77057
Phone: (713) 952-9782

#276
Blue Moose Lodge
Category: Pub, Sports Bar, Music Venues
Average price: Exclusive
Area: The Heights, Rice Military
Address: 5306 Washington Ave
Houston, TX 77007
Phone: (713) 861-5525

#277
The Gallery
Category: Venues, Event Space
Area: Gulfton
Address: 6303 Beverly Hill St
Houston, TX 77057
Phone: (713) 255-2889

#278
Opera in the Heights
Category: Performing Arts, Opera, Ballet
Area: The Heights
Address: 1703 Heights Blvd
Houston, TX 77008
Phone: (713) 861-5303

#279
Party Boy
Category: Party Supplies
Area: The Heights
Address: 1515 Studemont St
Houston, TX 77007
Phone: (713) 861-9080

#280
La Fuente Winery
Category: Winery
Average price: Modest
Area: Lazy Brook/Timbergrove
Address: 10606 Hempstead Rd
Houston, TX 77092
Phone: (713) 956-6219

#281
Deborah Colton Gallery
Category: Art Gallery
Area: West University
Address: 2445 North Blvd
Houston, TX 77098
Phone: (713) 869-5151

#282
National United States Armed Forces Museum
Category: Museum
Area: Pleasantville
Address: 8611 Wallisville Rd
Houston, TX 77029
Phone: (713) 673-1234

#283
Embassy Suites
Category: Hotel
Average price: Modest
Area: Downtown
Address: 1515 Dallas St
Houston, TX 77010
Phone: (713) 739-9100

#284
Buffalo Soldier National Museum & Heritage Center
Category: Museum
Area: Midtown
Address: 3816 Caroline
Houston, TX 77004
Phone: (713) 942-8920

#285
Savarese Promotions
Category: Professional Sports Team
Area: Downtown
Address: 1612 Austin St
Houston, TX 77002
Phone: (713) 659-0299

#286
Savory Celebration
Category: Personal Chefs, Caterer, Cooking School
Area: Highland Village
Address: 4242 Richmond Ave
Houston, TX 77027
Phone: (281) 601-4850

#287
Lancaster Hotel
Category: Hotel
Average price: Modest
Area: Fourth Ward, Downtown
Address: 701 Texas St
Houston, TX 77002
Phone: (713) 228-9500

Houston Travel Guide 2015 / Shops, Restaurants, Arts, Entertainment & Nightlife

#288
Cougar Field
Category: Stadium/Arena
Area: Third Ward
Address: 3100 Calhoun Rd
Houston, TX 77004
Phone: (713) 462-6647

#289
Houston Food Bank
Category: Community Service
Area: Pleasantville
Address: 535 Portwall St
Houston, TX 77029
Phone: (713) 223-3700

#290
Imperial Reception Hall
Category: Venues, Event Space
Area: Gulfton
Address: 6400 Southwest Fwy
Houston, TX 77074
Phone: (713) 789-9090

#291
Houston House of Creeps
Category: Music Venues
Average price: Exclusive
Area: Gulfgate/Pine Valley
Address: 2710 Carrolton
Houston, TX 77023
Phone: (979) 319-1208

#292
18 Hands Gallery
Category: Art Gallery
Average price: Expensive
Area: The Heights
Address: 249 W. 19th Street
Houston, TX 77008
Phone: (713) 869-3099

#293
Fajita Pete's
Category: Caterer, Tex-Mex
Average price: Modest
Area: Braeswood Place, West University
Address: 4050 Bellaire Blvd
Houston, TX 77025
Phone: (713) 723-8100

#294
War'Hous Visual Studios
Category: Art Gallery
Area: Museum District
Address: 4715 main st.
Houston, TX 77004
Phone: (832) 768-9515

#295
Sam Houston Ballroom and Conference Center
Category: Venues, Event Space, Caterer
Area: Sharpstown, Chinatown
Address: 6833 W Sam Houston Pkwy S
Houston, TX 77072
Phone: (281) 781-9983

#296
Houston Farm & Ranch Club
Category: Venues, Event Space
Area: Addicks/Park Ten
Address: 1 Abercrombie Dr
Houston, TX 77084
Phone: (281) 463-6650

#297
Wade Wilson Art
Category: Art Gallery
Average price: Exclusive
Area: Museum District, Montrose
Address: 4411 Montrose Blvd
Houston, TX 77246
Phone: (713) 521-2977

#298
Midtown Art Center
Category: Performing Arts
Area: Midtown
Address: 3414 La Branch St
Houston, TX 77004
Phone: (713) 521-8803

#299
The Orbit Room
Category: Dance Club
Area: EaDo
Address: 2524 McKinney St
Houston, TX 77003
Phone: (512) 758-9012

#300
Mango's
Category: Vegetarian, Music Venues, Pizza
Average price: Inexpensive
Area: Fourth Ward, Montrose
Address: 403 Westheimer Rd
Houston, TX 77006
Phone: (713) 522-8903

#301
Carl'o
Category: Food Stand, Food Truck, Caterer
Average price: Inexpensive
Area: The Heights
Address: 130 Heights Blvd
Houston, TX 77008
Phone: (713) 384-0067

#302
Antique & Interiors at the Pavilion
Category: Antiques, Art Gallery
Average price: Exclusive
Area: Upper Kirby, River Oaks
Address: 2311 Westheimer Rd
Houston, TX 77098
Phone: (713) 520-9755

#303
Mariposa At Reed Road
Category: Hotel, Apartments
Area: Sunnyside
Address: 2889 Reed Rd
Houston, TX 77051
Phone: (713) 738-1222

#304
Red Cat Jazz Caf'
Category: Jazz, Blues, Cajun, Creole
Average price: Modest
Area: Downtown
Address: 711 Franklin St
Houston, TX 77002
Phone: (713) 226-7870

#305
The Houstonian Hotel, Club & Spa
Category: Hotel, Day Spa, American
Average price: Expensive
Area: Memorial
Address: 111 N Post Oak Ln
Houston, TX 77024
Phone: (713) 680-2626

#306
A.D.
Category: Performing Arts
Area: Upper Kirby
Address: 2710 W Alabama St
Houston, TX 77098
Phone: (713) 526-2721

#307
Dave & Buster's
Category: Arcade, American
Average price: Modest
Area: Spring Branch
Address: 7620 Katy Fwy
Houston, TX 77024
Phone: (713) 263-0303

#308
Copy Dot Com
Category: Cards, Stationery
Average price: Inexpensive
Area: Montrose
Address: 1201 Westheimer Rd
Houston, TX 77006
Phone: (713) 528-1201

#309
Cinemark Movie 16
Category: Cinema
Area: Trinity/Houston Gardens, Kashmere Gardens
Address: 12920 NW Fwy
Houston, TX 77040
Phone: (713) 329-9402

#310
Platform Houston
Category: Special Education
Area: West University
Address: 5504 Morningside Dr
Houston, TX 77005
Phone: (832) 538-1441

#311
Houston Museum of African American Culture
Category: Museum
Area: Museum District
Address: 4807 Caroline St
Houston, TX 77004
Phone: (713) 526-1015

#312
Fred Astaire Dance Studio
Category: Performing Arts, Dance Studio
Area: Memorial
Address: 12649 Memorial Dr
Houston, TX 77024
Phone: (713) 827-8084

#313
Unique Style Productions
Category: DJs
Area: Lazy Brook/Timbergrove
Address: 5200 Mitchelldale St
Houston, TX 77092
Phone: (832) 475-0838

#314
Gremillion & Co.
Category: Art Gallery
Area: West University
Address: 2501 Sunset Blvd
Houston, TX 77005
Phone: (713) 522-2701

#315
Grizzaffi Coffee Catering
Category: Caterer
Area: Downtown
Address: 1500 Mckinney St
Houston, TX 77003
Phone: (832) 466-3325

#316
Talento Bilingue De Houston
Category: Performing Arts
Area: Warehouse District
Address: 333 S Jensen Dr
Houston, TX 77003
Phone: (713) 222-1213

Houston Travel Guide 2015 / Shops, Restaurants, Arts, Entertainment & Nightlife

#317
Museum of Southern History
Category: Museum
Area: Braeburn
Address: 7502 Fondren Road
Houston, TX 77074
Phone: (281) 649-3997

#318
Churrasco To Go
Category: Food Truck, Caterer
Average price: Modest
Area: Willow Meadows/Willowbend
Address: 239 Sharpstown Ctr
Houston, TX 77036
Phone: (832) 359-4543

#319
Wortham IMAX Theatre
Category: Cinema
Area: Museum District
Address: 1 Hermann Cir Dr
Houston, TX 77030
Phone: (713) 639-4629

#320
The Gardens Houston
Category: Venues, Event Space
Area: South Belt/Ellington
Address: 12001 Beamer Rd
Houston, TX 77089
Phone: (281) 481-0181

#321
Masquerade Theatre Box Office
Category: Performing Arts
Area: Oak Forest/Garden Oaks
Address: 3510 E T C Jester Blvd
Houston, TX 77018
Phone: (713) 861-7045

#322
Ashford Oaks
Category: Wedding Planning, Party & Event Planning
Area: Westchase
Address: 2022 Wilcrest Dr
Houston, TX 77042
Phone: (713) 784-6470

#323
Rudolph Projects ArtScan Gallery
Category: Art Gallery
Area: Montrose
Address: 1836 Richmond Ave
Houston, TX 77098
Phone: (713) 807-1836

#324
Pedal Party
Category: Party & Event Planning
Area: Sixth Ward
Address: 2000 Edwards St
Houston, TX 77007
Phone: (832) 429-6977

#325
Inprint
Category: Performing Arts, Education
Area: Montrose
Address: 1520 W. Main
Houston, TX 77006
Phone: (713) 521-2026

#326
Hotel ICON, Autograph Collection
Category: Hotel
Average price: Expensive
Area: Downtown
Address: 220 Main St
Houston, TX 77002
Phone: (713) 224-4266

#327
Alice Pratt Brown Hall
Category: Performing Arts,
Area: West University
Address: 6100 Main St
Houston, TX 77005
Phone: (713) 348-4854

#328
Sugar Bunch Creations
Category: Desserts, Caterer
Average price: Modest
Area: Midtown
Address: 3206 Jackson St
Houston, TX 77004
Phone: (832) 267-7876

#329
Main Street Theater
Category: Performing Arts
Area: West University
Address: 2540 Times Blvd
Houston, TX 77005
Phone: (713) 524-3622

#330
Brian O'Neill's Running Club
Category: Sports Club
Area: West University
Address: 5555 Morningside Dr
Houston, TX 77005
Phone: (713) 522-2603

#331
Watercolor Art Society - Houston
Category: Art Gallery
Average price: Inexpensive
Area: Montrose
Address: 1601 W Alabama St
Houston, TX 77006
Phone: (713) 942-9966

#332
Lone Star Veterans Association
Category: Community Service
Area: The Heights
Address: 170 Heights Blvd
Houston, TX 77007
Phone: (832) 393-8147

#333
Goldesberry Gallery
Category: Art Gallery
Area: Upper Kirby
Address: 2625 Colquitt St
Houston, TX 77098
Phone: (713) 528-0405

#334
Residence Inn Houston Downtown/Convention Center
Category: Hotel
Average price: Expensive
Area: Fourth Ward, Downtown
Address: 904 Dallas Street
Houston, TX 77002
Phone: (832) 366-1000

#335
Psychic For Love
Category: Psychics, Astrologers
Area: Memorial, Galleria/Uptown
Address: 6008 San Felipe
Houston, TX 77057
Phone: (888) 439-5479

#336
DJU Productions
Category: DJs,
Area: Spring Branch
Address: 5479 W Sam Houston Pkwy N
Houston, TX 77041
Phone: (713) 937-0134

#337
713 INC Art & Apparel
Category: Art Gallery
Average price: Modest
Area: Second Ward
Address: 4739 Canal St
Houston, TX 77011
Phone: (713) 545-6030

#338
Holiday Inn
Category: Hotel
Average price: Inexpensive
Area: Westchase
Address: 10609 Westpark Dr
Houston, TX 77042
Phone: (713) 532-5400

#339
Catherine Couturier Gallery
Category: Art Gallery
Area: Upper Kirby
Address: 2635 Colquitt St
Houston, TX 77098
Phone: (713) 524-5070

#340
Bellaire Town Square Family Aquatic Center
Category: Arts, Entertainment
Area: Bellaire
Address: 7008 S Rice Ave
Bellaire, TX 77401
Phone: (713) 662-8249

#341
McClain Gallery
Category: Art Gallery
Area: Upper Kirby
Address: 2242 Richmond Ave
Houston, TX 77098
Phone: (713) 520-9988

#342
Treebeards
Category: Cajun, Creole, Southern, Caterer
Average price: Inexpensive
Area: Fourth Ward, Downtown
Address: 315 Travis St
Houston, TX 77002
Phone: (713) 228-2622

#343
McMurtrey Gallery
Category: Art Gallery
Area: Upper Kirby
Address: 3508 Lake St
Houston, TX 77098
Phone: (713) 523-8238

#344
Julia Ideson Building
Category: Landmark/Historical
Area: Fourth Ward, Downtown
Address: 500 McKinney St
Houston, TX 77002
Phone: (713) 660-0772

#345
Ovations Night Club
Category: Music Venues
Average price: Modest
Area: West University
Address: 2536 Times Blvd
Houston, TX 77005
Phone: (713) 522-9801

Houston Travel Guide 2015 / Shops, Restaurants, Arts, Entertainment & Nightlife

#346
Monument au Fantome
Category: Local Flavor, Arts, Entertainment
Area: Downtown
Address: 910 Avenida De Las Americas
Houston, TX 77010
Phone: (713) 400-7336

#347
Tall Productions
Category: Video/Film Production, Videographers
Area: Spring Branch
Address: 9507 Weatherwood Dr
Houston, TX 77080
Phone: (281) 241-9510

#348
Kingdom Builders Center
Category: Venues, Event Space
Area: Central Southwest
Address: 6011 W Orem Dr
Houston, TX 77085
Phone: (713) 726-2500

#349
Fernando Marron Psychic Medium
Category: Psychics, Astrologers
Area: Second Ward
Address: 318 Eastwood St
Houston, TX 77011
Phone: (832) 813-9299

#350
The Concert Pub
Category: Sports Bar, American, Music Venues
Average price: Inexpensive
Area: Galleria/Uptown
Address: 5636 Richmond Ave
Houston, TX 77057
Phone: (713) 278-7272

#351
Spring Branch Meeting Rooms
Category: Venues, Event Space
Area: Spring Branch
Address: 2600 N Gessner
Houston, TX 77080
Phone: (281) 276-7734

#352
Houston International Festival
Category: Festival
Area: Fourth Ward, Montrose
Address: 4203 Montrose Blvd
Houston, TX 77006
Phone: (713) 654-8808

#353
Elegante Entertainment
Category: DJs, Performing Arts
Area: Lazy Brook/Timbergrove
Address: 10301 NW Fwy
Houston, TX 77092
Phone: (832) 465-1161

#354
Harlow's Food & Fun
Category: American, Arcade
Average price: Modest
Area: Greenway
Address: 3839 Weslyan
Houston, TX 77027
Phone: (713) 850-8555

#355
Jet Lounge
Category: Lounge, Venues, Event Space, Music Venues
Average price: Modest
Area: Downtown
Address: 1515 Pease St
Houston, TX 77002
Phone: (713) 659-2000

#356
Club Quarters
Category: Hotel
Average price: Modest
Area: Downtown
Address: 720 Fannin St
Houston, TX 77002
Phone: (713) 224-6400

#357
Houston Police Museum
Category: Museum
Area: Fourth Ward, Downtown
Address: 1200 Travis St
Houston, TX 77002
Phone: (281) 230-2353

#358
Darryl & Co.
Category: Party & Event Planning
Area: Independence Heights
Address: 483 W 38th St
Houston, TX 77018
Phone: (713) 863-0400

#359
Rice Cinema
Category: Cinema
Area: West University
Address: Rice Media Center
at Rice University Houston, TX 77005
Phone: (713) 348-7529

#360
Poissant Gallery
Category: Art Gallery
Area: The Heights, Rice Military
Address: 5102 Center St
Houston, TX 77007
Phone: (713) 868-9337

#361
Anya Tish Gallery
Category: Art Gallery
Average price: Exclusive
Area: Museum District, Montrose
Address: 4411 Montrose
Houston, TX 77005
Phone: (713) 524-2299

#362
The Sam Houston Hotel
Category: Hotel
Average price: Modest
Area: Downtown
Address: 1117 Prairie St
Houston, TX 77002
Phone: (832) 200-8800

#363
Summer Street Studios
Category: Art Gallery
Area: The Heights
Address: 2500 Summer St
Houston, TX 77007
Phone: (713) 448-9774

#364
De Santos Gallery
Category: Art Gallery
Average price: Expensive
Area: Montrose
Address: 1724-A Richmond Ave
Houston, TX 77098
Phone: (713) 520-1200

#365
Papa Mo's Deli
Category: Deli, Caterer, Sandwiches
Average price: Inexpensive
Area: The Heights
Address: 465B TC Jester Blvd
Houston, TX 77007
Phone: (713) 802-0043

#366
Houston Seance at La Carafe
Category: Performing Arts
Area: Downtown
Address: 813 Congress St
Houston, TX 77002
Phone: (832) 724-3045

#367
Houston Country Club
Category: Golf
Area: Memorial
Address: 1 Potomac Dr
Houston, TX 77057
Phone: (713) 465-8381

#368
Space 125 Gallery
Category: Art Gallery
Average price: Inexpensive
Area: River Oaks, Montrose
Address: 3201 Allen Parkway
Houston, TX 77019
Phone: (713) 527-9330

#369
Hotel Granduca
Category: Hotel
Average price: Expensive
Area: Galleria/Uptown
Address: 1080 Uptown Park Blvd
Houston, TX 77056
Phone: (713) 418-1000

#370
Secret Word Cafe
Category: Arts, Entertainment, Café
Average price: Modest
Area: Third Ward
Address: 2016 Dowling St
Houston, TX 77003
Phone: (832) 364-1162

#371
Upstage Theatre
Category: Performing Arts
Area: The Heights
Address: 1703 Heights Blvd
Houston, TX 77008
Phone: (713) 838-7191

#372
Na'-haus
Category: Art Gallery
Average price: Modest
Area: The Heights
Address: 223 E 11th St
Houston, TX 77008
Phone: (713) 931-9722

#373
The Mad Potter
Category: Party & Event Planning
Area: River Oaks, Montrose
Address: 1963 W Gray St
Houston, TX 77019
Phone: (713) 807-8900

#374
Aaron Brothers Art & Framing
Category: Art Supplies, Art Gallery
Average price: Modest
Area: Braeswood Place, West University
Address: 3057 W Holcombe Blvd
Houston, TX 77025
Phone: (713) 664-2395

#375
G Gallery
Category: Art Gallery
Average price: Exclusive
Area: The Heights
Address: 301 E 11th St
Houston, TX 77008
Phone: (713) 869-4770

#376
Crowne Plaza Hotel Northwest Brookhollow
Category: Hotel
Average price: Expensive
Area: Fairbanks/Northwest Crossing
Address: 12801 Norwest Frwy
Houston, TX 77040
Phone: (713) 462-9977

#377
Brazilian Arts Foundation
Category: Arts, Entertainment, Dance School
Area: The Heights
Address: 1133 E 11th St
Houston, TX 77009
Phone: (713) 862-3300

#378
Goode Company Barbeque
Category: Barbeque, Caterer, Gluten-Free
Average price: Modest
Area: Memorial
Address: 8911 Katy Fwy
Houston, TX 77024
Phone: (713) 464-1901

#379
Aurora Studios
Category: Art Gallery
Average price: Inexpensive
Area: The Heights
Address: 129 Aurora St
Houston, TX 77008
Phone: (713) 894-4480

#380
A La Carte Catering and Events
Category: Caterer
Area: River Oaks, Montrose
Address: 1302 Waugh Dr
Houston, TX 77019
Phone: (281) 408-4112

#381
Sirrom School of Dance
Category: Performing Arts
Area: West University
Address: 5570 Weslayan St
Houston, TX 77005
Phone: (713) 621-9818

#382
Couture House Rentals
Category: Women's Clothing, Bridal, Formal Wear
Average price: Inexpensive
Area: The Heights
Address: 1711 Durham Dr
Houston, TX 77007
Phone: (713) 253-2422

#383
Koelsch Gallery
Category: Art Gallery
Area: The Heights
Address: 703 Yale St.
Houston, TX 77007
Phone: (713) 626-0175

#384
Zen Art Space
Category: Art Gallery
Area: Galleria/Uptown
Address: 5175 Westheimer Rd
Houston, TX 77056
Phone: (713) 960-1159

#385
Monrreal & Co.
Category: Party & Event Planning
Area: Museum District
Address: 4740 Ingersoll St
Houston, TX 77027
Phone: (713) 338-1900

#386
Wings Over Houston Airshow
Category: Festival
Area: South Belt/Ellington
Address: 510 Ellington Field
Houston, TX 77034
Phone: (713) 266-4492

#387
Mixed Emotions Fine Art Inc.
Category: Art Gallery
Area: Fourth Ward, Midtown, Montrose
Address: 95 Tuam St
Houston, TX 77006
Phone: (713) 871-9666

#388
Houston Marriott West Loop By The Galleria
Category: Hotel
Average price: Expensive
Area: Galleria/Uptown
Address: 1750 West Loop South
Houston, TX 77027
Phone: (713) 960-0111

#389
Inman Gallery
Category: Art Gallery
Average price: Expensive
Area: Fourth Ward, Midtown
Address: 3901 Main St
Houston, TX 77002
Phone: (713) 526-7800

#390
West University Dance Centre
Category: Performing Arts
Area: Braeswood Place, West University
Address: 4007 Bellaire Blvd
Houston, TX 77025
Phone: (713) 664-2233

#391
Pioneer Memorial Log House Museum
Category: Museum
Area: Museum District
Address: 1513 Cambridge St
Houston, TX 77030
Phone: (713) 522-0396

#392
Prashe Decor
Category: Wedding Planning
Area: The Heights
Address: 600 N Shepherd Dr
Houston, TX 77007
Phone: (832) 377-3263

#393
Etta's Lounge
Category: Jazz, Blues, Bar
Area: MacGregor
Address: 5120 Scott St
Houston, TX 77004
Phone: (713) 528-2611

#394
Hanson Galleries
Category: Art Gallery
Average price: Expensive
Area: Galleria/Uptown
Address: 5000 Westheimer Rd
Houston, TX 77056
Phone: (713) 552-1242

#395
Surprises
Category: Art Gallery
Area: Highland Village
Address: 4302 Westheimer Rd
Houston, TX 77027
Phone: (713) 266-9400

#396
Bayou City Art Festival Downtown
Category: Festival
Area: Fourth Ward, Downtown
Address: 901 Bagby St
Houston, TX 77002
Phone: (713) 521-0133

#397
World Series of Dog Shows
Category: Festival
Area: Medical Center
Address: Reliant Center
Houston, TX 77054
Phone: (832) 667-1400

#398
Monkey Joe's
Category: Amusement Park, Playground
Area: Westchase
Address: 12523 Westheimer Rd
Houston, TX 77077
Phone: (281) 497-5637

#399
Houston Crawfish Festival
Category: Festival
Area: EaDo
Address: 1002 Palmer St
Houston, TX 77003
Phone: (281) 686-6138

#400
Palace Inn Greenspoint
Category: Hotel
Area: Greenspoint
Address: 13001 North Fwy
Houston, TX 77060
Phone: (281) 248-4002

#401
Jacob Calle
Category: Performing Arts
Area: Midtown
Address: 1509 Stuart St.
Houston, TX 77004
Phone: (832) 322-8107

#402
Halau Hoola Ka Mana O Hawaii
Category: Performing Arts, Cultural Center
Area: Sharpstown, Chinatown
Address: 7601 W Sam Houston Pkwy S
Houston, TX 77036
Phone: (817) 532-8224

#403
Hunter Gorham Fine Art Photography
Category: Art Gallery
Area: Montrose
Address: 1834 1/2 Westheimer Rd
Houston, TX 77098
Phone: (713) 492-0504

#404
Bryan Miller Gallery
Category: Art Gallery
Area: Fourth Ward, Midtown
Address: 3907 Main St
Houston, TX 77004
Phone: (713) 523-2875

Houston Travel Guide 2015 / Shops, Restaurants, Arts, Entertainment & Nightlife

#405
Biron Gymnastics
Category: Party & Event Planning
Area: Energy Corridor
Address: 1322 S Dairy Ashford St
Houston, TX 77077
Phone: (281) 497-6666

#406
Allan Rodewald Gallery
Category: Art Gallery
Area: Sixth Ward
Address: 1402 Dart St
Houston, TX 77007
Phone: (713) 501-6613

#407
Houston Railroad Museum
Category: Museum
Area: East Houston
Address: 7390 Mesa Dr
Houston, TX 77028
Phone: (713) 631-6612

#408
Offshore Technology Conference
Category: Event Planning
Area: Medical Center
Address: Reliant Center
Houston, TX 77054
Phone: (972) 952-9494

#409
International Ballroom
Category: Cinema
Area: Fondren Southwest, Fondren Gardens
Address: 14035 Main St
Houston, TX 77035
Phone: (713) 729-1400

#410
Morris Cultural Arts Center
Category: Arts, Entertainment,
Venues, Event Space
Area: Braeburn
Address: 7502 Fondren Rd
Houston, TX 77074
Phone: (713) 649-3000

#411
Houston City Club
Category: Venues, Event Space
Area: Lake Houston
Address: 1 City Club Dr
Houston, TX 77046
Phone: (713) 840-9001

#412
Techland Houston
Category: Performing Arts
Area: The Heights
Address: 2420 Center
Houston, TX 77007
Phone: (832) 518-5583

#413
Tres Market
Category: Caterer, American
Area: Memorial
Address: 12699 Memorial Dr
Houston, TX 77024
Phone: (713) 365-0722

#414
A.D.C.
Category: Performing Arts,
Dance Studio, Dance School
Area: Lawndale/Wayside
Address: 6606 Lawndale St, Ste 200
Houston, TX 77023
Phone: (832) 766-6095

#415
The Westin Houston, Memorial City
Category: Hotel
Average price: Expensive
Area: Memorial
Address: 945 Gessner Road
Houston, TX 77024
Phone: (281) 501-4300

#416
Classical Theatre Company
Category: Performing Arts
Area: Sixth Ward
Address: 1824 Spring St
Houston, TX 77007
Phone: (713) 963-9665

#417
Hollywood Frame Gallery
Category: Art Gallery, Framing
Area: West University
Address: 2427 Bissonnet St
Houston, TX 77005
Phone: (713) 942-8885

#418
Houston Dash
Category: Professional Sports Team
Area: Downtown
Address: 1001 Avenida de las Americas
Houston, TX 77010
Phone: (713) 276-7500

#419
Gems of Wisdom Radio
Category: Psychics, Astrologers
Area: Spring Branch
Address: 7800 Amelia Rd
Houston, TX 77055
Phone: (713) 534-7329

#420
Dominic Walsh Dance Theater
Category: Performing Arts
Area: Montrose
Address: 2311 Dunlavy St
Houston, TX 77006
Phone: (713) 652-3938

Houston Travel Guide 2015 / Shops, Restaurants, Arts, Entertainment & Nightlife

#421
Via Colori Street Painting Festival
Category: Festival, Performing Arts
Area: Fourth Ward, Downtown
Address: 901 Bagby St
Houston, TX 77002
Phone: (713) 523-3633

#422
The Fantasy Gallery
Category: Art Gallery
Area: Fourth Ward, Montrose
Address: 804 W Gray St
Houston, TX 77019
Phone: (713) 528-6569

#423
Heritage Custom Framing
Category: Art Gallery
Area: Galleria/Uptown
Address: 1928 Fountain View Dr
Houston, TX 77057
Phone: (713) 781-7772

#424
River Oaks Country Club
Category: Golf
Area: River Oaks
Address: 1600 River Oaks Blvd
Houston, TX 77019
Phone: (713) 529-4321

#425
L'atelier
Category: Art Gallery
Average price: Modest
Area: Montrose
Address: 2011 Waugh Dr
Houston, TX 77006
Phone: (713) 429-1307

#426
Club Venue
Category: Dance Club
Average price: Modest
Area: Fourth Ward, Downtown
Address: 719 Main St
Houston, TX 77002
Phone: (713) 236-8150

#427
The Artful Corner
Category: Art Gallery
Average price: Modest
Area: The Heights
Address: 3423 White Oak Dr
Houston, TX 77007
Phone: (713) 426-4278

#428
The Nice Winery
Category: Winery
Average price: Expensive
Area: Spring Branch
Address: 2901 W Sam Houston Pkwy N
Houston, TX 77043
Phone: (713) 744-7444

#429
The Wynden
Category: Venues, Event Space
Area: Galleria/Uptown
Address: 1025 S Post Oak Ln
Houston, TX 77056
Phone: (281) 768-6070

#430
226 Recordings
Category: Arts, Entertainment
Area: The Heights
Address: 226 West 19th Street
Houston, TX 77008
Phone: (713) 861-4497

#431
Lunar New Year Houston Celebration
Category: Festival
Area: Westwood
Address: 8388 W Sam Houston Pkwy
Houston, TX 77072
Phone: (713) 861-8270

#432
The Houston Zoo
Category: Zoo
Area: Museum District
Address: 6200 Hermann Park Dr
Houston, TX 77030
Phone: (713) 533-6500

#433
Shakespeare Festival
Category: Festival
Area: Third Ward
Address: 133 CWM
Houston, TX 77204
Phone: (281) 823-9103

#434
Divisi Strings
Category: Performing Arts
Area: Braeburn
Address: 7322 SW Fwy
Houston, TX 77074
Phone: (713) 229-8663

#435
Kirkwood Dance Studio
Category: Performing Arts
Area: South Belt/Ellington
Address: 10906 Beamer Rd
Houston, TX 77089
Phone: (281) 481-4983

Houston Travel Guide 2015 / Shops, Restaurants, Arts, Entertainment & Nightlife

#436
Gilbert & Sullivan Society of Houston
Category: Performing Arts
Area: Galleria/Uptown
Address: 1177 West Loop S
Houston, TX 77027
Phone: (713) 627-3570

#437
A Fare Extraordinaire
Category: Caterer
Area: Montrose
Address: 2035 Marshall St
Houston, TX 77098
Phone: (713) 527-8288

#438
HITS Theatre
Category: Performing Arts
Area: The Heights
Address: 311 W 18th St
Houston, TX 77008
Phone: (713) 861-7408

#439
Nizza Mosaic Studio & Gallery
Category: Art Gallery
Area: The Heights
Address: 1135 E 11th St
Houston, TX 77009
Phone: (281) 787-2472

#440
In A Flash Photography
Category: Photographers
Area: Montrose
Address: 1901 Brun St
Houston, TX 77019
Phone: (713) 562-0412

#441
Belly Dance Oasis
Category: Performing Arts, Dance Studio
Area: Museum District
Address: 805 Chelsea Blvd
Houston, TX 77002
Phone: (713) 530-4183

#442
Paper Source
Category: Cards, Stationery
Average price: Modest
Area: Memorial
Address: 795 Town And Country Blvd
Houston, TX 77024
Phone: (713) 984-8619

#443
Venus
Category: Dance Club, Gay Bar, Music Venues
Average price: Modest
Area: Midtown
Address: 2901 Fannin St
Houston, TX 77002
Phone: (713) 751-3185

#444
River Oaks Chamber Orchestra
Category: Performing Arts
Area: River Oaks, Montrose
Address: 1973 West Gray
Houston, TX 77019
Phone: (713) 665-2700

#445
Goode Company Barbeque
Category: Barbeque, Caterer, Gluten-Free
Average price: Modest
Area: West University
Address: 5109 Kirby Dr
Houston, TX 77098
Phone: (713) 522-2530

#446
Bayou City Performing Arts
Category: Performing Arts
Area: Upper Kirby
Address: 2990 Richmond Ave
Houston, TX 77098
Phone: (713) 521-7464

#447
Chevron Jingle Bell Run and Walk
Category: Sports Club
Area: Fourth Ward, Downtown
Address: 808 Pease
Houston, TX 77002
Phone: (713) 739-3675

#448
**Del Espadin Flamenco
& Spanish Dance Academy**
Category: Performing Arts, Dance School
Area: Gulfton
Address: 3939 Hillcroft St
Houston, TX 77057
Phone: (713) 977-3900

#449
**Houston Tidelanders
Barbershop Chorus**
Category: Performing Arts
Area: Downtown
Address: 705 Main St
Houston, TX 77002
Phone: (713) 223-8433

#450
Red Door
Category: Lounge, Dance Club,
Venues, Event Space
Average price: Modest
Area: Fourth Ward, Midtown
Address: 2416 Brazos
Houston, TX 77006
Phone: (713) 256-9383

#451
HMNS Museum Store
Category: Shopping, Museum
Average price: Modest
Area: Museum District
Address: 1 Hermann Circle Dr
Houston, TX 77004
Phone: (713) 639-4665

#452
Alonti Cafe & Catering
Category: American, Caterer
Average price: Inexpensive
Area: Greenspoint
Address: 12153 Greenspoint Dr
Houston, TX 77060
Phone: (281) 875-5934

#453
Nameless Sound
Category: Performing Arts
Area: Eastwood
Address: 1458 Lawson
Houston, TX 77023
Phone: (713) 928-5653

#454
Linens By Lisa
Category: Party Supplies
Area: Willow Meadows/Willowbend, Westbury
Address: 11144 South Post Oak Rd
Houston, TX 77035
Phone: (281) 498-0021

#455
Mother's Day Out
Category: Festival
Area: Midtown
Address: 1311 Holman St
Houston, TX 77004
Phone: (713) 529-3589

#456
Fred Astaire Dance Studio
Category: Dance Studio, Performing Arts, Dance Club
Area: Highland Village
Address: 3601 Westheimer Rd
Houston, TX 77027
Phone: (713) 871-1300

#457
Elegant Linens Events
Category: Party & Event Planning
Area: Westchase
Address: 12126 Westheimer Rd
Houston, TX 77077
Phone: (281) 531-0212

#458
Spring Valley Village Fall Festival
Category: Festival
Area: Memorial
Address: 1025 Campbell Rd
Houston, TX 77055
Phone: (713) 465-8308

#459
2 Day Postcards
Category: Printing Services, Cards, Stationery
Average price: Modest
Area: Fourth Ward, Museum District, Montrose
Address: 621 Richmond Ave
Houston, TX 77006
Phone: (713) 224-8808

#460
Thornwood Gallery
Category: Art Gallery
Area: Upper Kirby
Address: 2643 Colquitt St
Houston, TX 77098
Phone: (713) 528-4278

#461
The White Swan
Category: Music Venues
Average price: Inexpensive
Area: Second Ward
Address: 4419 Navigation Blvd
Houston, TX 77011
Phone: (713) 923-2837

#462
Houston Fire Museum
Category: Museum
Area: Fourth Ward, Midtown
Address: 2403 Milam St
Houston, TX 77006
Phone: (713) 524-2526

#463
AMC Gulf Pointe 30
Category: Cinema
Area: South Belt/Ellington
Address: 11801 So. Sam Houston Pkwy E
Houston, TX 77089
Phone: (281) 464-8801

#464
Darke Gallery
Category: Art Gallery
Area: The Heights, Rice Military
Address: 320 B Detering
Houston, TX 77007
Phone: (713) 542-3802

#465
Central Market Catering Department
Category: Caterer
Area: Highland Village
Address: 3815 Westheimer
Houston, TX 77027
Phone: (713) 386-1750

#466
Barbara Davis Gallery
Category: Art Gallery
Average price: Exclusive
Area: Museum District, Montrose
Address: 4411 Montrose
Houston, TX 77006
Phone: (713) 520-9200

#467
Parkerson Gallery
Category: Art Gallery
Area: Upper Kirby
Address: 3510 Lake St
Houston, TX 77098
Phone: (713) 524-4945

#468
La Fontaine Reception Hall
Category: Venues, Event Space
Area: Fairbanks/Northwest Crossing
Address: 7758 W Tidwell
Houston, TX 77040
Phone: (832) 464-7189

#469
Peel Gallery Shop
Category: Art Gallery, Home Decor
Average price: Modest
Area: Museum District, Montrose
Address: 4411 Montrose Blvd
Houston, TX 77006
Phone: (713) 520-8122

#470
Hotel Indigo Houston At The Galleria
Category: Hotel, Venues, Event Space
Average price: Modest
Area: Galleria/Uptown
Address: 5160 Hidalgo St
Houston, TX 77056
Phone: (713) 621-8988

#471
Hofheinz Pavilion
Category: Stadium/Arena
Area: Third Ward
Address: 3875 Holman St
Houston, TX 77204
Phone: (800) 433-3243

#472
Hail-A-Cab
Category: Taxis
Area: Northside Village
Address: 1406 Hays St
Houston, TX 77009
Phone: (713) 236-1111

#473
The Deck House Bar & Grill
Category: Sports Bar, American, Music Venues
Average price: Modest
Area: Gulfton, Galleria/Uptown
Address: 5810 Beverly Hill
Houston, TX 77057
Phone: (713) 784-0818

#474
Redbud Gallery
Category: Art Gallery
Area: The Heights
Address: 303 E 11th St
Houston, TX 77008
Phone: (713) 862-2532

#475
Evoke Photography & Video
Category: Photographers, Videographers
Area: West University
Address: 5407 Kelvin Dr
Houston, TX 77005
Phone: (713) 349-9508

#476
Planet Funk Academy
Category: Performing Arts
Area: River Oaks
Address: 5731 Logan Ln
Houston, TX 77007
Phone: (713) 802-1772

#477
Kenny & Ziggy's New York Delicatessen Restaurant
Category: Deli, Sandwiches, Caterer
Average price: Modest
Area: Galleria/Uptown
Address: 2327 Post Oak Blvd
Houston, TX 77056
Phone: (713) 871-8883

#478
Dean Day Gallery
Category: Art Gallery
Area: Upper Kirby
Address: 2639 Colquitt St
Houston, TX 77098
Phone: (713) 520-1021

#479
Jones Plaza
Category: Music Venues
Area: Fourth Ward, Downtown
Address: 601 Lousiana
Houston, TX 77002
Phone: (713) 237-1439

#480
S.H.A.P.E.
Category: Community Service
Area: Midtown
Address: 3903 Almeda Rd
Houston, TX 77004
Phone: (713) 521-0629

#481
Zuma Fun Center
Category: Mini Golf, Arcade
Area: Trinity/Houston Gardens, Kashmere Gardens
Address: 6767 SW Fwy
Houston, TX 77074
Phone: (713) 981-7888

#482
Port Of Galveston
Category: Arts, Entertainment
Area: Sixth Ward
Address: 123 Rosenberg
Houston, TX 77002
Phone: (281) 286-2484

#483
Moores Opera House
Category: Performing Arts
Area: Third Ward
Address: 3800 Cullen Blvd
Houston, TX 77004
Phone: (713) 743-3009

#484
Topgolf
Category: Golf, Bar, American
Average price: Modest
Area: Energy Corridor
Address: 1030 Memorial Brook Blvd
Houston, TX 77084
Phone: (281) 406-3176

#485
Cinemark Tinseltown USA
Category: Cinema
Area: El Dorado/Oates Prairie
Address: 11450 East Freeway
Jacinto City, TX 77029
Phone: (713) 330-3946

#486
Retro Gallery
Category: Art Gallery, Antiques, Home Decor
Average price: Exclusive
Area: Upper Kirby
Address: 2311 Westheimer Rd
Houston, TX 77098
Phone: (713) 582-1265

#487
Cafe Express
Category: American, Caterer
Average price: Modest
Area: Galleria/Uptown
Address: 1101 Uptown Park Blvd
Houston, TX 77056
Phone: (713) 963-9222

#488
Mildred's Umbrella Theater Company
Category: Performing Arts
Area: Midtown
Address: 3414 LaBranch
Houston, TX 77004
Phone: (832) 463-0409

#489
Opportunity Houston
Category: Arts, Entertainment
Area: Fourth Ward, Downtown
Address: 1200 Smith
Houston, TX 77002
Phone: (713) 844-3600

#490
Barnevelder Movement Arts Complex
Category: Venues, Event Space
Area: EaDo, Warehouse District
Address: 2201 Preston St
Houston, TX 77003
Phone: (713) 529-1819

#491
Asian Decor
Category: Furniture Store, Home Decor, Art Gallery
Area: West University
Address: 6132 Village Pkwy
Houston, TX 77005
Phone: (713) 270-9605

#492
Tri On The Run
Category: Bikes, Bike Rentals
Average price: Modest
Area: The Heights, Rice Military
Address: 518 Shepherd Dr
Houston, TX 77007
Phone: (832) 673-0600

#493
Bobbindoctrin Puppet Theatre
Category: Performing Arts
Area: River Oaks, Montrose
Address: 3201 Allen Pkwy
Houston, TX 77019
Phone: (713) 259-1304

#494
Houston Haunted Houses
Category: Arts, Entertainment
Area: Edgebrook
Address: 1500 Elton
Houston, TX 77034
Phone: (713) 946-2266

#495
Hilton Houston Plaza
Category: Hotel
Average price: Modest
Area: West University
Address: 6633 Travis St
Houston, TX 77030
Phone: (713) 313-4000

#496
Cougar Softball Field
Category: Stadium/Arena
Area: Third Ward
Address: 3100 Cullen Blvd
Houston, TX 77004
Phone: (713) 743-0000

#497
Holiday Inn Express
Category: Venues, Event Space, Hotel
Average price: Modest
Area: Braeswood Place
Address: 8080 S Main St
Houston, TX 77025
Phone: (713) 665-4439

#498
Heights Contemporary Fine Art Gallery & Event Space
Category: Venues, Event Space, Art Gallery
Area: The Heights
Address: 617 W 19th St
Houston, TX 77008
Phone: (713) 456-9513

#499
Cynthia Woods Mitchell Center for the Arts
Category: Performing Arts
Area: Third Ward
Address: 4800 Calhoun Rd
Houston, TX 77004
Phone: (713) 743-2255

#500
Sky High Sports
Category: Amusement Park, Trampoline Park
Area: Spring Branch
Address: 10510 Westview Dr
Houston, TX 77043
Phone: (713) 464-5867

TOP 500 NIGHTLIFE
The Most Recommended by Locals & Trevelers
(From #1 to #500)

Houston Travel Guide 2015 / Shops, Restaurants, Arts, Entertainment & Nightlife

#1
Miller Outdoor Theatre
Category: Performing Arts, Music Venues
Average price: Inexpensive
Area: Museum District
Address: 6000 Hermann Park Dr
Houston, TX 77030
Phone: (281) 373-3386

#2
Poison Girl
Category: Dive Bar
Average price: Inexpensive
Area: Montrose
Address: 1641 Westheimer Rd
Houston, TX 77006
Phone: (713) 527-9929

#3
Double Trouble Caffeine & Cocktails
Category: Coffee, Tea, Cocktail Bar
Average price: Modest
Area: Fourth Ward, Midtown
Address: 3622 Main St
Houston, TX 77006
Phone: (713) 874-0096

#4
Anvil Bar & Refuge
Category: Cocktail Bar
Average price: Modest
Area: Montrose
Address: 1424 Westheimer Rd
Houston, TX 77006
Phone: (713) 523-1622

#5
Flying Saucer Draught Emporium
Category: Pub
Average price: Modest
Area: Fourth Ward, Downtown
Address: 705 Main St
Houston, TX 77002
Phone: (713) 228-9472

#6
Agora
Category: Coffee, Tea, Wine Bar
Average price: Inexpensive
Area: Montrose
Address: 1712 Westheimer Rd
Houston, TX 77098
Phone: (713) 526-7212

#7
The Ginger Man
Category: Pub, Restaurant
Average price: Modest
Area: West University
Address: 5607 Morningside Dr
Houston, TX 77005
Phone: (713) 526-2770

#8
Warehouse Live
Category: Music Venues
Average price: Modest
Area: Downtown, EaDo
Address: 813 St Emanuel St
Houston, TX 77003
Phone: (713) 225-5483

#9
Little Woodrow's
Category: Bar
Average price: Inexpensive
Area: Fourth Ward, Midtown
Address: 2306 Brazos St
Houston, TX 77006
Phone: (713) 522-1041

#10
The Continental Club
Category: Dive Bar, Music Venues, Karaoke
Average price: Modest
Area: Fourth Ward, Midtown
Address: 3700 Main St
Houston, TX 77002
Phone: (713) 529-9899

#11
Boneyard Drinkery
Category: Bar, Dog Park
Average price: Inexpensive
Area: Lazy Brook, Timbergrove
Address: 8150 Washington
Houston, TX 77007
Phone: (832) 494-1600

#12
13 Celsius
Category: Wine Bar, Café
Average price: Modest
Area: Midtown
Address: 3000 Caroline St
Houston, TX 77004
Phone: (713) 529-8466

#13
Absinthe Brasserie
Category: Lounge
Average price: Modest
Area: Fourth Ward, Museum District, Montrose
Address: 609 Richmond Ave
Houston, TX 77006
Phone: (713) 528-7575

#14
Nouveau Antique Art Bar
Category: Bar, Venues, Event Space
Average price: Modest
Area: Fourth Ward, Midtown
Address: 2913 Main St
Houston, TX 77002
Phone: (713) 526-2220

#15
Liberty Station
Category: Bar
Average price: Modest
Area: Sixth Ward
Address: 2101 Washington Ave
Houston, TX 77007
Phone: (713) 640-5220

#16
Rosemont Social Club
Category: Cocktail Bar, Lounge
Average price: Modest
Area: Fourth Ward, Montrose
Address: 910 Westheimer Rd
Houston, TX 77006
Phone: (832) 530-4698

#17
Alice's Tall Texan Drive Inn
Category: Dive Bar
Average price: Inexpensive
Area: The Heights
Address: 4904 N Main St
Houston, TX 77009
Phone: (713) 862-0141

#18
The Pastry War
Category: Cocktail Bar
Average price: Modest
Area: Fourth Ward, Downtown
Address: 310 Main St
Houston, TX 77002
Phone: (713) 226-7770

#19
Captain Foxheart's Bad News Bar & Spirit Lodge
Category: Lounge, Cocktail Bar
Average price: Modest
Area: Downtown
Address: 308 Main St
Houston, TX 77002
Phone: (832) 555-4776

#20
Leon's Lounge
Category: Lounge
Average price: Modest
Area: Midtown
Address: 1006 McGowen St
Houston, TX 77002
Phone: (713) 659-5366

#21
The Big Easy Social and Pleasure Club
Category: Jazz, Blues
Average price: Inexpensive
Area: West University
Address: 5731 Kirby Dr
Houston, TX 77005
Phone: (713) 523-9999

#22
The Flat
Category: Lounge, American
Average price: Modest
Area: Montrose
Address: 1701 Commonwealth St
Houston, TX 77006
Phone: (713) 360-7228

#23
Wild West
Category: Dance Club
Average price: Inexpensive
Area: Gulfton, Galleria, Uptown
Address: 6101 Richmond Ave
Houston, TX 77057
Phone: (713) 266-3455

#24
Underdogs Pub
Category: Pub, Sports Bar
Average price: Inexpensive
Area: The Heights
Address: 4212 Washington Ave
Houston, TX 77007
Phone: (713) 410-5660

#25
The Davenport
Category: Lounge
Average price: Modest
Area: Upper Kirby
Address: 2117 Richmond Ave
Houston, TX 77098
Phone: (281) 888-1226

#26
Down the Street
Category: Cocktail Bar, Tapas
Average price: Modest
Area: The Heights
Address: 5746 Larkin St
Houston, TX 77007
Phone: (713) 880-3508

#27
Maple Leaf Pub
Category: Pub
Average price: Inexpensive
Area: Fourth Ward, Midtown
Address: 514 Elgin St
Houston, TX 77006
Phone: (713) 520-6464

#28
Big Star Bar
Category: Dive Bar
Average price: Inexpensive
Area: The Heights
Address: 1005 W 19th St
Houston, TX 77008
Phone: (281) 501-9560

#29
Voodoo Queen
Category: Dive Bar
Average price: Modest
Area: Second Ward
Address: 322 Milby St
Houston, TX 77003
Phone: (713) 555-5666

#30
Grand Prize Bar
Category: Bar
Average price: Inexpensive
Area: Museum District
Address: 1010 Banks St
Houston, TX 77006
Phone: (713) 526-4565

#31
3rd Floor
Category: Wine Bar, Cocktail Bar
Average price: Modest
Area: Fourth Ward, Midtown
Address: 2303 Smith St
Houston, TX 77006
Phone: (832) 384-1960

#32
Dirt Bar
Category: Dive Bar, Lounge
Average price: Inexpensive
Area: Downtown
Address: 1209 Caroline
Houston, TX 77002
Phone: (713) 426-4222

#33
The Community Bar
Category: Lounge, Gastropub, Sports Bar
Average price: Modest
Area: Fourth Ward, Midtown
Address: 2703 Smith St
Houston, TX 77006
Phone: (713) 526-1576

#34
Blue At Brenner's
Category: Lounge
Average price: Modest
Area: River Oaks
Address: 1 Birdsall St
Houston, TX 77007
Phone: (713) 868-4444

#35
Mongoose Versus Cobra
Category: Bar
Average price: Modest
Area: Fourth Ward, Midtown
Address: 1011 McGowen St
Houston, TX 77002
Phone: (713) 650-6872

#36
Numbers Night Club
Category: Music Venues, Dance Club
Average price: Inexpensive
Area: Fourth Ward, Midtown, Montrose
Address: 300 Westheimer Rd
Houston, TX 77006
Phone: (713) 521-1121

#37
Oporto Café
Category: Tapas Bar, Wine Bar, Portuguese
Average price: Modest
Area: Greenway
Address: 3833 Richmond Ave
Houston, TX 77027
Phone: (713) 621-1114

#38
Valhalla
Category: Bar
Average price: Inexpensive
Area: West University
Address: 6100 Main St
Houston, TX 77005
Phone: (713) 348-3258

#39
Catbirds
Category: Bar
Average price: Inexpensive
Area: Montrose
Address: 1336 Westheimer Rd
Houston, TX 77006
Phone: (713) 523-8000

#40
CRISP
Category: Italian, Wine Bar
Average price: Modest
Area: The Heights
Address: 2220 Bevis St
Houston, TX 77008
Phone: (713) 360-0222

#41
Little Dipper Lounge
Category: Cocktail Bar, Lounge
Average price: Modest
Area: Fourth Ward, Downtown
Address: 304 Main St.
Houston, TX 77002
Phone: (979) 319-1208

#42
Stage Lounge & Live Music
Category: Bar, Music Venues, Breakfast & Brunch
Average price: Modest
Area: Sharpstown, Chinatown
Address: 9889 Bellaire Blvd
Houston, TX 77036
Phone: (281) 846-1389

#43
notsuoH
Category: Bar, Music Venues
Average price: Inexpensive
Area: Fourth Ward, Downtown
Address: 314 Main St
Houston, TX 77002
Phone: (713) 409-4750

#44
Shoeshine Charley's Big Top Lounge
Category: Dive Bar, Music Venues
Average price: Inexpensive
Area: Fourth Ward, Midtown
Address: 3714 Main St
Houston, TX 77002
Phone: (832) 831-1565

#45
Public House Heights
Category: Pub
Average price: Modest
Area: The Heights
Address: 2802 White Oak
Houston, TX 77007
Phone: (713) 880-2337

#46
Etro Lounge
Category: Lounge, Dance Club
Average price: Modest
Area: Montrose
Address: 1424 Westheimer Rd
Houston, TX 77006
Phone: (713) 521-3876

#47
Reserve 101
Category: Lounge, Cocktail Bar
Average price: Modest
Area: Downtown
Address: 1201 Caroline St
Houston, TX 77002
Phone: (832) 831-2052

#48
Down House
Category: Bar, Café, Breakfast & Brunch
Average price: Modest
Area: The Heights
Address: 1801 Yale St
Houston, TX 77008
Phone: (713) 864-3696

#49
South Beach
Category: Dance Club, Gay Bar
Average price: Modest
Area: Fourth Ward, Montrose
Address: 810 Pacific St
Houston, TX 77006
Phone: (713) 529-7623

#50
D & T Drive Inn
Category: Dive Bar
Average price: Modest
Area: The Heights
Address: 1307 Enid St
Houston, TX 77009
Phone: (713) 868-6165

#51
Barbarella Houston
Category: Dance Club
Average price: Modest
Area: Midtown
Address: 2404 San Jacinto St
Houston, TX 77002
Phone: (832) 831-3620

#52
Petrol Station
Category: American, Bar
Average price: Modest
Area: Oak Forest, Garden Oaks
Address: 985 Wakefield Dr
Houston, TX 77018
Phone: (713) 957-2875

#53
Hearsay Gastro Lounge
Category: Lounge, American
Average price: Modest
Area: Downtown
Address: 218 Travis St
Houston, TX 77002
Phone: (713) 225-8079

#54
Fitzgerald's
Category: Dive Bar, Music Venues
Average price: Modest
Area: The Heights
Address: 2706 White Oak Dr
Houston, TX 77007
Phone: (713) 862-3838

#55
Red Door
Category: Lounge, Dance Club, Venues, Event Space
Average price: Modest
Area: Fourth Ward, Midtown
Address: 2416 Brazos
Houston, TX 77006
Phone: (713) 256-9383

#56
1919 Wine & Mixology
Category: Wine Bar
Average price: Modest
Area: Upper Kirby
Address: 2736 Virginia St
Houston, TX 77098
Phone: (713) 568-9197

#57
MKT BAR
Category: Bar, American, Music Venues
Average price: Modest
Area: Downtown
Address: 1001 Austin St
Houston, TX 77010
Phone: (832) 360-2222

#58
Winston's On Washington
Category: Bar, Breakfast & Brunch, American
Average price: Modest
Area: The Heights, Rice Military
Address: 5111 Washington Ave
Houston, TX 77007
Phone: (281) 501-9088

#59
Hay Merchant
Category: Bar, American
Average price: Modest
Area: Montrose
Address: 1100 Westheimer Rd
Houston, TX 77006
Phone: (713) 528-9805

#60
The Cellar Bar
Category: Karaoke, Music Venues, Pub
Average price: Inexpensive
Area: Upper Kirby
Address: 3140 Richmond Ave
Houston, TX 77098
Phone: (713) 528-6435

#61
Seasons 52
Category: American, Vegetarian, Wine Bar
Average price: Modest
Area: Highland Village
Address: 4410 Westheimer Rd
Houston, TX 77027
Phone: (713) 621-5452

#62
Eleven : Eleven Restaurant & Bar
Category: Seafood
Average price: Modest
Area: Fourth Ward, Montrose
Address: 607 W Gray St
Houston, TX 77019
Phone: (713) 529-5881

#63
The Boom Boom Room
Category: Wine Bar, Champagne Bar
Average price: Modest
Area: The Heights
Address: 2518 Yale St
Houston, TX 77008
Phone: (713) 868-3740

#64
Glitter Karaoke
Category: Karaoke, Bar
Average price: Modest
Area: Fourth Ward, Midtown
Address: 2621 Milam St
Houston, TX 77006
Phone: (713) 526-4900

#65
Sonoma Retail Wine Bar & Restaurant
Category: Wine Bar, American, Champagne Bar
Average price: Modest
Area: The Heights
Address: 801 Studewood St
Houston, TX 77007
Phone: (713) 864-9463

#66
Cezanne
Category: Bar, Music Venues, Jazz, Blues
Average price: Modest
Area: Montrose
Address: 4100 Montrose Blvd
Houston, TX 77006
Phone: (713) 522-9621

#67
Moon Tower Inn
Category: Dive Bar, Hot Dogs
Average price: Inexpensive
Area: Second Ward
Address: 3004 Canal St
Houston, TX 77003
Phone: (832) 266-0105

#68
Pinot's Palette
Category: Arts, Entertainment, Arts, Crafts, Nightlife
Average price: Modest
Area: Fourth Ward, Midtown, Montrose
Address: 2406 Taft St
Houston, TX 77006
Phone: (713) 523-4769

#69
R Bar
Category: Sports Bar
Average price: Inexpensive
Area: River Oaks
Address: 5535 Memorial Dr
Houston, TX 77007
Phone: (713) 426-4994

#70
Island Sizzler Jamaican Rum Bar & Grill
Category: Caribbean, Sports Bar
Average price: Inexpensive
Area: Medical Center
Address: 2114 Holly Hall St
Houston, TX 77054
Phone: (713) 378-5375

#71
Avant Garden
Category: Lounge, Venues, Event Space
Average price: Modest
Area: Fourth Ward, Montrose
Address: 411 Westheimer Rd
Houston, TX 77006
Phone: (832) 519-1429

#72
The Music Box Theater
Category: Comedy Club, Performing Arts, Music Venues
Average price: Modest
Area: Upper Kirby
Address: 2623 Colquitt
Houston, TX 77098
Phone: (713) 522-7722

#73
Celtic Gardens
Category: Pub, American
Average price: Modest
Area: Fourth Ward, Midtown
Address: 2300 Louisiana St
Houston, TX 77006
Phone: (713) 900-2500

#74
Walters Downtown
Category: Music Venues, Bar
Average price: Inexpensive
Area: Northside Village
Address: 1120 Naylor St
Houston, TX 77002
Phone: (713) 222-2679

#75
Meteor
Category: Gay Bar, Dance Club
Average price: Modest
Area: Fourth Ward, Midtown, Montrose
Address: 2306 Genesee St
Houston, TX 77006
Phone: (713) 521-0123

#76
Lola's Depot
Category: Dive Bar
Average price: Inexpensive
Area: Fourth Ward, Montrose
Address: 2327 Grant St
Houston, TX 77006
Phone: (713) 528-8342

#77
Under the Volcano
Category: Dive Bar, American
Average price: Modest
Area: West University
Address: 2349 Bissonnet St
Houston, TX 77005
Phone: (713) 526-5282

#78
Firehouse Saloon
Category: Bar, Music Venues
Average price: Modest
Area: Gulfton, Galleria, Uptown
Address: 5930 Southwest Fwy
Houston, TX 77057
Phone: (281) 513-1995

#79
Howl at the Moon
Category: Music Venues, Bar
Average price: Modest
Area: Fourth Ward, Midtown
Address: 612 Hadley St
Houston, TX 77002
Phone: (713) 658-9700

#80
House Of Blues
Category: Music Venues, Venues, Event Space, American
Average price: Modest
Area: Downtown
Address: 1204 Caroline St
Houston, TX 77002
Phone: (888) 402-5837

#81
The Fedora Lounge
Category: Lounge, Jazz, Blues
Average price: Modest
Area: West University
Address: 2726 Bissonnet St
Houston, TX 77005
Phone: (832) 581-3232

#82
Lucky's Pub
Category: Pub, Sports Bar
Average price: Modest
Area: Downtown, EaDo
Address: 801 St Emanuel
Houston, TX 77003
Phone: (713) 522-2010

#83
Boondocks
Category: Dive Bar, Music Venues
Average price: Inexpensive
Area: Montrose
Address: 1417 Westheimer Ave
Houston, TX 77006
Phone: (713) 522-8500

#84
Barringer Bar and Lounge
Category: Cocktail Bar, Lounge
Average price: Modest
Area: Fourth Ward, Downtown
Address: 410 Main St
Houston, TX 77002
Phone: (832) 786-1836

Houston Travel Guide 2015 / Shops, Restaurants, Arts, Entertainment & Nightlife

#85
Wakefield CrowBar
Category: Bar
Average price: Modest
Area: Oak Forest, Garden Oaks
Address: 954 Wakefield Dr
Houston, TX 77018
Phone: (713) 686-8388

#86
Onyx Club
Category: Adult Entertainment
Average price: Modest
Area: Galleria, Uptown
Address: 3113 Bering Drive
Houston, TX 77057
Phone: (713) 785-0444

#87
Porch Swing Pub
Category: Pub, American, Burgers
Average price: Modest
Area: The Heights
Address: 69 Heights Blvd
Houston, TX 77007
Phone: (713) 880-8700

#88
Absolve Wine Lounge
Category: Wine Bar
Average price: Modest
Area: The Heights
Address: 920 Studemont St
Houston, TX 77007
Phone: (281) 501-1788

#89
Bar 5015
Category: Bar
Average price: Modest
Area: Museum District
Address: 5015 Almeda Rd
Houston, TX 77007
Phone: (713) 522-5015

#90
Cedar Creek
Category: Bar, American, Burgers
Average price: Modest
Area: The Heights
Address: 1034 W 20th St
Houston, TX 77008
Phone: (713) 808-9623

#91
MAX's Wine Dive
Category: Wine Bar, American, Breakfast & Brunch
Average price: Modest
Area: Fourth Ward, Midtown, Montrose
Address: 214 Fairview St
Houston, TX 77006
Phone: (713) 528-9200

#92
Guava Lamp
Category: Lounge, Karaoke, Gay Bar
Average price: Modest
Area: Montrose
Address: 570 Waugh Dr
Houston, TX 77019
Phone: (713) 524-3359

#93
Boheme
Category: Wine Bar, Café, American
Average price: Modest
Area: Fourth Ward, Midtown, Montrose
Address: 307 Fairview St
Houston, TX 77006
Phone: (713) 529-1099

#94
Sherlock's Baker Street Pub
Category: Pub
Average price: Modest
Area: Westchase
Address: 10001 Westheimer Rd
Houston, TX 77042
Phone: (713) 977-1857

#95
Pub Fiction
Category: Pub, Sports Bar, American
Average price: Modest
Area: Fourth Ward, Midtown
Address: 2303 Smith St
Houston, TX 77006
Phone: (713) 400-8400

#96
Little Woodrow's
Category: Bar
Average price: Modest
Area: Downtown, EaDo
Address: 2019 Walker
Houston, TX 77003
Phone: (713) 222-2224

#97
Thirteen: The Heights Bar
Category: Bar, Karaoke
Average price: Inexpensive
Area: The Heights
Address: 1537 N Shepherd Dr
Houston, TX 77008
Phone: (713) 526-2626

#98
Midtown Bar & Grill
Category: Breakfast & Brunch, Bar, American
Average price: Modest
Area: Fourth Ward, Montrose
Address: 415 W Gray
Houston, TX 77019
Phone: (713) 528-2887

#99
Bayou Place
Category: Lounge, Dance Club
Average price: Expensive
Area: Fourth Ward, Downtown
Address: 534 Texas St
Houston, TX 77002
Phone: (281) 300-1568

#100
Mugsy's
Category: Pub, Sports Bar
Average price: Modest
Area: Upper Kirby
Address: 2239 Richmond Ave
Houston, TX 77098
Phone: (713) 522-7118

#101
McGonigel's Mucky Duck
Category: Pub, Music Venues, Irish
Average price: Modest
Area: Upper Kirby
Address: 2425 Norfolk St
Houston, TX 77098
Phone: (713) 528-5999

#102
Sonoma Wine Bar & Restaurant
Category: Wine Bar, American, Champagne Bar
Average price: Modest
Area: Upper Kirby
Address: 2720 Richmond Ave
Houston, TX 77098
Phone: (713) 526-9463

#103
Outlaw Dave's Worldwide Headquarters
Category: Bar
Average price: Modest
Area: The Heights
Address: 6502 Washington Ave
Houston, TX 77007
Phone: (713) 862-3283

#104
Burlap Barrel Pub
Category: Pub
Average price: Inexpensive
Area: Memorial
Address: 909 Town and Country Blvd
Houston, TX 77024
Phone: (713) 465-4977

#105
Local Pour Houston
Category: Bar, American, Music Venues
Average price: Modest
Area: River Oaks, Montrose
Address: 1952 W Gray St
Houston, TX 77019
Phone: (713) 521-1881

#106
Giau Bar N Bites
Category: Asian Fusion, Vietnamese, Lounge
Average price: Modest
Area: Sharpstown, Chinatown
Address: 9889 Bellaire Blvd
Houston, TX 77036
Phone: (713) 988-8988

#107
The Tasting Room
Category: Wine Bar, American
Average price: Modest
Area: Galleria, Uptown
Address: 1101-18 Uptown Park Blvd
Houston, TX 77056
Phone: (713) 993-9800

#108
Sambuca Jazz Café
Category: American, Lounge, Music Venues
Average price: Expensive
Area: Fourth Ward, Downtown
Address: 909 Texas St
Houston, TX 77002
Phone: (713) 224-5299

#109
Benjy's
Category: Lounge, American
Average price: Modest
Area: West University
Address: 2424 Dunstan Rd
Houston, TX 77005
Phone: (713) 522-7602

#110
The Alley Kat Bar & Lounge
Category: Cocktail Bar
Average price: Modest
Area: Fourth Ward, Midtown
Address: 3718 Main St
Houston, TX 77002
Phone: (713) 874-0722

#111
Hughes Hangar
Category: Lounge, Dance Club, Venues, Event Space
Average price: Modest
Area: The Heights
Address: 2811 Washington Ave
Houston, TX 77007
Phone: (281) 501-2028

#112
Royal Oak Bar and Grill
Category: Pub, American
Average price: Modest
Area: Montrose
Address: 1318 Westheimer Rd
Houston, TX 77006
Phone: (281) 974-4752

Houston Travel Guide 2015 / Shops, Restaurants, Arts, Entertainment & Nightlife

#113
Ziller
Category: Karaoke
Average price: Modest
Area: Spring Branch
Address: 10179 Westview Drive
Houston, TX 77043
Phone: (713) 722-7111

#114
Monnalisa Bar
Category: Lounge
Average price: Modest
Area: Memorial
Address: 800 Sorella Ct
Houston, TX 77024
Phone: (713) 973-1600

#115
Vintropolis
Category: Wine Bar
Average price: Modest
Area: Westchase
Address: 10001 Westheimer Rd
Houston, TX 77042
Phone: (713) 532-9463

#116
Darkhorse Tavern
Category: Pub
Average price: Inexpensive
Area: Sixth Ward
Address: 2207 Washington
Houston, TX 77007
Phone: (713) 426-2442

#117
Little Woodrow's
Category: Sports Bar
Average price: Inexpensive
Area: Braeswood Place, West University
Address: 4235 Bellaire Blvd
Houston, TX 77025
Phone: (713) 661-5282

#118
OTC Patio Bar
Category: Pub
Average price: Modest
Area: Upper Kirby
Address: 3212 Kirby Dr
Houston, TX 77098
Phone: (713) 489-0860

#119
Hunter's Pub
Category: Dive Bar
Average price: Inexpensive
Area: Willow Meadows, Willowbend, Meyerland
Address: 10549 S Post Oak Rd
Houston, TX 77035
Phone: (713) 283-5333

#120
Kay's Lounge
Category: Dive Bar, Music Venues, Pizza
Average price: Inexpensive
Area: West University
Address: 2324 Bissonnet St
Houston, TX 77005
Phone: (713) 521-0010

#121
Kung Fu Saloon
Category: Bar
Average price: Modest
Area: The Heights, Rice Military
Address: 5317 Washington Ave
Houston, TX 77007
Phone: (713) 864-0642

#122
Texas Hookah Lounge
Category: Hookah Bar, Lounge
Average price: Modest
Area: Montrose
Address: 1431 Westheimer Rd
Houston, TX 77006
Phone: (713) 401-9008

#123
Twin Peaks
Category: American, Sports Bar, American
Average price: Modest
Area: Upper Kirby
Address: 4527 Lomitas St.
Houston, TX 77098
Phone: (713) 520-7730

#124
Simone on Sunset
Category: Lounge, Wine Bar
Average price: Modest
Area: West University
Address: 2418 Sunset Blvd
Houston, TX 77005
Phone: (713) 636-3033

#125
Proof Rooftop Lounge
Category: Lounge
Average price: Modest
Area: Fourth Ward, Midtown
Address: 2600 Travis St
Houston, TX 77006
Phone: (832) 767-0513

#126
Batanga
Category: Tapas, Cocktail Bar, Latin American
Average price: Modest
Area: Fourth Ward, Downtown
Address: 908 Congress
Houston, TX 77002
Phone: (713) 224-9500

Houston Travel Guide 2015 / Shops, Restaurants, Arts, Entertainment & Nightlife

#127
The Boot
Category: Bar, Cajun, Creole, Seafood
Average price: Modest
Area: The Heights
Address: 1206 W 20th St
Houston, TX 77008
Phone: (713) 869-2668

#128
Station Theater
Category: Comedy Club
Average price: Inexpensive
Area: Sixth Ward
Address: 1230 Houston Ave
Houston, TX 77007
Phone: (903) 271-3203

#129
Pinot's Palette
Category: Art Classes, Wine Bar
Average price: Modest
Area: Memorial
Address: 12343 Kingsride Ln
Houston, TX 77024
Phone: (713) 973-2086

#130
Last Concert Café
Category: Tex-Mex, Music Venues, Dive Bar
Average price: Modest
Area: Downtown, Warehouse District
Address: 1403 Nance St
Houston, TX 77002
Phone: (713) 226-8563

#131
Mainstage
Category: Dance Club, Music Venues
Average price: Modest
Area: Fourth Ward, Midtown, Downtown
Address: 2016 Main St
Houston, TX 77002
Phone: (713) 751-3101

#132
Improv Comedy Club
Category: Comedy Club
Average price: Modest
Area: Spring Branch
Address: 7620 Katy Fwy
Houston, TX 77024
Phone: (713) 333-8800

#133
Blue Lagoon Club
Category: Bar, Dance Club
Average price: Inexpensive
Area: Spring Branch
Address: 1248 Witte Rd
Houston, TX 77055
Phone: (713) 468-9398

#134
Stanton's City Bites
Category: Burgers, American, Bar
Average price: Inexpensive
Area: Sixth Ward
Address: 1420 Edwards St
Houston, TX 77007
Phone: (713) 227-4893

#135
The Corkscrew
Category: Wine Bar
Average price: Modest
Area: The Heights
Address: 1308 W 20th St
Houston, TX 77008
Phone: (713) 230-8352

#136
Sassafras
Category: Wine Bar, Dive Bar
Average price: Modest
Area: Oak Forest, Garden Oaks
Address: 5022 Pinemont Dr
Houston, TX 77092
Phone: (832) 804-9079

#137
Paladora Lounge
Category: Lounge
Average price: Modest
Area: Medical Center
Address: 6580 Fannin Street
Houston, TX 77030
Phone: (713) 796-0080

#138
The Black Swan
Category: Pub, Lounge, Dance Club
Average price: Modest
Area: Galleria, Uptown
Address: Omni Hotel
Houston, TX 77056
Phone: (713) 871-8181

#139
The West End
Category: Lounge, American
Average price: Modest
Area: Galleria, Uptown
Address: 5320 Westheimer Rd
Houston, TX 77056
Phone: (713) 590-0616

#140
Neil's Bahr
Category: Bar
Average price: Inexpensive
Area: Downtown, EaDo
Address: 2006 Walker St
Houston, TX 77003
Phone: (281) 352-7456

Houston Travel Guide 2015 / Shops, Restaurants, Arts, Entertainment & Nightlife

#141
The Balcony Bar
Category: Sports Bar
Average price: Modest
Area: Downtown
Address: 1800 Texas Ave
Houston, TX 77003
Phone: (713) 398-6275

#142
Cozy Corner
Category: Dive Bar
Average price: Inexpensive
Area: Westbury
Address: 11530 Burdine St
Houston, TX 77035
Phone: (713) 723-4048

#143
F Bar
Category: Karaoke, Gay Bar, Dance Club
Average price: Modest
Area: Fourth Ward, Midtown, Montrose
Address: 202 Tuam St
Houston, TX 77006
Phone: (713) 522-3227

#144
Beta Theater
Category: Comedy Club, Performing Arts
Average price: Inexpensive
Area: Sixth Ward
Address: 1900 Kane St
Houston, TX 77007
Phone: (713) 591-5867

#145
The Men's Club
Category: Adult Entertainment
Average price: Modest
Area: Galleria, Uptown
Address: 3303 Sage Rd
Houston, TX 77056
Phone: (713) 629-7900

#146
Muldoon's the Patio
Category: Pub
Average price: Modest
Area: Galleria, Uptown
Address: 2611 Augusta Dr
Houston, TX 77057
Phone: (713) 706-4490

#147
Anderson Fair
Category: Music Venues
Average price: Modest
Area: Fourth Ward, Montrose
Address: 2007 Grant St
Houston, TX 77006
Phone: (832) 767-2785

#148
The Nook Cafe
Category: Coffee, Tea, Bakery, Music Venues
Average price: Inexpensive
Area: Third Ward
Address: 4701 Calhoun St
Houston, TX 77004
Phone: (832) 831-3620

#149
The Listening Room
Category: Music Venues
Average price: Modest
Area: The Heights
Address: 508 Pecore St
Houston, TX 77009
Phone: (713) 864-4260

#150
TC's Houston's Premiere Showbar
Category: Gay Bar, Performing Arts
Average price: Modest
Area: Fourth Ward, Montrose
Address: 817 Fairview
Houston, TX 77006
Phone: (713) 526-2625

#151
Crú A Wine Bar
Category: Wine Bar, American
Average price: Modest
Area: Upper Kirby
Address: 2800 Kirby Dr
Houston, TX 77098
Phone: (713) 528-9463

#152
Ej's
Category: Gay Bar, Pool Hall
Average price: Inexpensive
Area: Montrose
Address: 2517 Ralph St
Houston, TX 77006
Phone: (713) 527-9071

#153
Marfreless
Category: Lounge
Average price: Modest
Area: River Oaks, Montrose
Address: 2006 Peden St
Houston, TX 77019
Phone: (832) 954-7019

#154
Hans' Bier Haus
Category: Bar
Average price: Inexpensive
Area: West University
Address: 2523 Quenby St
Houston, TX 77005
Phone: (713) 520-7474

#155
Bayou Music Center
Category: Music Venues, Venues, Event Space
Average price: Modest
Area: Fourth Ward, Downtown
Address: 520 Texas Ave
Houston, TX 77002
Phone: (713) 230-1600

#156
The Oak Forest Chill Neighborhood Icehouse
Category: Bar
Average price: Inexpensive
Area: Oak Forest, Garden Oaks
Address: 3542 Oak Forest Dr
Houston, TX 77018
Phone: (713) 682-6900

#157
Rose Garden
Category: Dive Bar
Average price: Inexpensive
Area: The Heights
Address: 2621 Link Rd
Houston, TX 77009
Phone: (713) 863-8027

#158
Drink Houston
Category: Dance Club, Karaoke, Sports Bar
Average price: Modest
Area: Spring Branch
Address: 7620 Katy Fwy
Houston, TX 77024
Phone: (713) 471-1896

#159
Pimlico Irish Pub
Category: Pub
Average price: Modest
Area: River Oaks, Montrose
Address: 810 Waugh Dr
Houston, TX 77019
Phone: (713) 560-1721

#160
J. Black's Feel Good Kitchen & Lounge
Category: American, Lounge
Average price: Modest
Area: The Heights
Address: 110 S Heights Blvd
Houston, TX 77007
Phone: (713) 862-7818

#161
Lowbrow
Category: Bar, Breakfast & Brunch
Average price: Modest
Area: Montrose
Address: 1601 W Main St
Houston, TX 77006
Phone: (281) 501-8288

#162
D&W Lounge
Category: Dive Bar
Average price: Inexpensive
Area: EaDo, Eastwood
Address: 911 Milby
Houston, TX 77023
Phone: (713) 226-8777

#163
Houston House of Creeps
Category: Music Venues
Average price: Exclusive
Area: Gulfgate, Pine Valley
Address: 2710 Carrolton
Houston, TX 77023
Phone: (979) 319-1208

#164
Ritz Houston
Category: Adult Entertainment, Sports Bar
Average price: Expensive
Area: Hobby
Address: 10520 Gulf Fwy
Houston, TX 77034
Phone: (713) 944-6445

#165
Canyon Creek Cafe
Category: Burgers, Bar, Breakfast & Brunch
Average price: Modest
Area: Washington Corridor
Address: 6603 Westcott St
Houston, TX 77007
Phone: (713) 864-5885

#166
Revelry on Richmond
Category: Gastropub, Sports Bar
Average price: Modest
Area: Museum District, Montrose
Address: 1613 Richmond Ave
Houston, TX 77006
Phone: (832) 538-0724

#167
Treasures
Category: Adult Entertainment, Restaurant, Bar
Average price: Modest
Area: Galleria, Uptown
Address: 5647 Westheimer Rd
Houston, TX 77056
Phone: (713) 629-6200

#168
Eighteen Twenty Bar
Category: Lounge
Average price: Modest
Area: Downtown
Address: 1820 Franklin Ave
Houston, TX 77002
Phone: (713) 224-5535

#169
Onion Creek
Category: Coffee, Tea, Bar, Breakfast & Brunch
Average price: Modest
Area: The Heights
Address: 3106 White Oak Dr
Houston, TX 77007
Phone: (713) 880-0706

#170
Yes KTV
Category: Karaoke
Average price: Modest
Area: Sharpstown, Chinatown
Address: 9889 Bellaire Blvd
Houston, TX 77036
Phone: (832) 605-8566

#171
The Honeymoon Cafe & Bar
Category: Cocktail Bar, Café, Coffee, Tea
Average price: Modest
Area: Fourth Ward, Downtown
Address: 300 Main St
Houston, TX 77002
Phone: (281) 846-6995

#172
Clutch City Squire
Category: Dive Bar
Average price: Inexpensive
Area: Fourth Ward, Downtown
Address: 410 Main St
Houston, TX 77002
Phone: (713) 228-2800

#173
The Spot Club
Category: Dive Bar, Cocktail Bar
Average price: Inexpensive
Area: Lazy Brook, Timbergrove
Address: 1732 W 18th St
Houston, TX 77008
Phone: (713) 864-4485

#174
Dean's
Category: Dive Bar, Music Venues
Average price: Modest
Area: Fourth Ward, Downtown
Address: 316 Main St
Houston, TX 77002
Phone: (281) 624-5541

#175
Luke's Icehouse
Category: Sports Bar, Burgers
Average price: Modest
Area: The Heights, Rice Military
Address: 903 Durham Dr
Houston, TX 77007
Phone: (281) 888-7028

#176
Kalf Hookah Lounge
Category: Hookah Bar, Lounge
Average price: Inexpensive
Area: Gulfton
Address: 6300 Westpark Dr
Houston, TX 77057
Phone: (713) 975-0400

#177
Diallo's of Houston
Category: Dive Bar
Average price: Inexpensive
Area: MacGregor
Address: 3340 Dixie Dr
Houston, TX 77021
Phone: (713) 747-4223

#178
Seasons 52
Category: American, Vegetarian, Wine Bar
Average price: Modest
Area: Memorial
Address: 842 W Sam Houston Pkwy
Houston, TX 77024
Phone: (713) 464-5252

#179
The Houston Club
Category: Venues, Event Space, Bar
Average price: Expensive
Area: Fourth Ward, Downtown
Address: 910 Louisiana St
Houston, TX 77002
Phone: (713) 225-1661

#180
Azul Lounge
Category: Lounge
Average price: Modest
Area: Medical Center
Address: 9880 Buffalo Speedway
Houston, TX 77025
Phone: (713) 667-1512

#181
Marquis II
Category: Dive Bar
Average price: Inexpensive
Area: West University
Address: 2631 Bissonnet St
Houston, TX 77005
Phone: (713) 522-2090

#182
Synn Ultralounge
Category: Lounge, Hookah Bar, Venues, Event Space
Average price: Modest
Area: Highland Village
Address: 3302 Mercer St
Houston, TX 77027
Phone: (713) 294-5552

#183
Belvedere
Category: Dance Club, Lounge
Average price: Expensive
Area: Galleria, Uptown
Address: 1131 Uptown Park Blvd
Houston, TX 77056
Phone: (713) 552-9271

#184
Ruthie's Place
Category: Bar
Average price: Inexpensive
Area: Museum District, Montrose
Address: 1829 Richmond Ave
Houston, TX 77098
Phone: (713) 522-7240

#185
Bowlmor Houston
Category: Nightlife, Bowling, Arts, Entertainment
Average price: Expensive
Area: Memorial
Address: 925 Bunker Hill Rd
Houston, TX 77024
Phone: (713) 461-1207

#186
The Railyard
Category: Sports Bar
Average price: Inexpensive
Area: Highland Village
Address: 4200 San Felipe St
Houston, TX 77027
Phone: (713) 621-4000

#187
Camerata at Paulie's
Category: Wine Bar
Average price: Modest
Area: Montrose
Address: 1834 Westheimer Rd
Houston, TX 77098
Phone: (713) 522-8466

#188
Lucky Strike
Category: Bowling, Lounge, Pool Hall
Average price: Modest
Area: Downtown
Address: 1201 San Jacinto St
Houston, TX 77002
Phone: (713) 343-3300

#189
Hudson Lounge
Category: Lounge
Average price: Modest
Area: West University
Address: 2506 Robinhood St
Houston, TX 77005
Phone: (713) 523-0020

#190
The Stag's Head Pub
Category: Pub, Sports Bar
Average price: Modest
Area: Upper Kirby
Address: 2128 Portsmouth St
Houston, TX 77098
Phone: (713) 533-1199

#191
Super Happy Fun Land
Category: Performing Arts, Music Venues
Average price: Inexpensive
Area: EaDo, Eastwood
Address: 3801 Polk St
Houston, TX 77003
Phone: (713) 880-2100

#192
NJ's
Category: Dive Bar, Music Venues
Average price: Inexpensive
Area: Oak Forest, Garden Oaks
Address: 3815 Mangum Rd
Houston, TX 77092
Phone: (713) 682-3363

#193
Stone's Throw
Category: Cocktail Bar, Lounge
Average price: Modest
Area: Montrose
Address: 1417 Westheimer Rd
Houston, TX 77006
Phone: (832) 659-0265

#194
Galway Hooker Irish Pub
Category: Irish, Pub
Average price: Modest
Area: The Heights, Rice Military
Address: 5102 Washington Ave
Houston, TX 77007
Phone: (281) 989-3467

#195
Red Ox Bar & Grill
Category: Bar, Mexican
Average price: Modest
Area: Northside Village
Address: 811 Collingsworth St
Houston, TX 77009
Phone: (713) 227-3369

#196
Saint Dane's Bar & Grille
Category: Sports Bar, American
Average price: Inexpensive
Area: Fourth Ward, Midtown
Address: 502 Elgin St
Houston, TX 77246
Phone: (713) 807-7040

#197
Memorial Wine Cellar
Category: Wine Bar
Average price: Modest
Area: Memorial
Address: 7951 Katy Fwy
Houston, TX 77024
Phone: (713) 680-9772

#198
The Dogwood
Category: Bar, American
Average price: Modest
Area: Fourth Ward, Midtown
Address: 2403 Bagby St
Houston, TX 77006
Phone: (281) 501-9075

#199
Michael's Outpost Inc.
Category: Gay Bar
Average price: Inexpensive
Area: Museum District, Montrose
Address: 1419 Richmond Ave
Houston, TX 77006
Phone: (713) 520-8446

#200
Goro & Gun
Category: Tapas, Ramen, Cocktail Bar
Average price: Modest
Area: Fourth Ward, Downtown
Address: 306 Main St
Houston, TX 77002
Phone: (832) 708-6195

#201
Shot Bar
Category: Bar
Average price: Modest
Area: Fourth Ward, Midtown
Address: 2315 Bagby St
Houston, TX 77006
Phone: (713) 526-3000

#202
Ninja Ramen
Category: Cocktail Bar, Ramen
Average price: Modest
Area: The Heights
Address: 4219 Washington Ave
Houston, TX 77007
Phone: (281) 888-5873

#203
Emmit's Place
Category: Jazz, Blues, Music Venues, Lounge
Average price: Modest
Area: Willow Meadows, Willowbend
Address: 4852 Benning Dr
Houston, TX 77035
Phone: (713) 728-0012

#204
Lone Star Saloon
Category: Dive Bar
Average price: Inexpensive
Area: Fourth Ward, Downtown
Address: 1900 Travis St
Houston, TX 77002
Phone: (713) 757-1616

#205
The Drake
Category: Lounge, Dance Club
Average price: Modest
Area: Sixth Ward
Address: 1902 Washington Ave
Houston, TX 77007
Phone: (713) 869-8333

#206
Joke Joint Comedy Showcase
Category: Comedy Club
Average price: Modest
Area: South Belt, Ellington
Address: 11460 Fuqua St
Houston, TX 77089
Phone: (281) 481-1188

#207
Bohemeo's
Category: Coffee, Tea, Sandwiches, Bar
Average price: Inexpensive
Area: Eastwood
Address: 708 Telephone Rd
Houston, TX 77023
Phone: (713) 923-4277

#208
The Spot Lounge & Bar
Category: Bar
Average price: Inexpensive
Area: MacGregor
Address: 4709 Dowling St
Houston, TX 77004
Phone: (713) 523-1169

#209
Catty Corner Ice House
Category: Dive Bar
Average price: Inexpensive
Area: Oak Forest, Garden Oaks
Address: 895 Wakefield Dr
Houston, TX 77018
Phone: (713) 691-9197

#210
Pandora Lounge
Category: Dance Club, Lounge
Average price: Modest
Area: Sixth Ward
Address: 1815 Washington Ave
Houston, TX 77007
Phone: (832) 296-6220

Houston Travel Guide 2015 / Shops, Restaurants, Arts, Entertainment & Nightlife

#211
Caribbean Flavor Restaurant & Bar
Category: Caribbean, Bar
Average price: Modest
Area: Westchase
Address: 10850 Westheimer Rd
Houston, TX 77042
Phone: (832) 530-4317

#212
Front Porch Pub
Category: Pub
Average price: Modest
Area: Fourth Ward, Midtown, Montrose
Address: 217 Gray St
Houston, TX 77002
Phone: (713) 571-9571

#213
Molly's Pub
Category: Sports Bar, Sandwiches
Average price: Inexpensive
Area: Westchase
Address: 11128 Westheimer Rd
Houston, TX 77042
Phone: (713) 789-9580

#214
The House of Dereon Media Center
Category: Music Venues, Venues, Event Space
Average price: Exclusive
Area: Midtown
Address: 2202 Crawford St
Houston, TX 77002
Phone: (713) 772-5175

#215
5th Amendment
Category: Dance Club
Average price: Modest
Area: Fourth Ward, Midtown
Address: 2900 Travis
Houston, TX 77006
Phone: (832) 474-3394

#216
Sparrow Bar + Cookshop
Category: Bar, American
Average price: Expensive
Area: Fourth Ward, Midtown
Address: 3701 Travis
Houston, TX 77002
Phone: (713) 524-6922

#217
Tony's Corner Pocket
Category: Gay Bar
Average price: Inexpensive
Area: Fourth Ward, Midtown, Montrose
Address: 817 W Dallas
Houston, TX 77019
Phone: (713) 571-7870

#218
George Country Sports Bar
Category: Dive Bar, Sports Bar, Gay Bar
Average price: Inexpensive
Area: Fourth Ward, Montrose
Address: 617 Fairview St
Houston, TX 77006
Phone: (713) 528-8102

#219
Grooves of Houston
Category: Dance Club, Music Venues, Venues, Event Space
Average price: Modest
Area: Third Ward
Address: 2300 Pierce St
Houston, TX 77003
Phone: (713) 652-9900

#220
The Next Door
Category: Dive Bar
Average price: Inexpensive
Area: Montrose
Address: 2020 Waugh Dr
Houston, TX 77006
Phone: (713) 520-1712

#221
Pinot's Palette
Category: Wine Bar, Art Classes
Average price: Modest
Area: Gulfton, Galleria, Uptown
Address: 5539 Richmond Ave
Houston, TX 77056
Phone: (713) 975-7867

#222
Club Venue
Category: Dance Club
Average price: Modest
Area: Fourth Ward, Downtown
Address: 719 Main St
Houston, TX 77002
Phone: (713) 236-8150

#223
Reef
Category: Seafood, Lounge
Average price: Expensive
Area: Fourth Ward, Midtown
Address: 2600 Travis St
Houston, TX 77006
Phone: (713) 526-8282

#224
Ovations Night Club
Category: Music Venues
Average price: Modest
Area: West University
Address: 2536 Times Blvd
Houston, TX 77005
Phone: (713) 522-9801

Houston Travel Guide 2015 / Shops, Restaurants, Arts, Entertainment & Nightlife

#225
Harp
Category: Pub
Average price: Inexpensive
Area: Museum District, Montrose
Address: 1625 Richmond Ave
Houston, TX 77006
Phone: (713) 528-7827

#226
Friends Restaurant
Category: Korean, Pub
Average price: Modest
Area: Spring Branch
Address: 10104 Hammerly Blvd
Houston, TX 77080
Phone: (713) 461-9988

#227
Secret
Category: Adult Entertainment
Average price: Modest
Area: Northside, Northline
Address: 7928 N Shepherd Dr
Houston, TX 77088
Phone: (281) 591-8888

#228
55 Bar & Restaurant
Category: Bar, American
Average price: Modest
Area: West University
Address: 5510 Morningside Dr
Houston, TX 77005
Phone: (713) 590-0610

#229
Capitol Bar Midtown
Category: Lounge, Beer, Wine, Spirits, Sports Bar
Average price: Modest
Area: Fourth Ward, Midtown
Address: 2415 Main St
Houston, TX 77002
Phone: (713) 487-6854

#230
The Marque
Category: Lounge
Average price: Exclusive
Area: Memorial
Address: 798 Sorella Ct
Houston, TX 77024
Phone: (832) 726-1930

#231
Luxury Trio
Category: Jazz, Blues
Average price: Modest
Area: Westchase
Address: 10611 Candlewood
Houston, TX 77042
Phone: (713) 829-1553

#232
Harlem Knights
Category: Adult Entertainment
Average price: Inexpensive
Area: Eastex, Jensen
Address: 9834 Jensen Dr
Houston, TX 77093
Phone: (713) 699-9434

#233
Hard Rock Café
Category: Burgers, American, Music Venues
Average price: Modest
Area: Fourth Ward, Downtown
Address: 502 Texas Ave.
Houston, TX 77002
Phone: (713) 227-1392

#234
Gold Digger Cabaret
Category: Adult Entertainment
Average price: Inexpensive
Area: South Main
Address: 11305 Main St
Houston, TX 77025
Phone: (713) 666-6906

#235
Lumen Lounge
Category: Dance Club, Bar
Average price: Expensive
Area: West University
Address: 5000 Kirby
Houston, TX 77005
Phone: (713) 807-7567

#236
Mezzanine Sports Bar and Grill
Category: Sports Bar, Karaoke, American
Average price: Modest
Area: Upper Kirby
Address: 2200 Southwest Fwy
Houston, TX 77098
Phone: (713) 528-6399

#237
Jimmie's Ice House
Category: Dive Bar
Average price: Inexpensive
Area: The Heights
Address: 2803 White Oak Dr
Houston, TX 77007
Phone: (713) 862-7001

#238
Chymistry Bar and Lounge
Category: Lounge, Dance Club
Average price: Inexpensive
Area: South Acres, Crestmont Park
Address: 1002 Almeda Genoa
Houston, TX 77047
Phone: (832) 530-4255

#239
Warren's Inn
Category: Dive Bar
Average price: Inexpensive
Area: Fourth Ward, Downtown
Address: 307 Travis St
Houston, TX 77002
Phone: (713) 247-9207

#240
Sugarhill Bar & Lounge
Category: Lounge, Dance Club
Average price: Modest
Area: MacGregor
Address: 2533 Southmore Blvd
Houston, TX 77004
Phone: (832) 794-0743

#241
Provisions
Category: American, Bar
Average price: Modest
Area: Fourth Ward, Midtown, Montrose
Address: 807 Taft St
Houston, TX 77019
Phone: (713) 628-9020

#242
Midtown Drinkery
Category: Bar, American
Average price: Modest
Area: Fourth Ward, Midtown
Address: 2416 Brazos St
Houston, TX 77006
Phone: (713) 522-0118

#243
Bam Bou
Category: Dance Club
Average price: Expensive
Area: West University
Address: 2540 University Blvd
Houston, TX 77005
Phone: (713) 521-7228

#244
Brixx
Category: Lounge, Sports Bar
Average price: Modest
Area: The Heights, Rice Military
Address: 5110 Washington Ave
Houston, TX 77007
Phone: (713) 864-8811

#245
Warehouse Bar & Chill
Category: Bar, American
Average price: Modest
Area: Lazy Brook, Timbergrove
Address: 3333 W 11th St
Houston, TX 77008
Phone: (713) 802-2445

#246
Line & Lariat
Category: American, Lounge
Average price: Expensive
Area: Downtown
Address: 220 Main St
Houston, TX 77002
Phone: (832) 667-4470

#247
Chic's Cabaret
Category: Adult Entertainment
Average price: Exclusive
Area: Northshore
Address: 10255 East Fwy
Houston, TX 77029
Phone: (713) 670-8438

#248
B.U.S. Bar
Category: Sports Bar
Average price: Modest
Area: Downtown
Address: 1800 Texas St
Houston, TX 77003
Phone: (713) 222-2287

#249
Nox
Category: Dance Club, Lounge
Average price: Expensive
Area: The Heights
Address: 4701 Nett St
Houston, TX 77007
Phone: (713) 570-6699

#250
La Carafe
Category: Dive Bar
Average price: Modest
Area: Downtown
Address: 813 Congress St
Houston, TX 77002
Phone: (713) 229-9399

#251
Cafe Luxor
Category: American, Hookah Bar, Sports Bar
Average price: Modest
Area: The Heights
Address: 3730 Washington Ave
Houston, TX 77007
Phone: (713) 864-0000

#252
WXYZ Bar
Category: Bar
Average price: Modest
Area: Galleria, Uptown
Address: 5415 Westheimer Rd
Houston, TX 77056
Phone: (713) 622-7010

#253
Nyx Ultra Lounge
Category: Lounge, Karaoke
Average price: Modest
Area: Alief
Address: 10905 Bellaire Blvd
Houston, TX 77072
Phone: (832) 603-7145

#254
Chula's Sports Cantina
Category: Tex-Mex, Sports Bar
Average price: Modest
Area: Northshore
Address: 12008 East Fwy
Houston, TX 77029
Phone: (713) 455-7300

#255
Sunny's Bar
Category: Dive Bar, Pool Hall
Average price: Inexpensive
Area: Fourth Ward, Downtown
Address: 902 Capitol St
Houston, TX 77002
Phone: (713) 224-3200

#256
District Lounge
Category: Lounge
Average price: Modest
Area: The Heights
Address: 4606 Washington Ave
Houston, TX 77007
Phone: (713) 869-2787

#257
Faces Club
Category: Dive Bar
Average price: Inexpensive
Area: Spring Branch
Address: 1453 Witte Rd
Houston, TX 77080
Phone: (713) 463-9099

#258
Dua
Category: Vietnamese, Asian Fusion, Cocktail Bar
Average price: Modest
Area: Montrose
Address: 1201 Westheimer
Houston, TX 77006
Phone: (713) 524-5664

#259
Dding Ga Dding Ga
Category: Karaoke
Average price: Modest
Area: Spring Branch
Address: 9875 Long Point Rd
Houston, TX 77080
Phone: (713) 464-0992

#260
The Red Lion
Category: Pub
Average price: Modest
Area: River Oaks
Address: 2316 S Shepherd Dr
Houston, TX 77019
Phone: (713) 529-8390

#261
The Living Room
Category: Lounge
Average price: Expensive
Area: Galleria, Uptown
Address: 2670 Sage Rd
Houston, TX 77056
Phone: (713) 850-8200

#262
The Den Campus Pub
Category: Sports Bar, Pub
Average price: Inexpensive
Area: Third Ward
Address: 4835 Calhoun Rd
Houston, TX 77004
Phone: (281) 888-4299

#263
Lucky's Pub
Category: Sports Bar, Burgers, Pizza
Average price: Modest
Area: The Heights
Address: 2520 Houston Ave
Houston, TX 77009
Phone: (713) 862-2400

#264
V Live Houston Vintage SteakHouse
Category: Dance Club, Music Venues, Seafood Market
Average price: Modest
Area: Gulfton
Address: 6213 Richmond Ave
Houston, TX 77063
Phone: (682) 583-0753

#265
Libra Lounge
Category: Lounge
Average price: Inexpensive
Area: Medical Center
Address: 9880 Buffalo Speedway
Houston, TX 77025
Phone: (713) 667-1512

#266
Bronx Bar
Category: Bar
Average price: Modest
Area: West University
Address: 5555 Morningside Dr
Houston, TX 77005
Phone: (713) 520-9690

#267
Hardbodies
Category: Adult Entertainment
Average price: Modest
Area: Galleria, Uptown
Address: 2850 Fountain View Dr
Houston, TX 77057
Phone: (832) 200-5300

#268
Costa's
Category: Cocktail Bar, Dive Bar, Wine Bar
Average price: Modest
Area: Fourth Ward, Montrose
Address: 415 Westheimer Rd
Houston, TX 77006
Phone: (832) 831-1565

#269
Diem Lounge
Category: Lounge, Dance Club
Average price: Modest
Area: The Heights
Address: 4701A Nett St
Houston, TX 77007
Phone: (713) 498-9662

#270
Shiloh Club
Category: Dive Bar
Average price: Inexpensive
Area: The Heights
Address: 1321 Studewood St
Houston, TX 77008
Phone: (713) 880-2401

#271
Bambou
Category: Dance Club
Average price: Modest
Area: West University
Address: 2540 University Blvd
Houston, TX 77005
Phone: (713) 236-8150

#272
Griff's
Category: Sports Bar, Pub, American, Café
Average price: Inexpensive
Area: Fourth Ward, Montrose
Address: 3416 Roseland St
Houston, TX 77006
Phone: (713) 528-9912

#273
Melody House
Category: Karaoke, Lounge, Café
Average price: Modest
Area: Sharpstown, Chinatown
Address: 9889 Bellaire Blvd
Houston, TX 77036
Phone: (713) 772-8866

#274
Epic 22 Lounge
Category: Dive Bar
Average price: Inexpensive
Area: Third Ward
Address: 3000 Blodgett St
Houston, TX 77004
Phone: (713) 522-3742

#275
51fifteen Restaurant & Lounge
Category: Lounge, American
Average price: Expensive
Area: Galleria, Uptown
Address: 5115 Westheimer Rd
Houston, TX 77056
Phone: (713) 963-8067

#276
The Cover Girls Cabaret
Category: Adult Entertainment
Average price: Modest
Area: Carverdale
Address: 10310 W Little York Rd
Houston, TX 77041
Phone: (713) 937-7772

#277
Don Patron Bar & Grill
Category: Mexican, Bar
Average price: Modest
Area: Fourth Ward, Downtown
Address: 500 Dallas St
Houston, TX 77002
Phone: (713) 659-1050

#278
Maxwell's Club
Category: Dance Club
Average price: Inexpensive
Area: Braeswood Place, Medical Center
Address: 9255 S Main St
Houston, TX 77025
Phone: (281) 698-7618

#279
Red Cat Jazz Café
Category: Jazz, Blues, Cajun, Creole
Average price: Modest
Area: Downtown
Address: 711 Franklin St
Houston, TX 77002
Phone: (713) 226-7870

#280
The White Swan
Category: Music Venues
Average price: Inexpensive
Area: Second Ward
Address: 4419 Navigation Blvd
Houston, TX 77011
Phone: (713) 923-2837

#281
Lei Low
Category: Cocktail Bar, Lounge
Average price: Modest
Area: The Heights
Address: 6412 N Main St
Houston, TX 77009
Phone: (713) 380-2968

#282
Fifty Fifty Acorn Golf & Icehouse
Category: Golf, Bar
Average price: Inexpensive
Area: Oak Forest, Garden Oaks
Address: 5050 Acorn St
Houston, TX 77092
Phone: (832) 831-5327

#283
Nomad Tavern
Category: Nightlife
Average price: Inexpensive
Area: Spring Branch
Address: 2133 Bingle Rd
Houston, TX 77055
Phone: (713) 468-0020

#284
Rosinka Wine & Tea House
Category: Coffee, Tea, Café, Wine Bar
Average price: Inexpensive
Area: West University
Address: 2509 Rice Blvd
Houston, TX 77005
Phone: (832) 509-9464

#285
ComedySportz
Category: Comedy Club
Average price: Inexpensive
Area: Memorial
Address: 901 Town & Country Blvd.
Houston, TX 77024
Phone: (713) 868-1444

#286
JetLounge
Category: Lounge, Venues,
Event Space, Music Venues
Average price: Modest
Area: Downtown
Address: 1515 Pease St
Houston, TX 77002
Phone: (713) 659-2000

#287
Sunset Strip
Category: American,
Adult Entertainment, Sports Bar
Average price: Modest
Area: Lazy Brook, Timbergrove
Address: 2425 Mangum Rd
Houston, TX 77092
Phone: (713) 680-3500

#288
West Alabama Ice House
Category: Dive Bar
Average price: Inexpensive
Area: Montrose
Address: 1919 W Alabama St
Houston, TX 77098
Phone: (713) 528-6874

#289
Nikki's Irish Pub
Category: Pub
Average price: Modest
Area: Spring Branch, Memorial
Address: 10885 Katy Fwy
Houston, TX 77079
Phone: (713) 932-0800

#290
Mazaj Hookah Bar & Grill
Category: Middle Eastern, Hookah Bar
Average price: Modest
Area: Gulfton, Galleria, Uptown
Address: 5615 Richmond Ave
Houston, TX 77057
Phone: (713) 334-9977

#291
Sin City
Category: Adult Entertainment
Average price: Modest
Area: Westwood
Address: 10554 SW Fwy
Houston, TX 77074
Phone: (832) 299-4746

#292
Osteria Mazzantini
Category: Wine Bar, Italian
Average price: Expensive
Area: Galleria, Uptown
Address: 2200 Post Oak Blvd
Houston, TX 77056
Phone: (713) 993-9898

#293
Crocker Bar
Category: Gay Bar
Average price: Inexpensive
Area: Fourth Ward, Montrose
Address: 2312 Crocker St
Houston, TX 77006
Phone: (713) 529-3355

#294
Gold Cup
Category: Adult Entertainment,
Beer, Wine, Spirits
Average price: Expensive
Area: Fairbanks, Northwest Crossing
Address: 12747 Northwest Fwy
Houston, TX 77092
Phone: (713) 460-0171

Houston Travel Guide 2015 / Shops, Restaurants, Arts, Entertainment & Nightlife

#295
Swagger Lounge & Bar
Category: Sports Bar, Lounge
Average price: Modest
Area: Greenway, West University
Address: 3839 Southwest Fwy
Houston, TX 77027
Phone: (713) 840-7924

#296
Kris Bistro and Wine Lounge
Category: French, Wine Bar, Lounge
Average price: Modest
Area: Northside Village
Address: 7070 Allensby
Houston, TX 77022
Phone: (713) 358-5079

#297
Status Lounge And Cigar Bar
Category: Lounge
Average price: Modest
Area: Third Ward
Address: 3710 Dowling St
Houston, TX 77004
Phone: (713) 528-0069

#298
The Concert Pub
Category: Sports Bar, American, Music Venues
Average price: Inexpensive
Area: Galleria, Uptown
Address: 5636 Richmond Ave
Houston, TX 77057
Phone: (713) 278-7272

#299
Bosta Wine and Coffee
Category: Wine Bar, Coffee, Tea
Average price: Modest
Area: Museum District
Address: 1801 Binz St
Houston, TX 77004
Phone: (713) 533-9560

#300
GreenStreet
Category: Music Venues, Shopping Center
Average price: Modest
Area: Downtown
Address: 1201 Fannin St
Houston, TX 77002
Phone: (832) 320-1200

#301
The Brewery Tap
Category: Pub
Average price: Modest
Area: Downtown
Address: 717 Franklin St
Houston, TX 77002
Phone: (713) 237-1537

#302
Roeder's Pub
Category: Sports Bar
Average price: Modest
Area: Upper Kirby
Address: 3116 S. Shepherd Dr
Houston, TX 77098
Phone: (713) 524-4994

#303
The Dog House Tavern
Category: Sports Bar, Dive Bar
Average price: Inexpensive
Area: Fourth Ward, Midtown
Address: 2517 Bagby St
Houston, TX 77006
Phone: (713) 520-1118

#304
Blur
Category: Gay Bar
Average price: Modest
Area: Fourth Ward, Montrose
Address: 710 Pacific St
Houston, TX 77006
Phone: (713) 529-3447

#305
Club Uropa
Category: Dance Club
Average price: Modest
Area: Highland Village
Address: 3302 Mercer St
Houston, TX 77027
Phone: (713) 627-1132

#306
Venus
Category: Dance Club, Gay Bar, Music Venues
Average price: Modest
Area: Midtown
Address: 2901 Fannin St
Houston, TX 77002
Phone: (713) 751-3185

#307
Diamond Club Cabaret
Category: Adult Entertainment
Average price: Inexpensive
Area: Upper Kirby
Address: 3136 Richmond Ave
Houston, TX 77098
Phone: (713) 528-8116

#308
Hookah Bar and Oxygen Bar
Category: Lounge
Average price: Inexpensive
Area: Fourth Ward, Downtown
Address: 914 Prairie St
Houston, TX 77002
Phone: (713) 237-8987

Houston Travel Guide 2015 / Shops, Restaurants, Arts, Entertainment & Nightlife

#309
Komodo's Pub
Category: Pub, Dive Bar
Average price: Inexpensive
Area: Fourth Ward, Midtown, Montrose
Address: 2004 Baldwin St
Houston, TX 77002
Phone: (713) 655-1501

#310
Eddie V's Prime Seafood
Category: Steakhouse, Seafood, Jazz, Blues
Average price: Expensive
Area: Memorial
Address: 12848 Queensbury Ln
Houston, TX 77024
Phone: (832) 200-2380

#311
M.J. PoolHouse
Category: Pool Hall
Average price: Inexpensive
Area: Sharpstown, Chinatown
Address: 9889 Bellaire Blvd
Houston, TX 77036
Phone: (832) 275-2563

#312
El Big Bad
Category: Bar, American
Average price: Modest
Area: Fourth Ward, Downtown
Address: 419 Travis
Houston, TX 77002
Phone: (713) 229-8181

#313
Plonk! Beer & Wine Bistro
Category: Wine Bar, American
Average price: Modest
Area: Oak Forest, Garden Oaks
Address: 1214 W 43rd St
Houston, TX 77018
Phone: (713) 290-1070

#314
Christian's Tailgate Grill
Category: Sports Bar, Burgers, Karaoke
Average price: Modest
Area: Fourth Ward, Midtown, Montrose
Address: 2000 Bagby St
Houston, TX 77002
Phone: (713) 527-0261

#315
Prospect Park Sports Bar & Kitchen
Category: Sports Bar, American, Music Venues
Average price: Modest
Area: Gulfton, Galleria, Uptown
Address: 3100 Fountain View Dr
Houston, TX 77057
Phone: (832) 794-0743

#316
OTC Midtown Pizza Grill & Patio Bar
Category: Bar, Pizza, American
Average price: Modest
Area: Fourth Ward, Midtown, Montrose
Address: 2708 Bagby St
Houston, TX 77006
Phone: (713) 518-2132

#317
Big Woodrows
Category: Sports Bar, Cajun, Creole, Karaoke
Average price: Modest
Area: Galleria, Uptown
Address: 3111 Chimney Rock Rd
Houston, TX 77056
Phone: (713) 784-2653

#318
Mosaic Bar and Lounge
Category: Lounge, Tapas Bar, Sports Bar
Average price: Modest
Area: Museum District
Address: 5927 Almeda Rd
Houston, TX 77004
Phone: (713) 533-9915

#319
Rieles Bar Los
Category: Pub, Dance Studio
Average price: Modest
Area: Spring Branch
Address: 7922 Long Point Rd
Houston, TX 77055
Phone: (713) 465-3632

#320
RIPCORD
Category: Gay Bar
Average price: Inexpensive
Area: Fourth Ward, Montrose
Address: 715 Fairview St
Houston, TX 77006
Phone: (713) 521-2792

#321
Lounge Next Door at Ibiza
Category: Lounge
Average price: Modest
Area: Fourth Ward, Midtown
Address: 2450 Louisiana St
Houston, TX 77006
Phone: (713) 520-7300

#322
Pearl Lounge Houston
Category: Lounge, Pub
Average price: Inexpensive
Area: The Heights
Address: 4216 Washington Ave
Houston, TX 77007
Phone: (832) 740-4933

#323
The Hut
Category: Sports Bar
Average price: Inexpensive
Area: Harrisburg, Manchester
Address: 1107 Central St
Houston, TX 77012
Phone: (281) 888-9209

#324
Bacchus Coffee & Wine Bar
Category: Wine Bar, Coffee, Tea, Mediterranean
Average price: Inexpensive
Area: Montrose
Address: 2502 Dunlavy
Houston, TX 77006
Phone: (713) 529-2330

#325
Ron's Pub
Category: Pub
Average price: Inexpensive
Area: Galleria, Uptown
Address: 1826 Fountain View Dr
Houston, TX 77057
Phone: (713) 977-4820

#326
Phil and Derek's
Category: Wine Bar, Cajun, Creole
Average price: Modest
Area: Upper Kirby
Address: 2811 Bammel Ln
Houston, TX 77098
Phone: (713) 529-1314

#327
Third Coast Comedy Players
Category: Comedy Club
Average price: Inexpensive
Area: Oak Forest, Garden Oaks
Address: 2317 W 34th St
Houston, TX 77018
Phone: (713) 263-9899

#328
2-A-Days Sports Bar & Grille
Category: Sports Bar
Average price: Inexpensive
Area: South Belt, Ellington
Address: 10555 Pearland Pkwy
Houston, TX 77089
Phone: (713) 991-0453

#329
611 Club the
Category: Nightlife
Average price: Inexpensive
Area: Fourth Ward, Montrose
Address: 611 Hyde Park Blvd
Houston, TX 77006
Phone: (713) 528-1582

#330
Mango's
Category: Vegetarian, Music Venues, Pizza
Average price: Inexpensive
Area: Fourth Ward, Montrose
Address: 403 Westheimer Rd
Houston, TX 77006
Phone: (713) 522-8903

#331
The Gaslamp
Category: Lounge, Breakfast & Brunch
Average price: Modest
Area: Fourth Ward, Midtown
Address: 2400 Brazos
Houston, TX 77006
Phone: (713) 561-2990

#332
Vibe Lounge
Category: Lounge, Vietnamese, Karaoke
Average price: Modest
Area: Alief
Address: 6968 Wilcrest Dr
Houston, TX 77072
Phone: (281) 575-0440

#333
Dan Electro's Guitar Bar
Category: Dive Bar, Music Venues
Average price: Inexpensive
Area: The Heights
Address: 1031 E 24th St
Houston, TX 77009
Phone: (713) 862-8707

#334
Dutchman the
Category: Nightlife
Average price: Inexpensive
Area: Oak Forest, Garden Oaks
Address: 834 Wakefield Dr
Houston, TX 77018
Phone: (713) 691-0228

#335
Little Woodrow's
Category: Pub
Average price: Inexpensive
Area: West University
Address: 5611 Morningside Dr
Houston, TX 77005
Phone: (713) 521-2337

#336
Secrets
Category: Dance Club, Lounge, Adult Entertainment
Average price: Modest
Area: South Belt, Ellington
Address: 10900 Kingspoint Rd
Houston, TX 77075
Phone: (713) 941-7005

#337
Izakaya Wa
Category: Japanese, Tapas, Bar
Average price: Modest
Area: Memorial
Address: 12665 Memorial Dr
Houston, TX 77024
Phone: (713) 461-0155

#338
Richmond Arms Pub
Category: Pub, American
Average price: Modest
Area: Gulfton, Galleria, Uptown
Address: 5920 Richmond Ave
Houston, TX 77057
Phone: (713) 784-7722

#339
Home Plate Bar & Grill
Category: Sports Bar, Burgers, American
Average price: Modest
Area: Downtown
Address: 1800 Texas St
Houston, TX 77003
Phone: (713) 222-1993

#340
Vintage Lounge
Category: Lounge
Average price: Modest
Area: Upper Kirby
Address: 2108 Kipling St
Houston, TX 77098
Phone: (713) 522-4200

#341
Speakeasy Lounge
Category: Lounge
Average price: Modest
Area: Downtown
Address: 110 Main St
Houston, TX 77002
Phone: (713) 547-0655

#342
Glamour Girls Cabaret
Category: Adult Entertainment
Average price: Modest
Area: Fairbanks, Northwest Crossing
Address: 14428 Hempstead Rd
Houston, TX 77040
Phone: (713) 462-1700

#343
H & H Saloon
Category: Bar
Average price: Inexpensive
Area: Fairbanks, Northwest Crossing
Address: 9309 Clay Rd
Houston, TX 77080
Phone: (713) 504-0479

#344
Tragos Lounge
Category: Lounge
Average price: Modest
Area: Galleria, Uptown
Address: 5887 Westheimer Rd
Houston, TX 77057
Phone: (281) 919-4412

#345
Chacho's
Category: Mexican, Sports Bar
Average price: Inexpensive
Area: Medical Center
Address: 2700 S Loop 610 W
Houston, TX 77054
Phone: (832) 778-0500

#346
Sarang Bang
Category: Karaoke
Average price: Modest
Area: Spring Branch
Address: 9444 Long Point Rd
Houston, TX 77055
Phone: (832) 358-0035

#347
Charbar
Category: Dive Bar
Average price: Modest
Area: Fourth Ward, Downtown
Address: 305 Travis St
Houston, TX 77002
Phone: (713) 222-8177

#348
Gatsby Lounge Inside of The Mark
Category: Dance Club, Lounge
Average price: Modest
Area: Sixth Ward
Address: 1902 Washington Ave
Houston, TX 77007
Phone: (832) 443-5781

#349
Limelight
Category: Dance Club
Average price: Modest
Area: Midtown
Address: 2401 San Jacinto
Houston, TX 77002
Phone: (832) 443-5781

#350
Re: HAB Bar On The Bayou
Category: Bar
Average price: Inexpensive
Area: The Heights
Address: 1658 Enid St
Houston, TX 77009
Phone: (713) 225-1668

#351
Sage County
Category: Dive Bar, Lounge, Wine Bar
Average price: Modest
Area: Fourth Ward, Midtown
Address: 2416 Brazos
Houston, TX 77006
Phone: (832) 701-1978

#352
The Wine Cellar Houston
Category: Wine Bar, Mediterranean
Average price: Modest
Area: Fourth Ward, Downtown
Address: 540 Texas Ave
Houston, TX 77002
Phone: (713) 225-2400

#353
Chez Lounge
Category: Dive Bar
Average price: Modest
Area: South Main
Address: 10308 Main St
Houston, TX 77025
Phone: (281) 501-8850

#354
West Wind Club
Category: Dive Bar, Country Dance Hall
Average price: Inexpensive
Area: Fairbanks, Northwest Crossing
Address: 5905 Guhn Rd
Houston, TX 77040
Phone: (713) 462-7204

#355
4500 Washington Avenue
Category: Dance Club, Social Club
Average price: Modest
Area: The Heights
Address: 4500 Washington Ave
Houston, TX 77007
Phone: (917) 828-0740

#356
Solid Platinum
Category: Adult Entertainment
Average price: Inexpensive
Area: Oak Forest, Garden Oaks, Lazy Brook, Timbergrove
Address: 2732 W T C Jester Blvd
Houston, TX 77244
Phone: (713) 680-1414

#357
Rick's Den
Category: Bar
Average price: Modest
Area: Northside Village
Address: 1203 Cavalcade St
Houston, TX 77009
Phone: (713) 691-8273

#358
Club Riddims
Category: Dance Club
Average price: Modest
Area: Fondren Southwest
Address: 8220 W Bellfort St
Houston, TX 77071
Phone: (713) 779-0033

#359
BLVD 610
Category: Lounge
Average price: Modest
Area: Highland Village
Address: 3005 W Lp S
Houston, TX 77027
Phone: (832) 875-3997

#360
Turning Point Club
Category: Nightlife
Average price: Inexpensive
Area: Old Spanish Trail, South Union, MacGregor
Address: 3352 Old Spanish Trl
Houston, TX 77021
Phone: (713) 747-8043

#361
Vinoteca Quattro
Category: Bar
Average price: Modest
Area: Downtown
Address: 1300 Lamar St
Houston, TX 77010
Phone: (713) 650-1300

#362
Red Room
Category: Dance Club
Average price: Expensive
Area: Upper Kirby
Address: 2732 Virginia St
Houston, TX 77098
Phone: (713) 520-5666

#363
T K Bitterman's
Category: Dive Bar
Average price: Inexpensive
Area: Montrose
Address: 2010 W Alabama St
Houston, TX 77098
Phone: (713) 529-8979

#364
Rudyard's British Pub
Category: Music Venues, Pub, Comedy Club
Average price: Inexpensive
Area: Montrose
Address: 2010 Waugh Dr
Houston, TX 77006
Phone: (713) 521-0521

Houston Travel Guide 2015 / Shops, Restaurants, Arts, Entertainment & Nightlife

#365
The Deck House Bar & Grill
Category: Sports Bar, American, Music Venues
Average price: Inexpensive
Area: Gulfton, Galleria, Uptown
Address: 5810 Beverly Hill
Houston, TX 77057
Phone: (713) 784-0818

#366
K100 Cafe & Lounge
Category: Karaoke, Chinese, Lounge
Average price: Modest
Area: Sharpstown, Chinatown
Address: 6609 W Sam Houston Pkwy S
Houston, TX 77036
Phone: (281) 888-3098

#367
Medel's Icehouse
Category: Bar
Average price: Inexpensive
Area: EaDo, Second Ward
Address: 3509 Harrisburg Blvd
Houston, TX 77003
Phone: (713) 237-8930

#368
Buffalo Fred's Icehouse
Category: Bar
Average price: Modest
Area: The Heights
Address: 2708 N Shepherd Dr
Houston, TX 77008
Phone: (713) 863-9409

#369
The De Gaulle
Category: Champagne Bar, Lounge
Average price: Expensive
Area: The Heights
Address: 2811 Washington Ave
Houston, TX 77007
Phone: (832) 704-8964

#370
Darwin's Theory
Category: Pub
Average price: Modest
Area: The Heights
Address: 33 Waugh
Houston, TX 77007
Phone: (713) 992-0396

#371
Kc's Bar & Grill
Category: Sports Bar, Chicken Wings, American
Average price: Modest
Area: Lazy Brook, Timbergrove
Address: 1971 W T C Jester Blvd
Houston, TX 77008
Phone: (713) 864-3944

#372
Club Next on Main Street
Category: Dance Club
Average price: Modest
Area: Downtown
Address: 108 Main St
Houston, TX 77002
Phone: (713) 222-2333

#373
Scotty's Pub
Category: Pub
Average price: Inexpensive
Area: South Belt, Ellington
Address: 10943A Scarsdale Blvd
Houston, TX 77089
Phone: (832) 328-7593

#374
Witchcraft Tavern & Provision Co.
Category: Pub, Burgers
Average price: Modest
Area: The Heights
Address: 1221 W 11th St
Houston, TX 77008
Phone: (832) 649-3601

#375
Carrington's Billiards
Category: Pool Hall
Average price: Inexpensive
Area: Braeswood Place, Medical Center
Address: 9585 S Main St
Houston, TX 77025
Phone: (713) 669-0804

#376
Queen Vic Pub & Kitchen
Category: Pub, Tea Room, British
Average price: Modest
Area: Upper Kirby
Address: 2712 Richmond Ave
Houston, TX 77098
Phone: (713) 533-0022

#377
The Gorgeous Gael
Category: Irish Pub
Average price: Modest
Area: West University
Address: 5555 Morningside Dr
Houston, TX 77005
Phone: (832) 667-8321

#378
Chulas Sports Cantina
Category: Tex-Mex, Sports Bar
Average price: Modest
Area: Braeburn
Address: 9501 SW Fwy
Houston, TX 77074
Phone: (713) 777-3400

#379
Lusso Lounge
Category: Dance Club, Lounge
Average price: Exclusive
Area: Montrose
Address: 526 Waugh Dr
Houston, TX 77019
Phone: (713) 493-2574

#380
Taps House of Beer
Category: Bar
Average price: Modest
Area: The Heights, Rice Military
Address: 5120 Washington Ave
Houston, TX 77007
Phone: (713) 426-1105

#381
The 43rd Restaurant
Category: American, Lounge
Average price: Expensive
Area: Fourth Ward, Downtown
Address: 1415 Louisiana St
Houston, TX 77002
Phone: (713) 739-6550

#382
Grasshopper
Category: Nightlife
Average price: Expensive
Area: Fourth Ward, Downtown
Address: 506 Main St
Houston, TX 77002
Phone: (713) 222-1442

#383
Bayou City Bar & Grill
Category: American, Gay Bar
Average price: Inexpensive
Area: Fourth Ward, Montrose
Address: 2409 Grant St
Houston, TX 77006
Phone: (713) 522-2867

#384
Rumba Club
Category: Dance Club
Average price: Inexpensive
Area: South Belt, Ellington
Address: 11030 Kingspoint Rd
Houston, TX 77075
Phone: (713) 947-8622

#385
Zimm's Martini & Wine Bar
Category: Wine Bar, Lounge, Cocktail Bar
Average price: Modest
Area: Museum District, Montrose
Address: 4321 Montrose Blvd
Houston, TX 77006
Phone: (713) 521-2002

#386
Joke Joint Comedy Showcase
Category: Comedy Club
Average price: Modest
Area: South Belt, Ellington
Address: 11460 Fuqua Street,
Houston, TX 77089
Phone: (281) 481-1188

#387
Icon Sports Bar
Category: Sports Bar
Average price: Modest
Area: MacGregor
Address: 3333 Old Spanish Trl
Houston, TX 77021
Phone: (713) 741-1300

#388
Rick's Cabaret
Category: Adult Entertainment
Average price: Inexpensive
Area: Greenspoint
Address: 410 N. Sam Houston Pkwy
Houston, TX 77060
Phone: (281) 999-7891

#389
Jackson's Watering Hole
Category: Dive Bar
Average price: Modest
Area: Museum District, Montrose
Address: 1205 Richmond
Houston, TX 77006
Phone: (713) 528-2988

#390
iBar & Grill
Category: Bar
Average price: Inexpensive
Area: Inwood
Address: 7303 Breen Dr
Houston, TX 77088
Phone: (281) 820-0078

#391
Live! at Bayou
Category: Bar, Dance Club
Average price: Inexpensive
Area: Fourth Ward, Downtown
Address: 500 Texas Ave
Houston, TX 77204
Phone: (832) 279-8451

#392
Caddy Shack Bar And Grill
Category: Bar, American
Average price: Modest
Area: Sixth Ward
Address: 1809 Washington Ave
Houston, TX 77007
Phone: (713) 426-1812

#393
Reputation
Category: Dance Club, Lounge
Average price: Modest
Area: Fourth Ward, Midtown
Address: 2600 Travis St
Houston, TX 77006
Phone: (832) 767-4699

#394
Michael's International
Category: Adult Entertainment
Average price: Inexpensive
Area: Gulfton
Address: 6440 SW Fwy
Houston, TX 77074
Phone: (713) 784-5900

#395
The Sam Bar
Category: Lounge
Average price: Expensive
Area: Fourth Ward, Downtown
Address: 1117 Prairie St
Houston, TX 77002
Phone: (832) 200-8888

#396
Kiss Lounge
Category: Karaoke, Lounge, Sports Bar
Average price: Modest
Area: Alief
Address: 6198 Wilcrest Dr
Houston, TX 77072
Phone: (832) 293-3888

#397
Slick Willie's Family Pool Halls
Category: Pool Hall
Average price: Modest
Area: Pecan Park
Address: 6969 Gulf Fwy
Houston, TX 77087
Phone: (713) 641-2802

#398
Brewingz Sports Bar & Grill
Category: Chicken Wings, American, Sports Bar
Average price: Modest
Area: Fairbanks, Northwest Crossing
Address: 13816A Northwest Fwy
Houston, TX 77040
Phone: (713) 329-9464

#399
Club 1
Category: Dance Club
Average price: Modest
Area: Alief
Address: 6262 Wilcrest Dr
Houston, TX 77072
Phone: (281) 568-3660

#400
The Colorado Sports Bar & Grill
Category: Sports Bar, Pool Hall, Adult Entertainment
Average price: Modest
Area: Sharpstown
Address: 6710 Southwest Fwy
Houston, TX 77074
Phone: (713) 781-1122

#401
Hurricane Hut the
Category: Dance Club
Average price: Modest
Area: Gulfton, Galleria, Uptown
Address: 6130 Richmond Ave
Houston, TX 77057
Phone: (713) 278-8108

#402
Mad Bull Club the
Category: Nightlife
Average price: Inexpensive
Area: Fairbanks, Northwest Crossing
Address: 14114 Hempstead Rd
Houston, TX 77040
Phone: (713) 460-8403

#403
Scott Gertner's Sports Bar
Category: Sports Bar
Average price: Modest
Area: Galleria, Uptown
Address: 3100 Fountain View Dr
Houston, TX 77057
Phone: (713) 785-1840

#404
Prive Lounge
Category: Lounge
Average price: Modest
Area: Fourth Ward, Montrose
Address: 910 Westheimer Rd
Houston, TX 77006
Phone: (713) 522-2542

#405
Westchase Tavern
Category: Bar
Average price: Inexpensive
Area: Westchase
Address: 10630 Westheimer Rd
Houston, TX 77042
Phone: (713) 785-5567

#406
Toc Bar
Category: Bar
Average price: Modest
Area: Downtown
Address: 711 Franklin St
Houston, TX 77002
Phone: (713) 224-4442

#407
Junction Bar & Grill
Category: Sports Bar
Average price: Inexpensive
Area: Fourth Ward, Midtown, Montrose
Address: 160 W Gray St
Houston, TX 77019
Phone: (713) 523-7768

#408
Neon Boots Dancehall & Saloon
Category: Country Dance Hall,
Gay Bar, Music Venues
Average price: Inexpensive
Area: Lazy Brook, Timbergrove
Address: 11410 Hempstead Hwy
Houston, TX 77092
Phone: (713) 677-0828

#409
Legends
Category: Adult Entertainment
Average price: Modest
Area: Gulfton
Address: 6333 Richmond Ave
Houston, TX 77057
Phone: (713) 784-6333

#410
Big John's Sports Bar & Grill
Category: Sports Bar, American
Average price: Modest
Area: Chinatown, Alief
Address: 6150 Wilcrest and Harwin
Houston, TX 77072
Phone: (281) 498-3499

#411
Benjy's
Category: American, Lounge,
Breakfast & Brunch
Average price: Modest
Area: The Heights, Rice Military
Address: 5922 Washington Ave
Houston, TX 77007
Phone: (713) 868-1131

#412
Museum District Bistro & Lounge
Category: Southern, American, Jazz, Blues
Average price: Modest
Area: Museum District
Address: 1112 Southmore Blvd
Houston, TX 77004
Phone: (713) 520-0505

#413
Uptown Hookah
Category: Hookah Bar
Average price: Modest
Area: Gulfton, Galleria, Uptown
Address: 5706 Richmond Ave
Houston, TX 77056
Phone: (713) 785-4188

#414
Eddie V's Prime Seafood
Category: Seafood, Steakhouse, Jazz, Blues
Average price: Expensive
Area: Upper Kirby
Address: 2800 Kirby Dr
Houston, TX 77098
Phone: (713) 874-1800

#415
The Mercury Room
Category: Dance Club, Lounge
Average price: Modest
Area: Downtown
Address: 1008 Prairie St
Houston, TX 77002
Phone: (713) 225-6372

#416
Faces Ultra Lounge
Category: Lounge
Average price: Modest
Area: Museum District
Address: 5104 Almeda Rd
Houston, TX 77004
Phone: (713) 522-3223

#417
Brewingz Sports Bar & Grill
Category: Chicken Wings, American, Sports Bar
Average price: Modest
Area: Gulfgate, Pine Valley, Lawndale, Wayside
Address: 6006 Gulf Fwy
Houston, TX 77023
Phone: (713) 921-9464

#418
Heights Cigar Lounge
Category: Tobacco Shop, Lounge
Average price: Modest
Area: The Heights
Address: 240 W 19th St
Houston, TX 77008
Phone: (832) 487-9086

#419
Brick House Tavern + Tap
Category: American, Pub
Average price: Modest
Area: Fairbanks, Northwest Crossing
Address: 12910 Northwest Fwy
Houston, TX 77040
Phone: (713) 462-0576

#420
Desiree'nite Club
Category: Nightlife
Average price: Modest
Area: Central Southwest, South Acres,
Crestmont Park
Address: 13334 Almeda Rd
Houston, TX 77045
Phone: (713) 433-2563

#421
Copa Cabana
Category: Dance Club
Average price: Expensive
Area: Downtown
Address: 114 Main St
Houston, TX 77002
Phone: (713) 539-3555

#422
Jai Ho
Category: Indian, Middle Eastern, Bar
Average price: Modest
Area: Fondren Southwest
Address: 11786 S Wilcrest Dr
Houston, TX 77099
Phone: (281) 741-1858

#423
Cockpit Bar & Grill
Category: Bar, American
Average price: Inexpensive
Area: Hobby
Address: 8101 Airport Blvd
Houston, TX 77061
Phone: (713) 640-9898

#424
The Shamrock Inn
Category: Sports Bar, American
Average price: Inexpensive
Area: Braeburn, Sharpstown
Address: 9161 S Gessner Rd
Houston, TX 77074
Phone: (713) 777-5700

#425
Hooters
Category: Sports Bar, American, Chicken Wings
Average price: Modest
Area: West University
Address: 2519 Southwest Freeway
Houston, TX 77098
Phone: (713) 527-9464

#426
Little Woodrow's on Shepherd
Category: Pub
Average price: Modest
Area: The Heights, Rice Military
Address: 720 Shepherd Dr
Houston, TX 77007
Phone: (832) 804-9941

#427
McElroy's Pub
Category: Pub
Average price: Modest
Area: Upper Kirby
Address: 3607 S Sandman St
Houston, TX 77098
Phone: (713) 524-2444

#428
The B.U.S.
Category: Sports Bar
Average price: Modest
Area: Downtown
Address: 1410 Bell
Houston, TX 77002
Phone: (713) 659-4667

#429
Nick's Sports Bar & Grill
Category: American, Bar
Average price: Modest
Area: Westchase
Address: 1448 Wilcrest Dr
Houston, TX 77042
Phone: (713) 785-9900

#430
The Glass House
Category: Dance Club, Lounge
Average price: Exclusive
Area: The Heights, Rice Military
Address: 5219 Washington Ave
Houston, TX 77007
Phone: (713) 518-2132

#431
Ojos Locos
Category: Sports Bar, Mexican
Average price: Modest
Area: South Belt, Ellington
Address: 12200 Gulf Freeway
Houston, TX 77034
Phone: (832) 831-2052

#432
Juan Mon's International Sandwiches
Category: Sandwiches, Juice Bar, Cocktail Bar
Average price: Inexpensive
Area: Fourth Ward, Midtown, Montrose
Address: 1901 Taft St
Houston, TX 77006
Phone: (713) 528-5826

#433
Spotlight Karaoke
Category: Karaoke
Average price: Modest
Area: Galleria, Uptown
Address: 5901 Westheimer Rd
Houston, TX 77057
Phone: (713) 266-7768

#434
Bar Munich
Category: Sports Bar, German
Average price: Modest
Area: Fourth Ward, Midtown
Address: 2616 Louisiana St
Houston, TX 77006
Phone: (713) 523-1008

#435
Our Legends Cigar Bar
Category: Lounge
Average price: Modest
Area: Museum District
Address: 5312 Almeda Rd
Houston, TX 77004
Phone: (713) 522-5312

#436
Gloria's Latin Cuisine
Category: Tex-Mex, Dance Club, Salvadoran
Average price: Modest
Area: Fourth Ward, Midtown
Address: 2616 Louisiana St
Houston, TX 77006
Phone: (832) 360-1710

#437
Cash Box Karaoke
Category: Karaoke
Average price: Modest
Area: Chinatown, Alief
Address: 10600 Bellaire Blvd
Houston, TX 77072
Phone: (281) 879-1700

#438
Elysium Lounge
Category: Dance Club, Lounge
Average price: Expensive
Area: Fourth Ward, Midtown
Address: 2400 Brazos
Houston, TX 77002
Phone: (832) 970-3454

#439
Motown II
Category: Dance Club, Jazz, Blues, Lounge
Average price: Inexpensive
Area: Third Ward
Address: 2541 N MacGregor Way
Houston, TX 77004
Phone: (713) 521-0600

#440
Live Oak Bar and Grill
Category: Venues, Event Space, Restaurant, Sports Bar
Average price: Inexpensive
Area: Lazy Brook, Timbergrove
Address: 10444 Hempstead Rd
Houston, TX 77092
Phone: (713) 686-9625

#441
410 Bistro & Lounge
Category: Dance Club
Average price: Inexpensive
Area: Fourth Ward, Downtown
Address: 410 Main St
Houston, TX 77002
Phone: (713) 227-2010

#442
Pink Monkey
Category: Dance Club
Average price: Modest
Area: Downtown
Address: 709 Franklin St
Houston, TX 77002
Phone: (713) 227-7465

#443
The Original OKRA Charity Saloon
Category: Bar
Average price: Modest
Area: Fourth Ward, Downtown
Address: 924 Congress St
Houston, TX 77002
Phone: (713) 237-8828

#444
GAGE Lounge
Category: Cocktail Bar, Lounge, Tapas
Average price: Modest
Area: Fourth Ward, Midtown
Address: 2600 Travis St
Houston, TX 77006
Phone: (832) 649-2354

#445
Vinoteca Poscol
Category: Italian, Wine Bar
Average price: Modest
Area: Montrose
Address: 1609 Westheimer
Houston, TX 77006
Phone: (713) 529-2797

#446
Velvet Melvin Pub
Category: Pub
Average price: Inexpensive
Area: Upper Kirby
Address: 3303 Richmond Ave
Houston, TX 77098
Phone: (713) 522-6798

#447
Skol Casbar & Grille
Category: Bar, American
Average price: Modest
Area: Midtown
Address: 1701 Webster St
Houston, TX 77003
Phone: (713) 651-1011

#448
The Phoenix On Westheimer
Category: Sports Bar, Pub, American
Average price: Modest
Area: Montrose
Address: 1915 Westheimer Rd
Houston, TX 77098
Phone: (713) 526-3100

#449
Aura Houston
Category: Dance Club, Lounge
Average price: Exclusive
Area: The Heights
Address: 4701 Nett St
Houston, TX 77007
Phone: (713) 965-4275

#450
Russo's Coal Fired Italian Kitchen
Category: Pizza, Italian, Wine Bar
Average price: Modest
Area: Memorial
Address: 9403 Katy Freeway
Houston, TX 77024
Phone: (713) 647-9100

#451
KC Brickhouse Bar & Grill
Category: Sports Bar, American
Average price: Modest
Area: Lazy Brook, Timbergrove
Address: 10444 Hempstead Hwy
Houston, TX 77092
Phone: (713) 266-5730

#452
Ray Ray's Sports Bar
Category: Sports Bar
Average price: Inexpensive
Area: Northside Village
Address: 1101 Collingsworth St
Houston, TX 77009
Phone: (713) 228-1050

#453
The Giulietta Sociale Localita
Category: Lounge
Average price: Modest
Area: The Heights, Rice Military
Address: 5110 Washington Ave
Houston, TX 77007
Phone: (713) 864-8811

#454
2828 Lounge
Category: Lounge
Average price: Modest
Area: Upper Kirby
Address: 2828 Southwest Fwy
Houston, TX 77098
Phone: (713) 942-2111

#455
Christian's Tailgate
Category: Sports Bar, Burgers, Karaoke
Average price: Modest
Area: The Heights
Address: 2820 White Oak Dr
Houston, TX 77007
Phone: (713) 863-1207

#456
Kenneally's Irish Pub
Category: Pub, Pizza, Irish
Average price: Modest
Area: Montrose
Address: 2111 S Shepherd Dr
Houston, TX 77019
Phone: (713) 630-0486

#457
Calvino's Grill and Wine Bar
Category: Wine Bar, Italian, Pizza
Average price: Modest
Area: Trinity, Houston Gardens
Address: 12510 N Fwy
Houston, TX 77060
Phone: (281) 872-1800

#458
Blue Moose Lodge
Category: Pub, Sports Bar, Music Venues
Average price: Exclusive
Area: The Heights, Rice Military
Address: 5306 Washington Ave
Houston, TX 77007
Phone: (713) 861-5525

#459
Buffalo Wild Wings
Category: Sports Bar, American, Chicken Wings
Average price: Modest
Area: Fourth Ward, Midtown, Downtown
Address: 510 Gray St
Houston, TX 77002
Phone: (713) 650-0002

#460
The Black Labrador
Category: British, Pub
Average price: Modest
Area: Montrose
Address: 4100 Montrose Blvd
Houston, TX 77006
Phone: (713) 529-1199

#461
Ibiza
Category: Wine Bar, American, Basque
Average price: Expensive
Area: Fourth Ward, Midtown
Address: 2450 Louisiana St
Houston, TX 77006
Phone: (713) 524-0004

#462
Goode's Armadillo Palace
Category: Bar, Music Venues, American
Average price: Modest
Area: West University
Address: 5015 Kirby Dr
Houston, TX 77098
Phone: (713) 526-9700

#463
Straits Restaurant
Category: Asian Fusion, Lounge, Singaporean
Average price: Modest
Area: Memorial
Address: 800 Sorella Ct
Houston, TX 77024
Phone: (713) 365-9922

#464
Bombers Sports Bar
Category: Sports Bar
Average price: Inexpensive
Area: South Belt, Ellington
Address: 15327 Gulf Fwy
Houston, TX 77034
Phone: (832) 406-7463

#465
Bubba's Sportsbar & Grill
Category: Sports Bar, American
Average price: Modest
Area: The Heights
Address: 6225 Washington Ave
Houston, TX 77007
Phone: (281) 888-4215

#466
Allure Lounge
Category: Dance Club, Lounge
Average price: Modest
Area: Fourth Ward, Midtown
Address: 2707 Milam
Houston, TX 77006
Phone: (281) 493-9797

#467
D'Place Restaurant & Grill
Category: Sports Bar, African, Lounge
Average price: Modest
Area: Westwood
Address: 9817 Bissonnet St
Houston, TX 77036
Phone: (832) 907-6799

#468
Barney's Billiard Saloon
Category: Pool Hall
Average price: Inexpensive
Area: Lazy Brook, Timbergrove
Address: 1702 West Loop N
Houston, TX 77008
Phone: (713) 869-8061

#469
Grub Burger Bar - City Centre
Category: Burgers, Bar
Average price: Modest
Area: Memorial
Address: 799 Town & Country Blvd
Houston, TX 77024
Phone: (713) 827-7157

#470
Bistro Bar
Category: Lounge
Average price: Modest
Area: Memorial
Address: 800 W Sam Houston Pkwy N
Houston, TX 77024
Phone: (713) 973-1600

#471
Fat Boy's Bar & Grill
Category: American, Sports Bar, Comedy Club
Average price: Modest
Area: Medical Center
Address: 2596 S Loop W
Houston, TX 77054
Phone: (713) 669-1183

#472
Link Lounge
Category: Dance Club
Average price: Modest
Area: Midtown
Address: 2901 Fannin St
Houston, TX 77002
Phone: (713) 655-7600

#473
Coaches Pub
Category: Sports Bar, Chicken Wings
Average price: Modest
Area: Fourth Ward, Midtown
Address: 2204 Louisiana
Houston, TX 77002
Phone: (713) 751-1970

#474
RA Sushi Bar Restaurant
Category: Sushi Bar, Lounge
Average price: Modest
Area: Highland Village
Address: 3908 Westheimer Rd
Houston, TX 77297
Phone: (713) 621-5800

#475
Lizard's Pub
Category: Pub
Average price: Inexpensive
Area: Upper Kirby
Address: 2715 Sackett St
Houston, TX 77098
Phone: (713) 529-4610

#476
Rebels Honky Tonk
Category: Dance Club
Average price: Modest
Area: The Heights, Rice Military
Address: 5002 Washington Ave
Houston, TX 77007
Phone: (281) 851-5224

#477
Fox & Hound Smokehouse & Tavern
Category: Sports Bar, Pool Hall
Average price: Modest
Area: South Belt, Ellington
Address: 12802 Gulf Fwy
Houston, TX 77034
Phone: (281) 481-0068

#478
Molly's Pub
Category: Pub
Average price: Inexpensive
Area: Fourth Ward, Downtown
Address: 509 Main St
Houston, TX 77002
Phone: (713) 222-1033

#479
1st & Goal Sports Bar & Grill
Category: Sports Bar, American
Average price: Modest
Area: Galleria, Uptown
Address: 3101 Fountainview Rd
Houston, TX 77057
Phone: (832) 831-5841

#480
Citizen Lounge
Category: Lounge
Average price: Inexpensive
Area: The Heights
Address: 4606 Washington Ave
Houston, TX 77007
Phone: (713) 862-4448

#481
The Deck On Fountainview
Category: Sports Bar, American
Average price: Modest
Area: Galleria, Uptown
Address: 6002 Fairdale Ln
Houston, TX 77057
Phone: (713) 914-9990

#482
1400 Bar & Grill
Category: Sports Bar
Average price: Modest
Area: The Heights
Address: 1400 Shepherd Dr
Houston, TX 77007
Phone: (713) 869-8080

#483
Walker's Original BBQ
Category: Barbeque, Sports Bar
Average price: Modest
Area: Midtown
Address: 4104 Fannin St
Houston, TX 77004
Phone: (713) 522-1651

#484
Hefley's
Category: Barbeque, Sports Bar, Burgers
Average price: Modest
Area: Fourth Ward, Midtown, Montrose
Address: 138 W Gray St
Houston, TX 77019
Phone: (713) 527-8100

#485
Embers American Grille
Category: American, Wine Bar
Average price: Modest
Area: Memorial, Galleria, Uptown
Address: 5709 Woodway
Houston, TX 77057
Phone: (832) 242-1888

#486
Salento
Category: Coffee, Tea, Wine Bar, American
Average price: Modest
Area: West University
Address: 2407 Rice Blvd
Houston, TX 77005
Phone: (713) 528-7478

#487
BreWingz Sports Bar & Grill
Category: Chicken Wings, Sports Bar, American
Average price: Modest
Area: Hobby
Address: 8490 S Sam Houston Pkwy E
Houston, TX 77075
Phone: (713) 987-5410

#488
Harvest Organic Grille
Category: Bar, American, Live/Raw Food
Average price: Modest
Area: Galleria, Uptown
Address: 1810 Fountain View Dr
Houston, TX 77057
Phone: (713) 243-0900

#489
Monarch Restaurant & Lounge
Category: American, Lounge
Average price: Expensive
Area: Museum District
Address: 5701 Main St
Houston, TX 77005
Phone: (713) 527-1800

#490
Vine Wine Room
Category: Wine Bar
Average price: Modest
Area: Memorial
Address: 12420 Memorial Dr
Houston, TX 77024
Phone: (713) 463-8463

#491
The Tasting Room
Category: Wine Bar, American, Breakfast & Brunch
Average price: Modest
Area: Memorial
Address: 818 Town and Country Blvd
Houston, TX 77024
Phone: (281) 822-1500

#492
TGI Friday's
Category: Sports Bar, American
Average price: Modest
Area: South Belt, Ellington
Address: 12895 Gulf Fwy
Houston, TX 77034
Phone: (281) 481-0932

#493
Montrose Mining Company
Category: Gay Bar
Average price: Inexpensive
Area: Fourth Ward, Montrose
Address: 805 Pacific St
Houston, TX 77006
Phone: (713) 529-7488

#494
Wasfi's Grill and Hookah
Category: Hookah Bar, Mediterranean, Middle Eastern
Average price: Modest
Area: Galleria, Uptown
Address: 6110 Richmond Ave
Houston, TX 77057
Phone: (713) 782-1789

#495
Underbelly
Category: American, Wine Bar
Average price: Expensive
Area: Montrose
Address: 1100 Westheimer Rd
Houston, TX 77006
Phone: (713) 528-9800

#496
Wild Plum Bar
Category: Lounge
Average price: Modest
Area: Galleria, Uptown
Address: 2400 W Loop S
Houston, TX 77027
Phone: (713) 586-2444

#497
Buffalo Wild Wings
Category: American, Sports Bar, Chicken Wings
Average price: Modest
Area: West University
Address: 2525 Rice Boulevard
Houston, TX 77005
Phone: (713) 521-1100

#498
P J's Sports Bar
Category: Sports Bar
Average price: Inexpensive
Area: Fourth Ward, Montrose
Address: 614 W Gray St
Houston, TX 77019
Phone: (713) 520-1748

#499
Capone's Bar and Oven
Category: Italian, Bar, Pizza
Average price: Modest
Area: Highland Village
Address: 4304 Westheimer Rd
Houston, TX 77027
Phone: (713) 840-0010

#500
MAX's Wine Dive
Category: Wine Bar, American, Breakfast & Brunch
Average price: Modest
Area: The Heights, Rice Military
Address: 4720 Washington Ave
Houston, TX 77007
Phone: (713) 880-8737

Printed in Great Britain
by Amazon.co.uk, Ltd.,
Marston Gate.